Rome Through the Mist

Rome Through the Mist

Walks Among the Fountains of the Eternal City

Joe Gartman

Photographs by Patricia Gartman

Jefferson, North Carolina

ISBN (print) 978-1-4766-8924-1
ISBN (ebook) 978-1-4766-4756-2

LIBRARY OF CONGRESS AND BRITISH LIBRARY
CATALOGUING DATA ARE AVAILABLE

Library of Congress Control Number 2023001732

On the cover: The Trevi Fountain (author's photograph)

Printed in the United States of America

Toplight is an imprint of McFarland & Company, Inc., Publishers

Box 611, Jefferson, North Carolina 28640
www.toplightbooks.com

Table of Contents

Acknowledgments

Our thanks to Marsha and Bob Nickerson, Benita and San-joy Bhattacharya, and Armida (Liz) Shore for reviewing and commenting on the photographs.

Thanks also go to Paul Grosvenor for proofreading the manuscript.

Introduction

When you go to Rome for the first time, and you have only a few days, let's be honest: you're not going to tramp around looking at fountains. You'll want to see the famous sights, and I don't blame you. You'll probably get to the Trevi Fountain, at least; be sure to toss that coin in the water, and someday, say the gods of tradition, you'll be back. Since you're reading this book, I'd guess the city intrigues you and you'd like to know it better, so feel free to follow these paths with me in imagination—until the next time…

Or perhaps you've already gotten to know Rome well—you're an old hand, you've found those secret places that the guidebooks miss, you know where to find the best *carbonara* and *carciofi alla Giudia*, you've laughed scornfully when faced with broken escalators and *spazzatura* and shifty-eyed pickpockets, and, despite it all, you still want to learn and understand more. I don't blame you, either. Well, then, here's another way to get to know this inexhaustibly surprising city.

After all, Rome's aqueducts and fountains nourished the city's glory for millennia and made possible all the many layers of history we love to peel away and savor. The city's fountains have stories to tell, and the streets, squares, paths, buildings, walls, and gardens in which we'll find them will fill in the details. We'll find our way by street and lane and landmark, leaving the GPS coordinates to those in a hurry. It may be that on our way we'll stop and talk awhile, or perhaps we'll stray a little off our path to visit something odd or precious or beautiful. So why not take a stroll or two through time and listen to the voices of the waters?

Since you're going to be experiencing Rome a bit more intimately than most foreign visitors, I have a few practical and cultural hints you might like to consider, to smooth your way when you're off the tourist track, as well as some thoughts about how you might use this book. Let's call them **Practicalities**:

Bus and Metro tickets (tickets are good on buses, trams, and the Metro) are available in Metro stations from ticket machines and, in some stations, from ticket booths. More conveniently, they can be purchased from tobacco shops (called *tabacchi*), which seem to be everywhere—except when you run out of bus tickets. Be sure to validate your ticket when you get on the bus or tram, or you can be fined when a transit inspector climbs aboard and inspects your ticket. The little validators are found near the front and the rear of the bus, mounted on poles. As I write, the basic bus ticket is for one Metro ride and/or 100 minutes on the bus (validate every time you board), and there are also tickets good for two, three or seven days. There's an *abbonamento mensile* (monthly pass) and even an annual *abbonamento*. ATAC, the city's transit authority, has a habit of changing its various plans, so check its website (www.atac.roma.it) to see what's available when you go.

There are three Metro lines in operation: line A (red or orange on maps), line B (blue) and line C (green). Lines A and B cross at Termini Station, the main train station in Rome. Termini is the only interchange between the two lines. Line C is under construction as I write, with a completed section that runs from Monte Compatri, about 20 miles southeast of Rome in the Alban Hills, to the San Giovanni station (line A and now line C) in Rome.

Taxis are available at taxi stands or by telephone and are not usually hailed from the street.

Street signs are usually found mounted on, or embedded in, the walls of buildings near intersections. Legibility varies, and in some cases I suspect there was never a sign there at all. Also, *piazza* is an elusive term in Italian. It usually signifies a square or marketplace, though sometimes it's just a wide spot in the road (these may be called "largos" instead). Confusingly, the streets surrounding a piazza, or leading to or from a piazza, will often share the piazza's name. So a street leading to or from, say, "Piazza della Cancelleria" might also be named "Piazza della Cancelleria," which makes it tough to know where you're going or when you've arrived.

As you walk, you'll notice that streets change their names frequently, for no apparent reason. I suppose that a history reaching back almost 3,000 years provides lots of events and people who need to be celebrated with a block or two of cobblestone. (By the way, the cobblestones used in the historic parts of Rome are called *sanpietrini*, or "little Saint Peters," because they were first used in the sixteenth century in Saint Peter's Square. They're pyramid shaped, with a flat, four-sided bottom, and are installed, pointy side down, in a bed of tight-packed sand. Stiletto heels beware!)

Street crossings: Roman pedestrians, like many big-city dwellers, are aggressive walkers, and Roman drivers are aggressive drivers. Be careful crossing the street, and don't assume you're safe just because you're in a crosswalk.

Toilets: The practice of dashing into a bar, ordering an espresso (*caffé* or *caffé normale*), gulping the thimbleful of coffee you didn't really want, and then visiting the facilities before someone else gets there is a time-honored tradition in Rome. You can find public toilets in department stores and shopping centers, and sometimes in or near tourist sites, but in the neighborhoods, the caffé at the bar is probably your only option. Fortunately, most bars are family owned and friendly, though don't be surprised if the toilet seat is missing.

Museums and churches: Most museums in Rome are closed on Mondays. Some important museums, though, are open. The Vatican Museums and the Capitoline Museums are open, as is the Ara Pacis Museum, and most open-air venues, like the Forum and the Palatine Hill, are usually open every day. Some of the larger, well-known churches, like Saint Peter's Basilica or Santa Maria in Trastevere, are normally open all day, morning to evening, except Sundays and major religious holidays. (St. Peter's usually closes on Wednesday mornings for the pope's audience, but it reopens around 1:00 p.m.) Most other churches open around 8:00 or 9:00 in the morning, close around noon for a couple of hours, and then reopen for two or three hours in the afternoon. The actual hours vary wildly, so, if possible, check before you go. This website, from the Rome tourist agency, lists web addresses (or at least telephone numbers) for most churches in Rome: http://060608.it/en/. Select "culture and leisure" and then "historic places of worship."

Dining: Restaurants, sit-down pizzerias, and trattorias usually open for dinner around 7:30 p.m. Some also open for lunch for two or three hours around noon. You'll find a great variety of takeaway pizza storefronts, market stalls, and neighborhood bars ("bars" are cafés, really, rather than taverns, usually serving coffee, sandwiches and pastries along with beer and wine) that are open all day. Some bars will also have a *tavola calda* (hot table) at lunchtime.

For coffee, drinks, or a snack in a bar, you'll often take a look at the available items in a glass case and then go to the cash desk, pay for what you want, and bring the receipt to the bar to be served, standing up. If you want to sit at a table, expect to pay significantly more. This practice is no longer universal but is still common. Ask before sitting down, unless your feet hurt and you just don't care.

Language: If you speak Italian, even badly, you're home free. Romans are, I've found, quite willing to forgive wonky grammar and barbaric pronunciation. And even if you don't speak the language, wherever tourists commonly go, you'll find English spoken. Outside of those areas, though (especially in residential neighborhoods), you may find that the owner of a bar or a mom-and-pop *alimentari* (grocery) doesn't speak your language. You can always resort to pointing and a quick game of practical charades, of course, and you'll be all right. But if you can muster a few pleasantries and sentences from a phrasebook that tell approximately what you need, you'll be a hero.

Using this book: There are fifteen walking tours in this book, *one per chapter*. Some are mere strolls around a particularly interesting or fountain-rich area. Some are longer and more strenuous. You can, of course, combine walking tours, so, when it is appropriate, there are detailed walking directions to continue from one chapter to the following chapter. There are maps for each chapter. When you are walking between the fountains covered within a chapter, you can use the appropriate map to supplement the written directions, but please remember that the maps are *not* drawn to scale and are really just meant to orient yourself within the tour. If you follow the written directions carefully, you should be fine. The letters "S" and "E" on the maps indicate the start and end of each walk's itinerary. A large capital M denotes a Metro station. Actual distances are greater than they appear on the maps, of course.

If you finish one chapter and still feel energetic, feel free to continue to the next with the walking directions provided, but you won't find maps for the routes *between* chapters.

Of course, you could use the GPS app on your phone. But don't, unless it's an emergency. Let's return to a pre-digital world, for a few precious hours, and experience the real city around us.

I have to admit that I didn't write this book just to tell you how to get from the Triton Fountain to the Trevi or from the Fountain of the Moor to the Mask in via Giulia. The walking directions in the book are interrupted frequently with stories, legends, descriptions, history and background about what you find at the fountains and on the paths between them; that's why it's better to follow the book, rather than your phone or a tourist map. (In fact, it might be more accurate to say that the stories, legends, descriptions and so on are occasionally interrupted by walking directions, but I'm putting them—the directions, that is—in italics, so you can easily find them. If you'd like to carry a regular map for security, pick one up at a newspaper kiosk or a bookstore, and keep it in your pocket until you actually need it.)

Fountains: Rome may be the "Eternal City," but that doesn't mean that nothing changes. You may hike to a fountain and find that the water's been turned off or that it's surrounded by plywood plastered with signs announcing that Bulgari or Fendi is sponsoring a three-year renovation. Just be comforted by the fact that there's another intriguing piece of Rome's watery history not far away.

There is one well-loved type of fountain you'll be glad to know about. It is made of cast iron and looks a bit like a fire hydrant with a long piece of pipe curving downward. A constant stream of water issues from the pipe, close to the ground, and into a drain. These fountains are called *nasoni* ("big noses"), after the curved pipes. Don't bend double to drink from the end of the pipe—just stop the end with a finger, and a jet of water will suddenly spurt upward from a small hole right where the pipe bends, soaking your shirt. This is for your convenience in drinking. There are hundreds of *nasoni* in the city.

You'll notice that some fountains are marked with the letters SPQR. As you probably know, these letters stand for *Senātus Populusque Rōmānus* ("The Senate and the People of Rome"). This motto originated in the days of the Roman Republic, more than two millennia ago, but most of the fountains on which you find it today were created after 1870, when papal rule ended in Rome and the new Italian nation stamped SPQR on public facilities, rather than the coats of arms of various popes. In some cases, though, older fountains were "updated" with the motto.

Not all fountains have a universally acknowledged name. The really famous ones do, of course, but less familiar fountains have surprisingly varied identities. I have tried to use the most common English (and the most common Italian) name for each fountain, though I concede that this nomenclature can be a matter of dispute.

I bought a book, years ago, by a man called Marvin Pulvers. The book is worth many hundreds of dollars nowadays. It's called *Roman Fountains*, and it contains pictures, most taken before the era of digital photography, of more than 2,000 fountains in Rome. I salute Marvin Pulvers and his epic photographic quest, but I can hardly carry his book from one room to another. This book only covers 80 fountains, but at least you can lift it. What I'm trying to say is—I'm awfully sorry if I missed your favorite fountain.

So much for the Practicalities!

Finally, before we set foot in today's Rome, let's take a quick detour into antiquity, and consider the vanished city, the vanished fountains, and the vanished people whose ghosts we may meet on our travels.

By the early fourth century AD, Rome's eleven aqueducts brought a million cubic meters of water into the city daily, from springs and seeps in the surrounding hills. There were elaborate public baths (which Romans of every class enthusiastically patronized), and over 1,300 neighborhood fountains provided nearby water sources for household use. (Some wealthy aristocrats even had running water in their homes!) There was irrigation water for public and private gardens. There were perhaps fifty monumental fountains, showpieces celebrating the city's watery abundance, and, at the height of the Imperial Age, there was even enough water to flood specially built arenas for spectacular mock naval battles.[1]

While the Western Roman Empire flourished, the aqueducts were well maintained, but, in the fourth and fifth centuries AD, as the decline of Rome began, the aqueducts fell more and more into disrepair; by the time the Goths cut most of the functioning aqueducts in 537 AD, there were fewer than 100 working fountains in the city. One aqueduct, the *Aqua Virgo*, still reliably carried a little water to the Campus Martius, but the rest of the fountains essentially dried up. There were attempts to patch the aqueducts in the Middle Ages, with meager success. Sadly, the glory of abundant water and majestic fountains did not return to Rome for nearly a thousand years.

It was not until the fifteenth century that a series of popes began to reclaim and repair some of the ancient aqueducts and to construct new ones to serve the city. Perhaps they built them for the glory of God, perhaps for their own glory, but, gradually, the people of Rome were served once more by a multitude of fountains. Some were grand showpieces, with waterfalls and cataracts and geysers erupting skyward. Some were beautiful, some bizarre. There were fountains in the forms of boats, or soup tureens, or stacks of cannonballs, as well as fountains decorated with turtles, sensuous naiads, Egyptian obelisks, and lions, of course—lots of lions.

But of all the fountains in Rome, the one that speaks most eloquently about the city's historical relationship with water is neither majestic nor beautiful, nor is it particularly bizarre. It is functional, though, in the truest sense of the word.

Just off via del Corso, in via Lata, there is a marble figure of a little man carrying a cask. The sculpture is set in a wall niche, somewhat below the shoulder height of most passersby, and from a hole in the cask a stream of water spouts invitingly. It is *Acqua Vergine* water, which from ancient times has been called the purest and sweetest in the city. Many pedestrians hurrying by on the busy Corso stop for a drink, as they have done for more than 400 years.

The little man's face is terribly battered. Considering that all he has done for centuries is offer refreshment to one and all, the reason for the apparent vandalism is a mystery. Some have suggested that his cap was similar to one favored by Martin Luther and that he was therefore attacked by Counter-Reformation zealots. But why would Martin Luther have carried a cask of water?

The figure is called *Il Facchino*—the Porter. But he should probably be called *Il Acquaerolo* (the Water Carrier), because he represents all the *acquaeroli* who, after the aqueducts were cut, collected water from the Tiber, let it stand in a vat or tub until the sediment settled, drew off the relatively clear liquid, and sold it all over Rome.[2] This was the water that most Romans used for drinking, boiling their vegetables, washing, and every other domestic purpose. Presumably the *acquaeroli* collected their supply upstream from the point where the *Cloaca Maxima* (ancient Rome's main sewer) flowed into the river just south of the island called Isola Tiberina. The

Il Facchino (The Porter): For centuries after Rome fell and the aqueducts failed, *acquaeroli* like Facchino carried water from the Tiber River throughout the city. Only Facchino remains now, dispensing pure *Acqua Vergine* water for free.

acquaeroli also brought barrels of water in their ox carts to construction sites, to slake the thirst of workers and animals, and for use in mixing mortar. They were the primary water distribution system for the city from medieval times until, in 1453, the ancient *Aqua Virgo* (renamed the *Acqua Vergine* and restored under a succession of popes from Nicholas V to Pius V) once more flowed freely into an early, very simple version of the Trevi Fountain in the Piazza dei Crociferi.

More aqueducts followed: The *Acqua Felice* was completed in 1587, using parts of two ancient aqueducts. Its construction was spurred by the iron will of Pope Sixtus V, a dynamic man of action who was born Felice Peretti. He named the new watercourse after himself. Not to be outdone, in 1612 Pope Paul V restored the *Aqua Traiana*, created by Emperor Trajan in the second century AD, and renamed it the *Acqua Paola*.

The waters were at last flowing into the Eternal City again, and the fountains followed, bringing water to every corner of Rome, until, of all the *acquaeroli*, the only one left was *Il Facchino*.

❧ 1 ❧

Triton and Trevi
and a Fountain Quartet
Piazza Barberini Area

LET'S BEGIN IN PIAZZA BARBERINI.

It's a cinch to find. There are at least seven bus lines with stops at or near the piazza—check the route signs at bus stops all over town, or use Rome's Transit Authority website (www.atac.roma.it) to calculate your route. Or you can simply take the Metro, Rome's subway system, to the Barberini Station (line A). We'll start our

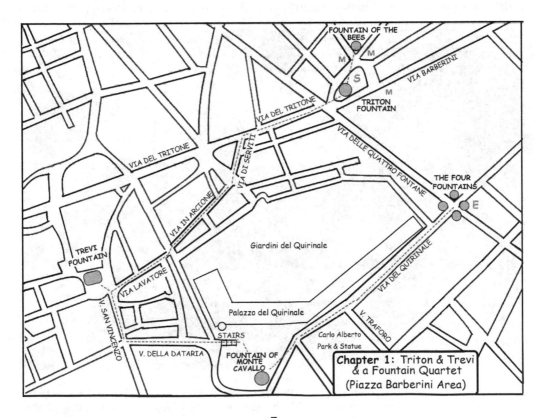

Chapter 1: Triton & Trevi & a Fountain Quartet (Piazza Barberini Area)

walk after we've had a look at Piazza Barberini and the two fountains associated with it.

In this piazza, you'll encounter someone who will become more and more familiar as you explore Rome's neighborhoods, palaces, churches, and, of course, fountains. His name is Gian Lorenzo Bernini, and it is impossible to escape him for long in Rome. Piazza Barberini is dominated by the giant Triton he designed, spouting water high from his conch shell, while at the corner where via Veneto enters the piazza there's another famous fountain by Bernini, the *Fontana delle Api* (Fountain of the Bees). Just a few steps from the piazza, on via delle Quattro Fontane, is the entrance to Palazzo Barberini, which Bernini designed and built (with help from Francesco Borromini) for his friend and patron, Pope Urban VIII. It's now the *Gallerie Nazionale d'Arte Antica*. Here, there are masterpieces by Caravaggio, Raphael, Guido Reni, and, of course, you know who. And, as you stand in the piazza facing the Triton, you'll see a grand eight-story hotel proudly proclaiming its name in giant neon letters on the roof: BERNINI.

The Triton Fountain—La Fontana del Tritone (1643)
ARCHITECT: GIAN LORENZO BERNINI

The Triton Fountain's base is a large travertine pool, in which four twisting dolphins, with gaping mouths half-submerged in the water, sinuously support a huge

The Triton Fountain: Bernini set this mighty Triton atop the fountain in Piazza Barberini for his patron and friend, Pope Urban VIII. The hotel is decorated for Christmas in this photograph, but it celebrates the great artist all year long.

bivalve's shell on their upturned tails. Kneeling astride the "hinge" of the shell, Triton (in Greek myth, a son of Poseidon and Amphitrite, god and goddess of the sea) holds a conch to his lips; to judge by old engravings, he blew a much higher plume of water several centuries ago than he does today. The dolphins' entwined tails also hold a papal tiara, crossed keys, and a scroll carved with three bees, the insignia of the Barberini family.

Urban VIII was very pleased with the fountain, and quite proud of it, symbolizing as it did the power and grandeur of the Barberini family, but there was a problem: too many farmers and carters and other tradesmen watered their horses in the lower pool. While this utilitarian response to the noble fountain rankled a bit, the pope was sensible enough to know that if you lead a horse to water, it very likely *will* drink, so he asked Bernini to design a smaller fountain to be installed nearby that would serve this purpose. Bernini, of course, was not satisfied with merely hanging a stone trough and a metal spigot from a convenient wall. He set to work and designed another landmark fountain, a small masterpiece called *La Fontana delle Api.*

You'll find our next fountain at the northwest corner of Piazza Barberini, decorating a bus stop where via Veneto enters the piazza. If you're facing the Triton, aim for the corner of the piazza to your left and behind him.

The Triton Fountain from atop the Hotel Bernini on a cool November day.

The Fountain of the Bees—La Fontana delle Api (1644)
Architect: Gian Lorenzo Bernini

Sticking with his theme of bivalves and bees, Bernini sculpted a marble scallop shell, partly opened, with one half attached upright to the wall of a house and the other half (below the "hinge") resting on a stone base to act as the basin from which animals could drink. Three streams of water issue from pipes just below three

The Fountain of the Bees: As you can see, Bernini's little seashell fountain attracts lots of bees. That's because three bees appear prominently in Pope Urban VIII's coat of arms, which is why this fountain is called *La Fontana delle Api.*

oversized bees near the bottom of the upright shell. Above the bees, an inscription in Latin reads, "Urban VIII Pont. Max., who made a fountain for the public ornamentation of the City, also made this small fountain to be of service to private citizens. In the year 1644, XXI of his pontificate." There were a couple of problems with the fountain, though: First, the inscription originally read, "In the year 1644, XXII of his pontificate." Trouble was, 1644 *wasn't* the twenty-second year of the pope's reign; it was the twenty-first. Also, the fountain was installed in via Sistina, near the edge of Piazza Barberini, and, what with horses, wagons, and carts stopping there, it tended to impede traffic.

The first problem was addressed by carefully chiseling out the second I from "XXII," but the traffic problem wasn't solved until 1887, when the fountain was removed from its wall. It was evidently stored in a warehouse somewhere, where it deteriorated severely. It emerged in 1919, having undergone extensive repair, and was installed near the opposite edge of the piazza from its original location, this time at the bus stop just outside the piazza, on via Veneto. Now, rather than thirsty horses, people drink or fill their water bottles here, in addition to using the fountain's base as a rather uncomfortable perch while waiting for buses.

(I should mention here that the City of Rome has recently amended a set of regulations, dating from 1946, that deal with public behavior. A few rules relate to the protection of public fountains and forbid, among other things, throwing objects in them, bathing pets in them, climbing on them, wading or swimming in them, and

The Fountain of the Bees: Besides bees, *La Fontana delle Api*'s sparkling pool, at a child-friendly height, attracts other little visitors.

damaging them. In some cases, sitting on them may be prohibited as well, though the degree of enforcement seems to vary, with highly touristed fountains receiving the most attention.)

Although the *Fontana delle Api* is just a few steps from the Triton Fountain, its water comes from a completely different source. The Triton is fed by the *Acqua Felice*, the aqueduct sponsored by Pope Sixtus V and completed in 1586. By contrast, the little Fountain of the Bees receives its water from the *Acqua Pia Antica Marcia*, which was completed by Pope Pius IX just before the soldiers of a united Italy captured the city in 1870, bringing papal rule in Rome to an end.

Just beyond the bus stop on via Veneto, you'll see the church of *Santa Maria della Concezione*, whose crypt is decorated with the skulls and bones of four thousand Capuchin friars. Mark Twain visited here in 1867 and was conducted through the displays by a Capuchin brother who, Twain thought, seemed to be musing about where his own skull and ribs could be displayed to best advantage when the time came.[1] If you'd like to see the extraordinary designs that can be made of such unlikely material, the crypt is open to visitors. Check www.cappucciniviaveneto.it for opening hours and ticket prices.

Despite his seeming ubiquity, Bernini did not design *all* the iconic fountains within easy walking distance of Piazza Barberini, so perhaps we should continue our examination of this star-studded cluster with the most famous of all Roman fountains ... the Trevi.

From Piazza Barberini, leave the Triton behind at the end of the piazza opposite the Bernini Hotel and take his namesake street, via del Tritone. The popular Pepy's

The Fountain of the Bees: A different kind of swarm surrounds the fountain from time to time when the tour groups arrive. The fountain is deservedly famous, but there are many others that the tour groups never discover.

Bar (known for its elegantly artistic finger sandwiches, called tramezzini*) will be on your left. A few minutes' walk will take you to the second street on the left, via dei Serviti. You'll see the narrow front façade of the triangular* Il Messaggero *building, headquarters of an important Italian newspaper. Follow via dei Serviti about 100 yards to where it intersects via del Traforo. Cross via del Traforo at the crosswalk, and continue straight ahead into via in Arcione (although, halfway along, it changes its name to via del Lavatore), which will lead you to Piazza di Trevi, and the fountain, in five or ten minutes.*

The Trevi Fountain—La Fontana di Trevi (1762)
ARCHITECTS: NICOLA SALVI, GIUSEPPE PANNINI, AND PIETRO BRACCI

If, late at night, you had been loitering in the narrow streets around the Piazza di Trevi back in the late 1950s, you might have made your way to the fountain by following the roar of the water and, like Marcello Mastroianni and Anita Ekberg in *La Dolce Vita*, found a dark, deserted square, with the basin's water reflecting the pale gleam of a streetlamp and winking a raffish invitation to take a refreshing dip. Now, though, even in the wee hours of the morning, you'll probably never have the fountain to yourself. The moody scene of darkened streets and echoing footsteps, with

The Trevi Fountain: A face in the crowd—sometimes it's hard to remember that the crush of people surrounding Rome's most iconic fountain, the Trevi, is composed of individuals.

two empty people finding little solace in the waters of the Trevi, is an unforgettable image, as well as an unrepeatable one.

Mastroianni died December 19, 1996, and that evening a quiet crowd waited as darkness fell, and black drapes were slowly unfurled over the pale marble fountain.

The Trevi Fountain: She's just tossed that coin over her shoulder and into the Trevi's pool— guaranteeing a return to Rome.

A band played; the city's mayor, Francesco Rutelli, spoke briefly; and then the tumbling water stopped flowing, leaving the small piazza in silence.

The piazza is rarely silent nowadays, nor is it dark. The city lights the fountain at night, the better to keep an eye on things. The Trevi Fountain is one of the most powerful tourist magnets in Rome, after the Vatican, the Coliseum, and possibly the Roman Forum. Many of the visitors who toss a coin in the water to ensure a return to Rome never saw the 1954 film *Three Coins in the Fountain*, which popularized the old tradition. But the floor of the basin is still regularly carpeted with small change—about €3,000 worth in a typical day. The money, collected early in the morning by workers from the Catholic charity *Caritas*, is used to fund a market called *Emporio Caritas*, supplying free food to the needy. Not long ago, sorting and valuing coins from dozens of currencies was a daunting task. Nowadays, with so many countries using the euro, the job is much easier.

The word *mostra* in Italian means "show" or "exhibition." Historically applied to large and elaborate fountains that mark the arrival point of an aqueduct, the name is appropriate for the *Fontana di Trevi*—it certainly puts on a show! Here the waters of the *Acqua Vergine* make their debut in Rome, performing on a grand stage with a supporting cast including the god Oceanus, 16 feet tall, poised in the center of a triumphal arch, above a rocky reef through which the waters of the Vergine plunge and tumble noisily into a wide basin. He is riding on a giant seashell pulled by rearing, winged sea horses (not to be confused with the tiny, spiny marine animals of the genus *Hippocampus*). Two Tritons, sons of Poseidon (one of whom is blowing a fanfare through a conch shell), struggle to control the eager steeds.

Oceanus is flanked by statues of two women representing Abundance (the Roman goddess Abundantia) on his left and Health (the Greek goddess Hygieia) to his right. Above the goddesses are reliefs of Marcus Agrippa supervising the construction of the *Aqua Virgo* (now the *Acqua Vergine*) and of a maiden showing Roman legionnaires the springs that became the source of the aqueduct's water—the *Aqua Virgo* was named in her honor.

The arch, the sculpted figures, the dramatic, stony reef with its cataracts and rapids, the basin whose water changes shades of blue with every passing cloud, are all framed (as if by a theatrical backdrop) by the façade of the Palazzo Poli, an aristocratic mansion dating from the sixteenth century. And in fact the whole of Piazza di Trevi is rather like a theater, with the fountain as the stage. There are steps leading down from the pavement to the edge of the basin, forming a near semi-circle around the fountain, almost like the seating at an ancient Roman arena.

The Trevi Fountain of today is the latest in a series of fountains marking the *mostra* of the *Acqua Vergine*. Leon Battista Alberti built the first one for Pope Nicholas V in 1453. It was nearby in the Piazza dei Crociferi. Pope Pius IV hired Giacomo della Porta to create one in the Piazza di Trevi, and he finished a relatively modest, wall-mounted fountain in 1570. (You'll meet Giacomo della Porta often in this book. Besides numerous fountains, he designed many important buildings and completed his friend Michelangelo's Dome of Saint Peter's.)

The present monumental fountain's creation dates from 1730. Pope Clement XII invited several architects to create designs for a new fountain; in the end, he awarded

The Trevi Fountain: The papal inscription honors Pope Clement XII, who commissioned the fountain in 1740, but it was Clement XIII who unveiled it 32 years later.

the job to a relative unknown, Nicola Salvi. (The pope financed the project with the proceeds from a popular papal lottery!)

Water first reached the new Trevi in 1743, although the fountain was far from complete. Nicola Salvi died in 1751, his health allegedly ruined by too much time spent in the damp conduits leading to the site. He was succeeded as the fountain's architect by Giuseppe Pannini, who saw the project to completion. The great sculptor Pietro Bracci (and several others) carved the monumental figures Salvi had designed, and the completed fountain was unveiled in 1762 by Pope Clement XIII, 32 years after Nicola Salvi won the design contest.

The fountain's name is said to derive from the Latin *Trivium*, meaning "the crossing of three streets," possibly referring to the former crossroads of via dei Crociferi, via Poli and via delle Muratte. And although the Trevi still uses water from the *Acqua Vergine* aqueduct, nowadays the water is stored in a tank and recycled. A modern supplemental aqueduct from the same general source as *Acqua Vergine* was completed in 1937 and named the *Acqua Vergine Nuova*, which supplies a number of other fountains.

If you'd like a bird's-eye view of the Trevi, ask the staff at the Hotel Fontana, right on the piazza. They'll take you to a top-floor "bar" with one table—but it has a view!—where you can enjoy a drink and take all the pictures you want. The price is commensurate with the view!

The Trevi Fountain: The fountain's ability to attract tourists by the millions means that the narrow, once-quiet surrounding streets are filled with souvenir stalls.

The route to our next stop, the Fountain of Monte Cavallo, begins in front of the little Baroque Church of Santi Vincenzo e Anastasio a Trevi, overlooking the Trevi Fountain at the corner of via del Lavatore and via di San Vincenzo. The church is unusual for a couple of reasons: the viscera (removed before embalming) of twenty-two popes, from Sixtus V to Leo XIII, are stored here in urns, and on either side of the attic story is a bare-breasted caryatid supporting a pillar capital on her head—a rare theme for church architecture.

Follow via di San Vincenzo past the church. Or, if you are willing to take a small detour underground, you can visit some well-preserved second-century apartments and an ancient Castellum Aquae—*a holding tank (complete with water) of the original* Aqua Virgo *aqueduct—both 30 feet beneath the street. They were discovered in 1999 during renovations of the old Trevi Cinema. The investors behind the theater renovations decided instead to fund excavation of this curious archeological site, which is called the* Vicus Caprarius *(City of Water). It's cool on a hot day and fascinating anytime. Check the website, www.vicuscaprarius.com, for opening times.*

Skip this paragraph if you want to continue without the detour. *To visit the Vicus Caprarius, turn left into a narrow alley, Vicolo dei Modelli, just past the church, and then turn right on Vicolo del Puttarello. The entrance is at number 25. After your visit, return to via di San Vincenzo by turning right as you exit from the Vicus*

Caprarius onto Vicolo del Puttarello and then, at the end of the street, right again on Vicolo del Babuccio, which ends at via di San Vincenzo.

To resume, whether you visited the Vicus or not: Continuing on via di San Vincenzo, you'll come almost immediately to via della Dataria, where you will turn left. After about 200 yards, in front of a grand flight of stairs, the street curves to the right. Rather than following the curve, go up the stairs. The building on the left is an annex to the Quirinal Palace, the official residence of the president of Italy (and previously the pope's summer palace). The annex, called the Palazzo della Panetteria because the papal bakery was nearby, ends where you'll see a squat, round tower at the top of the stair. This is where the actual presidential palace begins.

The tower was built in 1626 by Pope Urban VIII for defensive purposes, but two centuries later, in 1809, Napoleon's forces stormed the palace. The tower didn't seem to help, because they kidnapped the then-current pope, Pius VII, who had excommunicated Napoleon for annexing the Papal States. Napoleon evidently held a grudge, because he kept Pius a prisoner until 1814.

Past Urban VIII's tower, you will enter a vast square, the Piazza del Quirinale, and across it, to your right, you'll see a fountain ensemble made from several ancient works of stunning virtuosity.

Let us consider the long history of the Quirinal Hill before we meet the famous fountain:

The Quirinal is the highest of the seven hills of Rome, and, in a city where the summers can be uncomfortably hot, property at an altitude with reliable breezes is of course quite desirable. So, ever since the days of the Roman Republic, the hilltop has been valuable real estate. Temples were built there, and luxurious villas of wealthy patricians crowded the site. Constantine, the first Christian emperor, had a large bath complex created there, convenient for his upper-crust neighbors. Needless to say, elegant art was part of the design, so much so that a superb colossal sculptural group consisting of two muscular male nudes, each controlling a spirited, prancing horse (though the reins have long since disappeared), survived even through the long medieval years and into the Renaissance. In fact, the horses were so magnificent that the Quirinal gained the popular name *Monte Cavallo*. (*Cavallo* is "horse" in Italian.)

The two horse tamers are thought to be the *Dioscuri*, Castor and Pollux, born to an adventurous young woman named Leda after she was visited by Zeus in the form of a swan—though in some versions of the story Castor was the son of a mortal father and Pollux was the demigod son of Zeus (Leda evidently had a complicated love life!). Anyhow, after two very eventful mythic lives, the brothers can still be seen in the northern sky as the constellation *Gemini* (the Twins).

Cardinal Ippolito d'Este liked the neighborhood well enough to purchase some property from the Carafa family and build himself a summer getaway there. Ippolito was a son of Lucrezia Borgia and Duke Alfonso I of Ferrara. He had a knack for garden design and created a pleasant space on the hill, which he called Villa d'Este. But he soon was appointed governor of Tivoli, sold his villa to Pope Gregory XIII, and created an even more delightful Villa d'Este in Tivoli, with gardens famous for hundreds of spectacular, ingenious, and bizarre fountains (http://www.villadestetivoli.info).

Pope Gregory enlarged and expanded the property on Monte Cavallo into a true palace, and for centuries the Quirinal Palace was an official residence of the popes. Gregory XIII died in 1585, aged eighty-three, with a considerably more important legacy: he created (or at least commissioned the creation of) the Gregorian calendar—a reworking of the Julian calendar of Julius Caesar—which we still use today.

The Fountain of Monte Cavallo—La Fontana di Monte Cavallo, aka La Fontana dei Dioscuri (ca. 1819, assembled from ancient pieces)

ARCHITECTS: UNKNOWN EGYPTIAN OBELISK MAKER (FIRST CENTURY AD); UNKNOWN ROMAN SCULPTOR (FOURTH CENTURY AD); DOMINICO FONTANA (SIXTEENTH CENTURY AD); GIOVANNI ANTINORI (EIGHTEENTH CENTURY AD); RAFFAELE STERN (NINETEENTH CENTURY AD)

Gregory was succeeded as pope by Felice Peretti, who took the name Sixtus V. Sixtus sponsored the construction of a much-needed new aqueduct for Rome, which he named after himself: *Acqua Felice*. And, since he had a new source of water, he

The Monte Cavallo Fountain: Castor and Pollux, twin sons of Leda and Zeus, have stood with their horses on the Quirinal for 18 centuries, so admired that they survived while thousands of other marbles were burned to make lime.

looked out the window of the Quirinal Palace one day and decided to use the twins and their horses as the setting for a fountain.

The horses and their owners had their backs to the palace, but the pope's architect, Dominico Fontana, managed to turn them so that they were at least obliquely facing the building, and he put a large basin with a jet in the center between them. This rather pleasing arrangement (to judge by old engravings)[2] lasted for nearly 200 years until, in 1786, Pope Pius VI heard that an ancient Egyptian obelisk had been excavated near the Mausoleum of Augustus and decided it would look swell between the twins.

The massive marble twins and their horses were moved apart to allow the obelisk to be installed, a task that took four years; in the process, Fontana's basin was destroyed, and the Quirinal was without a fountain for the next thirty-two years, until in 1818 another Pope Pius (this time number VII) hired Raffaele Stern to create a new one.

Happily, Stern found a splendid solution. There was a huge granite basin of ancient Roman origin being used as a watering trough in the Campo Vaccino—in those days the Roman Forum was used for grazing cattle, so it was called the "Field of Cows"—and Stern had it moved to the Quirinal, where it still serves as the unifying focus of the mighty ensemble that is *La Fontana di Monte Cavallo*.

The Monte Cavallo Fountain: The magnificent horse sculptures that accompany the twins gave the Quirinal its other name: *Monte Cavallo.*

Before setting out for our next stop, take a look at the southeast corner of the piazza, behind Castor and Pollux. You'll see the rounded corner of a building with a small balcony attached, surmounted by the flags of Italy and the European Union. This is the former stable block—the *scuderie*—for the Quirinal Palace. It almost looks like the boys are leading their horses out of the stables for a gallop, but, actually, the building is now used for special art exhibitions, so if you see a line of people around the corner, check it out—it might be something worth seeing! Go to https://www.scuderiequirinale.it to see what's on.

Our next destination is a crossroads with a fountain at each corner. It's called, not surprisingly, Le Quattro Fontane—*the Four Fountains.*

Exit from Piazza del Quirinale from the open side, between the fountain and the Quirinal Palace. Go left on via del Quirinale. The side façade of the palace will be on your left, and on your right is a pleasant green park, the Villa Carlo Alberto. You'll see an equestrian statue of Carlo Alberto—Charles Albert of Savoy—in the middle of the park. He was king of Sardinia in the first half of the nineteenth century and father of Victor Emmanuel II, the first king of a united Italy.

A little farther along, past a Carabinieri *headquarters on the right, a semi-circular flight of shallow steps spills from the pedimented, columned entrance of*

The Monte Cavallo Fountain: In antiquity, this huge granite basin was part of the Marforio Fountain in the Forum; later, it was a cattle trough in the Campo Vaccino. Since 1818, it has been the centerpiece of the Monte Cavallo Fountain.

Sant'Andrea al Quirinale, the superb Baroque church that Bernini built for the Jesuits. (I warned you that Bernini was hard to avoid in Rome.) This church is said to have been his favorite of all the churches he designed.

The green, treed area next door is the church's Novitiate Garden, and a few more steps will take you to the intersection where via del Quirinale meets via delle Quattro Fontane. You have arrived at the Four Fountains!

The Four Fountains—Le Quattro Fontane (1588–1593)
ARCHITECTS: PIETRO DA CORTONA AND DOMENICO FONTANA

Felice Peretti, who became Pope Sixtus V, was a man of legendary vigor who used to enjoy long walks along the street named for him, via Felice. Coming from what is now Piazza Barberini, there is an uphill stretch that, on a warm day, might cause an old gentleman, no matter how vigorous, to wish for a drink from a handy fountain. So perhaps it was thirst that first inspired Sixtus with a whimsical thought: The area at the top of the hill, where via Felice met via Pia, was being developed—what if all four buildings at the intersection had their corners truncated, making the crossing a sort of octagonal piazza? And what if all four of the flattened corners were decorated with niches containing elegantly carved fountains? After all, water mains from his *Acqua Felice* were already in place.

The pope's whim became reality, and people who ascend via Felice (now via

The Four Fountains: On the left is the Fountain of Juno; on the right, the Fountain of Diana—two of the fountains making up the *Quattro Fontane*. In the center, via delle Quattro Fontane leads downhill to Piazza Barberini.

delle Quattro Fontane) from Piazza Barberini to its intersection with via Pia (now via del Quirinale south of the corner and via XX Settembre to the north), or, as you have, along via del Quirinale, will come to the four fountains, each with a recumbent allegorical figure within a grotto-like niche.

The northernmost fountain, set in a niche against an outbuilding of the Barberini Gardens, shows the goddess Diana, the huntress—if you look carefully, you can make out the crescent moon (her traditional attribute) in her hair. She's dozing, or perhaps enjoying a daydream of chasing some unfortunate animal through the woods. In her left hand are what may be a couple of small pears (a punning reference to Pope Sixtus V's name, Peretti), and she is leaning on the *trimonzio sistino*, a stylized image of three mountains (a symbol of Sixtus' papacy). The sculpture allegorically represents *Loyalty*, obviously to the pope. The artist who sculpted the figure is not known, though a seventeenth-century etching attributes it to Pietro da Cortona.[3]

In the southern corner, against Francesco Borromini's marvelous little church, *San Carlo alle Quattro Fontane*, is the god of the Tiber River. He's reclining beneath a small tree in front of a grotto filled with stalactites. With his left arm he cradles a cornucopia while pouring water from an amphora with his right. At his feet, a

The Four Fountains: Ignored by a group of pedestrians chatting on the corner, Diana the Huntress snoozes peacefully, no doubt dreaming of racing along with her hounds on the trail of a wild boar.

The Four Fountains: The river god of the Tiber dispenses water on the left; Juno does the same on the right. In the center, Borromini's beautiful little Baroque church, *San Carlo alle Quattro Fontane*, needs its face washed.

she-wolf peeks out from the grotto, and if you get close enough, you can see little Romulus and Remus hiding in the darkness beneath her. If the church is open, step through the door in the center of the undulating façade and be amazed by the intricate geometry of the interior, especially the ethereal dome that seems to float above you, a delicate pattern of elaborately interconnected coffers. This is Baroque style at its most refined.

The eastern fountain features, perhaps, the god of the Arno. The identification with Florence's river can be inferred from the presence of a lion lurking behind the figure's shoulder; one of Florence's traditional symbols is the Marzocco, a lion with the image of a lily in its paws. Whoever the god is, he appears to be leaning on the lion, who looks at him a bit quizzically. Behind the figure there are aquatic plants, perhaps rushes of some sort. This river deity seems to be copying the pose of the Tiber, only backward. He also clutches a cornucopia, but with his right arm, and pours water into his basin with his left.

The figure in the western fountain is probably Juno, and she is usually thought to symbolize strength or fortitude. She's wearing a crown, and she, too, has a lion with her, who must be a literary sort of feline, because he keeps a paw resting on a book while ejecting a stream of water from his mouth into a basin. A peacock flutters its wings (but does not spread its tail) at the goddess' feet. You may recall the old fable, in which the peacock, jealous of the nightingale, begged Juno to replace his raspy voice with a musical one. Juno advised him to be content with the beauty of his feathers.

The Four Fountains: This fellow may be the god of the Arno, if the lion is Marzocco, Florence's traditional lion mascot, who usually holds a lily. I don't see a lily; instead, the lion hiding behind this god's shoulder seems a bit of a shrinking violet.

Some authorities argue that the two goddesses represent rivers, just as the male gods do, but since no one seems to be able to make a plausible identification of just which rivers they personify, I have my doubts. And no one seems to know with certainty who designed and carved the south, east, and west fountains, though Domenico Fontana appears to be the favorite with most scholars. Domenico Fontana, by the way, was the younger brother of Giovanni Fontana, and these two appropriately named architect/engineers had a great impact on the Roman water supply. Giovanni supervised the creation of the *Acqua Felice* aqueduct, and Domenico designed the great Fountain of Moses, which we'll visit in Chapter 2.

The Four Fountains had a much-needed cleaning sometime between 2014 and 2016, but I'm sorry to say that, when I last saw it, the lovely façade of Borromini's church was as grimy as when I first saw it.

From the Four Fountains intersection, three of Rome's thirteen standing obelisks can be seen (if it's a clear day). Look northwest, toward Piazza Barberini, along via Quattro Fontane. At the end of the street in the distance is the *Sallustiano* obelisk, in Piazza Trinità dei Monti above the Spanish Steps. Looking the opposite direction, southeast, along via Quattro Fontane, you will see the *Esquiline* obelisk, behind the church of *Santa Maria Maggiore*. And finally, looking back southwest on via del Quirinale, is the Quirinal obelisk you just visited, between the twins on *Monte Cavallo*.

Here is where our first walk ends. If you don't want to walk to the next group

The Four Fountains: Here's Juno again. She has a lion, too, along with a peacock, her traditional attribute. This one is flapping its wings but appears to have lost its tail.

of fountains in Chapter 2, you can take via delle Quattro Fontane downhill, passing between the two female goddesses, and back to Piazza Barberini. You'll see the entrance to Palazzo Barberini on the right as you walk. The next fountain walk begins in Piazza Repubblica, one stop away from Barberini on the Metro (line A).

If you'd rather postpone fountain hopping to another day, you can use the Metro or buses to get to your lodgings (check www.atac.roma.it) or take a taxi from the stand on the east side of Piazza Barberini.

Or, to walk from the Four Fountains to Piazza Repubblica, you can take via delle Quattro Fontane, passing between the two male river gods in the opposite direction from Piazza Barberini, to via Nazionale; turn left, and continue straight (sempre dritto, *as the Italians say)—altogether, a little over a third of a mile to Piazza Repubblica. Via Nazionale is a busy street usually choked with traffic. You'll pass plenty of shops and several hotels. As you draw nearer, you'll see our next fountain at the end of the street. A block away from Piazza Repubblica at Hotel Quirinale, I often stop for a restorative glass of wine—the bar is quiet and peaceful.*

❧ 2 ❧

Sensuous to Sacred

Piazza Repubblica Area

The walk begins in Piazza della Repubblica.

Piazza della Repubblica is easily reached by Metro, with its own stop on the "A" line.

The piazza's central feature is one of Rome's grandest fountains, featuring water nymphs reveling in the mighty water display. The fountain that showers them sits where once the giant, semi-circular *exedra* (meeting room or theater) of Diocletian's early fourth-century baths stood. In fact, Piazza della Repubblica, until fairly recently, was called Piazza dell'Esedra. You can see the outline of the *exedra* in the curved shape of two handsome arcaded buildings overlooking the fountain; built by Gaetano Koch in 1898, they face, beyond the fountain, the *Basilica di Santa Maria degli Angeli e dei Martiri*. This great church is actually a part of the ruined tepidarium of Diocletian's enormous complex, repurposed by none other than Michelangelo! Let us begin with the fountain in the piazza, and then visit three other historic fountains nearby.

The Fountain of the Naiads—La Fontana delle Naiadi (1888)
Architects: Alessandro Guerrieri and Mario Rutelli

What was once the most notorious of Rome's fountains can be found in the center of Piazza della Repubblica, surrounded by a giant traffic circle droning with almost constant traffic. If you can safely negotiate crossing the roadway and reach the perimeter of the fountain, you can get a close-up view of the reasons for the fountain's naughty reputation: four giant statues of naked water nymphs, three of them in various stages of dreamy abandon while riding on the backs of aquatic animals, while the fourth struggles to control a giant sea horse.

The story of the fountain's creation is a bit complicated. It, too, is the *mostra* of a major aqueduct, just like the Trevi. Its aqueduct is the *Acqua Pia Antica Marcia*, a relative newcomer to Rome, having been commissioned by Pope Pius IX and named

28

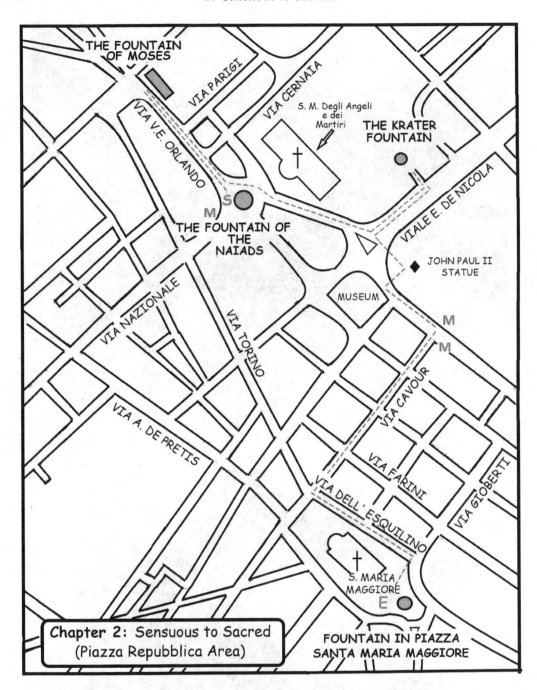

THE FOUNTAIN OF MOSES

VIA PARIGI

VIA CERNAIA

S. M. Degli Angeli e dei Martiri

THE KRATER FOUNTAIN

VIA V.E. ORLANDO

VIALE E. DE NICOLA

M S

THE FOUNTAIN OF THE NAIADS

JOHN PAUL II STATUE

MUSEUM

VIA NAZIONALE

VIA TORINO

M

M

VIA CAVOUR

VIA A. DE PRETIS

VIA FARINI

VIA GIOBERTI

VIA DELL' ESQUILINO

S. MARIA MAGGIORE

E

Chapter 2: Sensuous to Sacred (Piazza Repubblica Area)

FOUNTAIN IN PIAZZA SANTA MARIA MAGGIORE

for him, in 1870, just before he lost control of Rome to the forces of the *Risorgimento. Acqua Pia* has ancient roots, though, since it is a partial reconstruction of an aqueduct that served Rome long ago in the days of the ancient republic. The original *Aqua Marcia* was built around 140 BC under the supervision of a magistrate named Quintus Marcius Rex and named for him. It carried excellent water from about 55 miles east of Rome and was such a marvel of durability that it could still supply the great Baths of Diocletian four and a half centuries later!

Top: The Fountain of the Naiads, seen from via delle Terme di Diocleziano. Glaucus, the demigod fisherman, is in the center, while the Naiad of the Lakes is below, with the Naiad of the Subterranean Waters to the right. *Bottom:* The Naiad of the Oceans, trying to wrestle a wild sea horse into submission.

Originally, the fountain in the piazza was large and imposing, but rather plain. It was so boring, in fact, that before the German kaiser Wilhelm II arrived for a state visit in 1888, four plaster lions were hurriedly placed around the basin to add some interest to the scene. But this half-hearted solution didn't go over well with the people, so the city council hired a Sicilian sculptor named Mario Rutelli to replace the lions with something more interesting—and he did.

There are four figural groups: a "Naiad of the Oceans," trying to wrestle a rearing horse into submission; a "Naiad of the Rivers" happily entangled in the coils of a huge water snake; a "Naiad of the Subterranean Waters" lounging pleasurably on the back of a monstrous amphibian; and a "Naiad of the Lakes" playfully prone on the back of a king-sized bird. (Actually, the nymph of the oceans is a "nereid" rather than a "naiad," since she is a daughter of the sea rather than a lake, river, or marsh. Think of nereids as saltwater nymphs and naiads as the fresh-water variety.)

Rutelli's replacements turned out to be a bit *too* interesting for some people at the time (particularly the clergy), so after they were installed, the figures were hidden behind a wooden screen while the city council debated whether to keep them or start over. Finally, on the last Sunday of Carnival in 1901, a crowd of celebrants carried Rutelli in triumph from his hotel to the fountain, tore down the fence, and introduced the naiads to Rome. Despite some lingering complaints, the fountain has been one of the city's most popular sights ever since.[1]

The Fountain of the Naiads: The Naiad of the Rivers, entangled in the coils of a giant water snake.

Rutelli's first attempt at the central figure was not so popular, however. Three men, an octopus, and a dolphin spouting water high in the air were entwined in a confusing tangle. The Romans nicknamed it *Rutelli's fritto misto*, or "mixed fish-fry," and Rutelli soon replaced this group with a single figure: Glaucus, the mythical fisherman who became a sea god, holding another spouting dolphin. The *fritto misto* was deposited in Piazza Vittorio Emanuele on the Esquiline Hill, where you can still see it today. It was neglected for many years but has recently been given a bit of restoration.

The four nymphs bear a strong resemblance to one another. The identity of Rutelli's model (or models) has been debated for years. In the 1960s, the writer H.V. Morton traveled to a hilltop town called Anticolo Corrado, near Rome, between the source of the *Aqua Marcia* and the city. The town was famous in the nineteenth century because many of its inhabitants (said to descend from Saracens) would come to Rome and congregate at the foot of the Spanish Steps, where they might be hired, for their exotic looks, to pose for one of the many British or American artists working in the area.

Morton, in his book *The Fountains of Rome*, says that he was told by villagers in Anticolo Corrado that a local girl, Vittoria Placidi, was the original of all four of the nymphs.[2] But Mario Rutelli's great-grandson, the politician Francesco Rutelli (twice

The Fountain of the Naiads: The Naiad of the Subterranean Waters, relaxing on the back of a giant lizard.

mayor of Rome in the 1990s), stated in an interview that the sculptor used a number of models. (However, he did admit that his great-grandfather might have led one or two of the models to believe that she was his only muse.)[3]

The villagers told Morton that Vittoria had died long before her beauty could fade. In any case, even if she was only one of Rutelli's inspirations, her allure still lives on in Piazza della Repubblica.

Our next stop is a grand fountain that serves as the mostra *for an aqueduct completed in the late sixteenth century and unveiled with great fanfare and some embarrassment in 1587. To get there, you must exit Piazza Repubblica onto via Vittorio Emanuele Orlando. Just make sure you're leaving on the side of the fountain featuring the Naiad of the Rivers. She's the one reclining on her back, with her left arm raised to grasp the tail of her reptilian friend. You'll see "Le Grand Hotel" ahead on the right. (It's actually the St. Regis, but Cesar Ritz opened it in 1894 as the Grand Hotel.) After 200 yards or so, you'll see the fountain on your right, with a row of lions spitting water into a pool. By the way, past the fountain and across via Venti Settembre is the church of* Santa Maria della Vittoria. *Bernini alert! Inside is his sculpture—nowadays it would be called an installation—of Saint Teresa of Avila in ecstasy as an angel pierces her heart with an arrow, while golden beams of light illuminate the scene and sculpted onlookers gaze from balconies. But first, the fountain:*

The Fountain of the Naiads: The Naiad of the Lakes, far more interested in wildfowl ornithology than a naiad should be.

The Fountain of Moses—La Fontana dell'Acqua Felice (1587)
ARCHITECT: DOMINICO FONTANA

Officially, it's *La Fontana dell'Acqua Felice*, because it is the terminus, the *mostra*, of the aqueduct that Felice Peretti—Pope Sixtus V—named after himself. Running underground and then on the ancient arches of *Aqua Alexandrina*, *Aqua Claudia* and *Aqua Marcia*, the waters of *Acqua Felice* flow from an aquifer about 15 miles east of central Rome, and though it borrowed the use of some ancient structures, it was a brand-new water source for Rome, unlike the restored *Acqua Vergine*.

The fountain is an impressive structure, though the best view of it is across Largo Santa Susanna as you stand in a sea of parked motorbikes in Piazza di San Bernardo. At this distance, you can admire the three great marble arches from which the waters gush forth triumphantly. You can imagine the joy of those at the unveiling, in 1587, as the first "new water" flowed into Rome since the days of the Caesars.

The three arches are "blind"—they are not passageways and are blocked by walls. In the left arch, as you face the fountain, there is a scene carved in relief: *Aaron Leading the Jews to Drink*, by Giovanni Battista della Porta, which shows the Israelites enjoying the miraculous water Moses brought out of the rock. In the right arch,

The Fountain of Moses: Beyond all the bikes is *La Fontana dell'Acqua Felice*—it's the building with the three arches. In English, it's usually called the Moses Fountain. Now, where did I park my *motociclo*?

some writers have seen Gideon testing his soldiers before battling the Midianites (it's a biblical story from the book of Judges if you're curious), but most believe it's actually *Joshua Leads the Jews Across the Dry Jordan River*, by Flaminio Vacca.

But there was almost universal agreement about the middle arch, in which there is a monumental statue of Moses, gesturing downward with his right hand—it originally held a rod—with which he summons water (now flowing beneath his feet) from a rock.[4] With his left hand he props two stone tablets on his hip. The tablets presumably contain the Ten Commandments, which is a bit of a problem since his meeting with God on Mt. Sinai took place years after Moses—or, rather, God—brought forth water from the stone. Still, it wasn't just a chronological mix-up that caused a cascade of catcalls when the statue was revealed to the public.

You can read in many histories how the sculptor, Prospero Antichi, created the figure of Moses from a block of marble lying flat on the ground, rather than an upright stone; as a result, he got the proportions wrong, so that the statue, when raised, turned out to show Moses as a huge, squat, ungainly figure with a menacing, rather manic expression on his face. The story claims that Antichi was so distraught at the universal criticism that he begged Pope Sixtus to allow him to rework the statue, but the fierce old pontiff refused. Unable to face such disgrace, the poor man wasted away and died.

I'm happy to report that this story is probably untrue; in fact, Antichi may not have even been the sculptor; some sources give the credit (or blame) to Leonardo Sormani.[5] I like the ferocious and portly Moses, actually. Who can blame a prophet

The Fountain of Moses: Moses is in the middle arch, with biblical scenes in the side arches. In 1587, the figure of Moses caught a lot of criticism—too fat, too grumpy looking—but everybody loves the lions.

for having a second helping of manna now and then and being a bit frazzled and impatient if he has to lead a whole tribe of people across a barren desert where the only water seems to be locked up in stones?

The Romans now seem to regard the fountain with affection in spite of its perceived imperfections. In fact, it's actually a pleasure to stroll along the sidewalk fronting the water-filled basins below the arches. There are four Egyptian-style basalt lions, each one contentedly relaxing, paws crossed, beneath the four columns that separate the fountain's arches. Each lion spits a curving stream of water into his basin while eyeing passersby with a somewhat self-satisfied expression.

The lions are copies, made by Adamo Tadolini, a talented follower of Antonio Canova, in 1850. Tadolini made four lions, based on two originals that were carved in Egypt in the fourth century BC for Pharaoh Nectanebo II. The originals were brought to Rome as spoils of war sometime in antiquity to decorate the ancient Temple of Isis near the Pantheon. Excavated in the fifteenth century, they stood in front of the Pantheon until they were "borrowed" to adorn the Fountain of Moses in 1587. They are now in the Vatican Museums, in the Cortile della Pigna, below the Pigna Fountain, where they are no longer required to spout water. But Tadolini's splendid copies carry on the tradition. (By the way, you'll have a chance to visit the studio that Tadolini shared with Canova, and even enjoy a meal there, in Chapter 3.)

An inscription on the entablature above the arches also expresses a bit of well-deserved self-satisfaction: "Pope Sixtus V, of the Marches, conducted this water from a junction of several streams in the neighborhood of Colonna, at the

The Fountain of Moses: The lions are copies of Egyptian originals made for Pharaoh Nectanebo II in the fourth century BC. Are they identical? Actually, the two on the left are mirror images of the two on the right.

The Fountain of Moses: These excellent copies look so content, you might think they have been here forever, but they're less than 200 years old. The originals, now in the Vatican Museums, were carved about 2,500 years ago.

left of the Praenestine road, by a winding route, twenty miles from its reservoir and twenty-two from its source, and called it Felix, after the name he himself bore before his pontificate. He commenced the work in the first year of his pontificate, and finished it in the third, 1587."

The next fountain is an unusual one, a giant wine vessel converted to a moss-covered fountain in the middle of a quiet garden. To reach it, retrace your steps to the Fountain of the Naiads; then bear left around the fountain, passing between the church, Santa Maria degli Angeli e dei Martiri, *and the Naiad of the Subterranean Waters, who is reclining on her side, hands clasped behind her head, atop her giant lizard. Continue out of Piazza Repubblica, bearing slightly left into viale Luigi Einaudi. Be sure to take advantage of the wide left-hand sidewalk bordering the busy street. After about 500 feet, at a major intersection, bear left again, staying on the sidewalk, and you'll be on via Enrico de Nicola. Ever since you left Piazza Repubblica, you've been passing the ancient red-brick buildings of Diocletian's baths on your left. Notice the tall metal fence protecting them. After another few hundred feet, you'll find a gate in the fence marked* Terme di Dioclenziano. *This is the entrance to the part of the National Roman Museum featuring the Baths of Diocletian. Enter through the gate and continue straight ahead, under a trellis draped with vines, and you'll be in the garden forecourt of the baths. You'll see the fountain beneath the trees. Beyond it is the museum's ticket office—handy should you decide to spend the rest of the day exploring the gigantic complex. Otherwise, relax on a garden bench and admire the fountain.*

The Krater Fountain in the Baths of Diocletian—
Il Cratere Colossale (third century AD?)
ARCHITECT: UNKNOWN

There were many public bath complexes in ancient Rome. Diocletian built one of the largest on the Viminal Hill, and, as we've seen, Piazza Repubblica takes the shape of one of the bath's *exedrae*. This particular *exedra* was a huge semi-circular room on one side of the baths, where bathers (as many as 3,000 people used the baths every day) could relax on benches, read, or visit with friends after working out in an exercise area and bathing in a series of hot and cold pools. The baths were built between 298 and 306 AD and, of course, were named for Emperor Diocletian. Visiting the baths could take a whole day if visitors took advantage of all the facilities: the structure spread out over thirty-two square acres! Water came from the great *Aqua Marcia* aqueduct, which was already more than 400 years old by the time the baths were completed. The baths continued to operate until the sturdy old aqueduct was cut by the Ostrogoths in 537 AD.

In Renaissance times, parts of the ancient buildings were converted to religious uses. The round church of *San Bernardo alle Terme*, not far from the Fountain of Moses, was once a circular tower in the walls of the bath complex. In the sixteenth century, Michelangelo converted the frigidarium of the baths into the

The Krater Fountain: This giant version of the traditional Greek *krater*, or "mixing vessel,"
also served as a fountain in antiquity. Ordinary-sized kraters were used to mix wine with
water.

church of *Santa Maria degli Angeli e dei Martiri.* Next to the church was a small cloister and a charterhouse for a community of Carthusian monks. The cloister occupied part of what once was a large *natatio,* a kind of swimming pool in the ancient baths. The charterhouse's main cloister, called the Michelangelo Cloister, is much larger.

Today, the Baths of Diocletian are part of the National Roman Museum (https:// museonazionaleromano.beniculturali.it), and, in addition to viewing parts of the monumental architectural site, visitors can enjoy an Epigraphical Museum (10,000 ancient Roman inscriptions!) and a Protohistorical Museum with thousands of artifacts from life in the area before Romulus and Remus. From the great days of the Roman Republic and the Empire, there are over 400 splendid sculptures displayed, including (in the Michelangelo Cloister) seven colossal stone animal heads from the area of Trajan's Market.

Ancient columns and statuary, as well as handy shaded stone benches, greet visitors on their way to the ticket office. Marking the path is a large *krater,* or "mixing vessel" in Greek. Such vessels were used traditionally to mix water and wine—a common practice in antiquity. This vessel could have produced enough watered-down wine to provide a happy weekend and a hungover Monday for a small city! Today, the Krater sits on a mossy pedestal and dispenses delicate arcs of water (unmixed with wine) into a quiet circular pool.

Actually, the Krater was used as a fountain even in ancient times, though no one seems to know where it stood in antiquity. In medieval times, it was located in front of the basilica of *Santi Apostoli* on the western slope of the Quirinal Hill. Vessels like it are extremely rare, and this one is unique. There is another monumental vase used as a fountain, in front of the Church of Santa Cecilia in Trastevere, but its design is quite different. The Krater has decorated the garden of the Baths of Diocletian since the 1890s.

The last fountain on our itinerary today is historic, but the church in whose forecourt it lives is even more historic and might not exist now except for a snowstorm in August long ago.

So, exit the Krater Fountain's garden from the gate through which you entered. Turn right on via Enrico de Nicola's sidewalk, and, after about 100 yards, just before the road takes a wide turn to the right, look for a crosswalk to your left. Cross the street toward a large green-patinated bronze statue of Pope John Paul II.

Once across, turn right, passing in front of the statue and head for the grand Palazzo Massimo straight ahead. There are three roadways to cross before you reach the wide paved area in front of the palace. Fortunately, there are crosswalks for each one. Turn left in front of the palazzo, unless you'd like to visit the museum inside the building. (Look for the entrance around the corner to your right, but come back here afterward.) It's worth the detour, and here's a short preview:

The Palazzo Massimo is one part of the National Roman Museum. There are four different parts of the museum, each telling the engrossing story of Rome through art and archeology. You may have already visited the Baths of Diocletian; besides the Palazzo Massimo, there are two other sites: *Crypta Balbi,* an excavated Roman neighborhood and theater, and *Palazzo Altemps,* a sixteenth-century mansion stuffed to the gills with art, especially sculpture. They are separate venues within central Rome.

The Palazzo Massimo contains ancient Roman frescoes, mosaics, sculptures and even re-creations of aristocratic and imperial homes, decorated with art taken from the structures on the Palatine Hill. A whole room, frescoed with flowers, birds, and fruit trees, came from the villa that belonged to Livia, Augustus' wife. Her husband is in the building, too, in marble, dressed in his priestly *Pontifex Maximus* robes. (It's interesting that his ancient pagan title, which means "Chief High Priest," is still used—by the pope!) Another unforgettable masterpiece, a Hellenic sculpture of a battered, exhausted boxer, speaks to the unchanging reality of human anguish. You won't forget him. If you can spare it, your time in the palazzo will not be wasted.

Whether or not you've visited the museum, continue along the sidewalk as above. Cross via d'Azeglio, and on your right will be a block-long building with a series of arches along its front, forming an arcade that shelters a number of bars and shops. It's safer to walk inside the arches, out of the traffic. Once past the arcade, the first street on the right is via Cavour. Turn right here, and, after four blocks, you will see a tall obelisk, topped with a cross, in the center of a large piazza. Behind the obelisk is the papal basilica of Santa Maria Maggiore, *though you're looking at the apse end. Our fountain is around the church, at the front.*

So, turn left and follow Piazza dell'Esquilino along the left side of the church. After about 200 yards (yes, it's a big church!), you'll see on your right a tall, fluted column, with Mary on top—you'll recognize her from her halo. The column stands in Piazza Santa Maria Maggiore, and the fountain is at the column's base.

First, let me introduce the great church:

According to tradition, the Virgin Mary appeared to Pope Liberius in a dream one summer night in 356 AD. She told him that he should build her a church in Rome and that a miraculous sign would tell him where to build it. The next day, August 5, snow fell on the Esquiline Hill, and the pope, recognizing that snow in August in Rome was definitely a miracle, marked out the dimensions of the church in the snow. A wealthy patrician named Giovanni, to whom Mary had also appeared in a dream, financed the construction of the church, which became known as *Santa Maria delle Neve* (Saint Mary of the Snows).

However, archeological investigation indicates that the basilica was built under Pope Sixtus III, who, when it was completed in 431, dedicated it to Mary. However, there is an interesting line in the ancient chronicle called *Liber Pontificalis*, which contains biographies of the popes who came after Saint Peter. About Pope Liberius, the chronicle says, "*fecit basilicam nomini suo iuxta Macellum Liviae*," or, roughly, "he made this basilica named for him around the Market [or slaughterhouse] of Livia."[6] The Market of Livia was a trading area on the Esquiline Hill from the time of Augustus.

Santa Maria Maggiore is one of the four patriarchal basilicas of Rome. It is the largest church in Rome dedicated to the Virgin Mary (hence the name Santa Maria *Maggiore*) and the only one of the four that retains some of its early Christian decoration. Despite many renovations over the centuries, the nave and the two flanking aisles are divided by the same monumental columns as the original church, and flanking the apse are mosaics from the fifth century. The mosaics in the apse itself, depicting the coronation of the Virgin as queen of heaven, date from the thirteenth century. There are many other notable works of art in the church, and the tomb of one of Rome's most influential artists is marked by a very modest marble slab on the floor. "IOANNES LAVRENTIVS BERNINI" is carved in the stone: *Gian Lorenzo Bernini.*

Speaking of tombs, Pope Paul V is buried in a funerary chapel off the left aisle. Sixtus V's tomb is found off the right aisle; his *Cappella Sistina* (not to be confused with the Sistine Chapel in the Vatican) also houses the tomb of Pope Pius V. These three popes share a distinction important to us: each of them sponsored the creation or reconstruction of the three first aqueducts that brought water back to Rome in the Renaissance.[7]

About the piazzas at either end of the church: At the apse end is Piazza Esquilino, in the middle of which is the obelisk you saw earlier, nearly 85 feet high with its pedestal. It isn't Egyptian, though. It was made by the Romans and once guarded Augustus' mausoleum, along with a twin obelisk on the other side of the mausoleum's main door. It was installed here behind the church in 1587 by Pope Sixtus V. But the fountain we seek is in the other piazza.

The Fountain in Piazza Santa Maria Maggiore—
La Fontana di Piazza Santa Maria Maggiore (1613–1615)
ARCHITECT: CARLO MADERNO

Facing the front of the church is Piazza di Santa Maria Maggiore. There was a simple fountain in the middle of the square in medieval times, which served as a water source for people living around the church—at least when water was flowing in Rome's usually crippled aqueducts. However, in 1613, Pope Paul V decided to change all that. First, he commissioned Carlo Maderno to move a huge, fluted column (which had stood since antiquity in the Forum, at the Basilica of Maxentius) and erect it in the center of the piazza. Maderno topped the column with a statue of Mary, made from bronze melted down from a structure that once surrounded the famous "Pigna" fountain in the courtyard of Old Saint Peter's. (We will visit the Pigna Fountain when we explore the Vatican area.)

Then Maderno attached a fountain, in the shape of a large oval basin of marble, to one side of the column's base. At the ends of the basin were once carved dragons, from which water spouted; at the middle point of each of the sides, Maderno placed carved eagles, with spread wings, which also spouted water into small side basins. Below the eagles were small grotesque faces, and in the center of the large basin, a small, round bowl on a stout pedestal rising from the pool dispensed water from holes in its sides. Sometime in the nineteenth century, the dragons disappeared, and the small bowl was replaced by a larger one; however, the fountain still provides visitors with water, and pilgrims with a noble welcome, as it has for four centuries.

We've reached the end of our second tour. If you do not wish to begin the next chapter's walk immediately, here are some suggestions for returning to your lodgings:

Top: The Fountain in Piazza Santa Maria Maggiore sits beneath its tall column. The pink building is the Upim Department Store. If you were standing here, the great church would be on your left. *Bottom:* The upper basin of the fountain, with the front façade of the *Basilica di Santa Maria Maggiore* in the background. Barricades and soldiers are a common sight nowadays near historic buildings.

The Fountain in Piazza Santa Maria Maggiore: The fountain and its column, seen from the porch of the basilica. The column once graced the Basilica of Maxentius, in Rome's pre–Christian days; Pope Paul V moved it here and topped it with a statue of Mary.

An entrance to the Termini Metro can be found where you first turned onto via Cavour on your way to the fountain. Piazza dei Cinquecento, next to Termini, is a major city bus terminal. There are tram and bus stops on via Farini and via Napoleone III, one block to your right along via Gioberti as you face the church. You can also check for a bus route to your lodgings at www.atac.roma.it, or look for a taxi next to the left flank of the church as you face the front façade.

If you want to start the next itinerary immediately, I recommend that you take the Metro (line A) from Termini, as above, to the Spagna stop, rather than walking to Piazza di Spagna.

3

Queen Christina's Cannonball
to Audrey Hepburn's Sleepover

Piazza di Spagna Area

THE WALK BEGINS IN PIAZZA DI SPAGNA.

If you took the Metro to the Spagna stop to begin this itinerary, take the station exit marked Piazza di Spagna. At the end of the rather long tunnel, you'll find yourself in Vicolo del Bottino, a short alleyway leading from the Metro exit to Piazza di Spagna. Turn left at the end of the alley. Ahead, you'll probably see a crowd of people clustered thickly in the middle of the piazza; you may even get a glimpse of something looking like a low marble fountain. It's La Barcaccia (the Little Boat Fountain), but never mind—you can look at it later when you will have a better view. On the left there are stairs leading uphill toward a church at the top; they're the Spanish Steps, of course. Before you climb them, though, a little background:

Several years ago, I bought a book of antique views of Rome, at a bookstall near the Baths of Diocletian. In it, there is an engraving from 1640, showing the church of *Trinità dei Monti* at the top of a rather muddy slope, with winding, footworn trails leading to the church's double staircase.[1] Clearly parishioners had created their own switchback routes to avoid the steep central approach from the piazza at the bottom of the hill. The piazza was not known as Piazza di Spagna in those days—it was named after the church (Piazza della Trinità dei Monti)—and the Spanish Steps had not yet replaced the muddy slope. But the fountain known as *La Barcaccia* was already there, having been designed and built by Pietro Bernini (probably with help from his son Gian Lorenzo) in 1627.

Since the Baroque stairs that were finally built between 1723 and 1725, linking the church with the piazza below, were designed by an Italian, Francesco de Sanctis, and financed by a French diplomat named Étienne Gueffier, why are they called the Spanish Steps? Well, it's for the same reason that Piazza della Trinità dei Monti assumed the name "Piazza di Spagna" after 1647, when the Palazzo Monaldeschi, at the southern end of the piazza, became the home of the Spanish Embassy to the Holy See. The embassy, bordering the square, gave the Spanish moniker to the piazza, and the piazza's name was adapted to the stairs. However, the Romans don't call

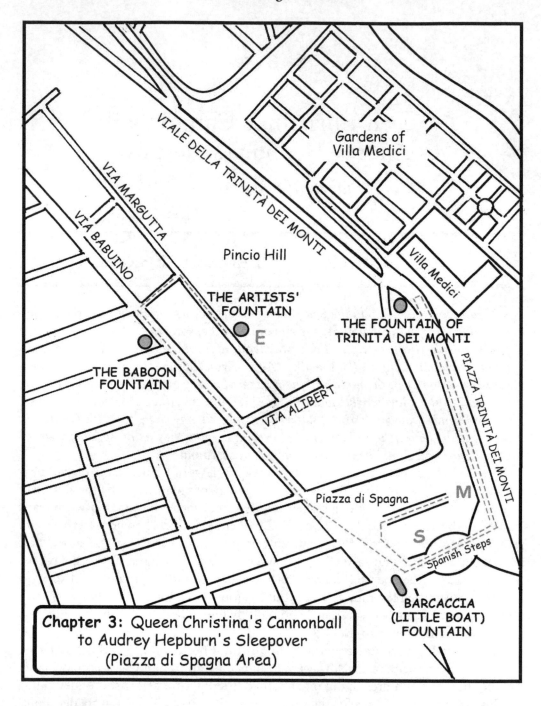

Chapter 3: Queen Christina's Cannonball
to Audrey Hepburn's Sleepover
(Piazza di Spagna Area)

the stairs the "Spanish Steps"; they call the staircase the *Scalinata della Trinità dei Monti*—unless they're giving directions to a tourist, of course.

Since a recent cleaning in 2019, the city administration has outlawed sitting on the steps, so as you go up, don't sit down! Near the top, the stairs divide into two flights around a convex wall; take the left flight, and when you reach the street above, you'll notice to your right a tall obelisk. It's not Egyptian, though. Called the Obelisco

Sallustiano, it's a Roman copy made in the first century BC *for the private garden of an important early historian and wealthy aristocrat named Sallust.*

At the top of the steps, turn left and proceed along the street, Piazza della Trinità dei Monti, for a few hundred yards. You'll find a quiet fountain among a group of handsome oak trees on the left, across the street from the façade of Villa Medici.

The Fountain of Trinità dei Monti—La Fontana di Trinità dei Monti, aka the Villa Medici Fountain (1587)
ARCHITECT: ANNIBALE LIPPI

This fountain, which sits on the edge of the Pincian Hill, in front of the Villa Medici, is also sometimes called *La Fontana della Palla di Cannone* (the Fountain of the Cannonball). There is in fact a spherical object in the center of its ancient granite basin, which *might* have begun its existence as a cannonball, but I cannot guarantee that the traditional story of how it came to be in the fountain is true. It seems (so goes the tale) that Queen Christina of Sweden was staying in Castel Sant'Angelo.

The Fountain of Trinità dei Monti: Named for the church at the top of the Spanish Steps, it actually stands a few hundred yards away, among a quiet group of oak trees, in front of the Villa Medici.

(You'll recall that Christina had converted from Protestantism to Catholicism and moved to Rome in 1655.) Anyway, she had an appointment with a friend of hers, a French painter named Charles Errand, the director of the French Academy in Rome; when Errand failed to arrive on time at Castel Sant'Angelo, Christina fired a cannon from the roof of the castle and scored a direct hit on the front door of Villa Medici. The ball was placed in the fountain in commemoration of her marksmanship. (As well it should—I don't know exactly how far it is from Castel Sant'Angelo to Villa Medici as the cannonball flies, but it must be half a mile at least!)

There once was a panoramic view of Rome from the terrace here, but the view is now largely blocked by trees, though there is still a limited vista. Villa Medici itself is worth a look (by appointment—consult www.villamedici.it) and has a colorful history. In ancient Roman times, the site was part of the Gardens of Lucullus, and then for centuries it was covered by grapevines. In the mid–sixteenth century, Cardinal Ricci di Montepulciano had the present villa designed and built by Annibale Lippi. Later, the enthusiastic collector Ferdinand de' Medici, grand duke of Tuscany, acquired the property, and its extensive gardens became home to a collection of ancient sculptures and fountains. Most of the sculptures ultimately found their way to Florence and the Uffizi—luckily before Napoleon occupied Rome and transferred

The Fountain of Trinità dei Monti: The "cannonball" in the center of the Fountain of Trinità dei Monti. A popular legend says that Queen Christina of Sweden's lunch date was late picking her up, so she woke him up by firing a cannon from Castel Sant'Angelo and hit the door of Villa Medici.

the French Academy in Rome to the villa. Otherwise, the priceless sculptures would probably be at the Louvre in Paris.[2]

Today, Villa Medici still belongs to the French Academy, and it houses young artists-in-residence who receive board and lodging for six to eighteen months while honing their skills. It is sometimes open to the public for special events and exhibitions.

The fountain is featured in Respighi's symphonic poem, *The Fountains of Rome*, in the fourth movement of the piece, "The Villa Medici Fountain at Sunset."

I suggest that now we return to the top of the Spanish Steps, under the obelisk. At this point, if you're interested and it happens to be open, you have a chance to visit the Trinità dei Monti church. It belongs to the French government, the site having been purchased by King Charles VIII of France just before he invaded Italy in 1494.

When you're ready, descend the Spanish Steps, and you'll have an excellent bird's-eye view of that crowded fountain you glimpsed in Piazza di Spagna; you can also enjoy mingling with the happy crowd in the piazza, always keeping in mind that pickpockets like to mingle, too.

The Little Boat Fountain—La Barcaccia (1627)
Architect: Pietro Bernini (assisted by Gian Lorenzo Bernini?)[3]

In the eighteenth and nineteenth centuries, Piazza di Spagna was sometimes called "the English ghetto" because of its popularity with British grand tourists and

La Barcaccia (the "Little Boat Fountain"). Made by Gian Lorenzo Bernini's dad, Pietro, it always draws a crowd in Piazza di Spagna.

expatriates, and it's still popular. So it is no surprise that, at number 23, you'll find that Babington's Tea Room (established by two Englishwomen in 1893) is still in business. As you face the steps, it's in the building just to the left. In the building to the right of the stairs, at number 26, is the flat where the great poet John Keats died in 1821; he was twenty-five years old. The building now houses the Keats-Shelley Memorial House (www.ksh.roma.it), a museum dedicated to the two poets. At number 31 is the house museum of the artist Giorgio de Chirico (https://fondazionedechirico. org/), godfather of surrealism. And at number 46 you'll find McDonald's if you need a Big Mac—but don't eat it on the steps. *Severamente vietato!* (Strictly forbidden!)

La Barcaccia, the "Little Boat Fountain," is a low, shallow fountain consisting of a large oval basin, within which there is a smaller basin in the form of a boat with a high, carved prow at either end. In the middle of the boat is an even smaller basin elevated on a marble stem; water spouts upward from a metal nozzle in the small basin, which fills and then overflows into the "boat," which in turn overflows into the large basin. The effect, to me, is rather like seeing Captain Nemo's lifeboat sinking in a bathtub.

The boat was commissioned by Pope Urban VIII, so it is not surprising that the prows of the boat are decorated, in carved relief, with papal tiaras and insignia bearing the Barberini bees. On the inner surface are carved sun discs with human faces, which also spout water into the boat. It is *severamente vietato* to wade into the water, and bollards connected by a low metal railing protect the fountain, which has

La Barcaccia: Whimsical and a bit childlike, *La Barcaccia* looks like it would be fun for kids to wade in on a hot summer day. Alas, that is definitely *severamente vietato*—strictly forbidden!

been vandalized from time to time. Early one morning, though, before the crowds arrived, I saw a fellow retrieving coins from the fountain with a long, flexible pole with, apparently, some kind of adhesive or magnetic substance on the tip. The occupants of a nearby police car watched him for nearly half an hour before rather gently chasing him away—with, it appeared, his catch safely in his pocket.

As I previously mentioned, it has recently been decreed by the Roman authorities that the long-standing tradition—honored for nearly three centuries—of sitting on the Spanish Steps is no longer permitted. As I write this book, it seems the prohibition is being enforced, so the stone semi-circle of legal seating on one side of the fountain is likely to be very crowded!

There is a tradition that Pietro Bernini designed the fountain in the form of a boat to memorialize a fishing vessel that allegedly washed ashore in the piazza during a great flood in 1598. Contemporary accounts suggest that the floodwaters may have actually reached the level of the piazza, so it is possible for a boat to have been stranded there, though I know of no historical confirmation that it happened.

When *La Barcaccia* was built, the *Acqua Vergine* had just been restored, but the water pressure to Piazza di Spagna was not forceful enough to power a tall, showy fountain. So the unique design of the little, sinking boat was a perfect answer to the problem—and its whimsical spirit helped spark the many imaginative Baroque fountains that followed.

Standing by La Barcaccia, *facing the Spanish Steps, turn left and follow the*

La Barcaccia: **Another thing that has recently been outlawed in Piazza di Spagna, as in all city streets and squares in Rome, are the open-topped horse-drawn carriages called *botticelle*.**

leftmost edge of Piazza di Spagna (it's lined with fashionable shops), exiting the piazza straight ahead into a pleasant street, rather upscale, with occasional storefronts bearing familiar names from the fashion world (Givenchy, Armani, Miu Miu) and any number of jewelry, perfume, and footwear shops. You can find restaurants, cafés, art galleries—in short, everything you need for an afternoon of retail therapy. The street's name, however, doesn't seem to fit the rather posh ambience, at least at first glance. This is via del Babuino—"The Street of the Baboon." You'll soon see the "baboon" himself, after a few hundred yards, but first some explanation is in order.

At number 150/a, via del Babuino, you'll find the Caffè Canova Tadolini, in a modest, faded-yellow building. The café is quite historic: it once was the Roman atelier of the great sculptor Antonio Canova and his most promising pupil, Adamo Tadolini. (Tadolini, by the way, made the wonderful copies of the Egyptian lions of the Fountain of Moses when the originals were sent to the Vatican.) When Canova died, the property was left to Tadolini, and the building was owned by the Tadolini family as late as 1967. It still houses works (mostly plaster models) by both Canova and Tadolini, and if you stop there for coffee or a meal, you can take your refreshment while rubbing shoulders with plaster popes and potentates, gods and goddesses, and figures from Greek and Roman myth. You will also find the cast of a shapely female torso hanging on one wall. It was made by Canova when he was carving one of his most famous—or notorious—sculptures: the semi-nude portrait of Pauline Bonaparte, Napoleon's younger sister, posing as Aphrodite. You can see the finished work in Galleria Borghese.

On the sidewalk in front of the café, nestled against the wall, reclining on a rough stone pedestal, is a strange figure, covered (except for his head) with some sort of apparently immortal green moss or lichen. Or maybe it's paint.

The Baboon Fountain—Il Babuino (second century AD?)
Architect: Unknown

In 1571, a nobleman named Alessandro Grandi was granted the right to tap a generous supply of water from the newly renovated *Acqua Vergine*. It seemed only fair, since he had helped raise funds for the work. Even so, he was required to share some of the water with the public by building a fountain on the street behind his palace. He found an ancient sculpture of Silenus (one of the god Dionysus' followers) and placed it on a stony base, with a basin in front of it. The basin was fed by water flowing through two openings in the stone, and—*voila!*—his fountain was complete.

Silenus, by the way, was one of Dionysus' most unappealing followers, of whom there were many—but, in some accounts (including Ovid's *Metamorphoses*), he was the god's foster father, because after Dionysus was reborn from Zeus' thigh, Hermes had given him into Silenus' care. So, even though Silenus was infamous for his continual drunkenness, Dionysus was, you might say, "stuck with him."

The Romans who lived on the street, which was then called via Paolina, didn't recognize the old, battered statue as the legendary dipsomaniac, but they certainly

The Baboon Fountain: *Il Babuino*, **"the Baboon," relaxes atop his fountain, in front of Caffè Canova Tadolini, in via del Babuino.**

thought he was ugly and nicknamed him *Il Babuino*. The name stuck. Despite his unattractive appearance, his neighbors grew to like him, especially when he became one of the famous "Talking Statues" of Rome. (There were traditionally six of these statues, collectively called the "Congress of Wits." Impertinent and usually scurrilous comments about the aristocracy and the clergy that ruled Rome, sometimes in rhyme, were hung or pasted on the statues.) In time, Babuino became so popular that the street was named for him!

In 1584, the city of Rome sent a notice to one Simone Grazzini (who apparently then owned the palace) demanding that he repair the fountain within eight days, or else his water supply would be cut off. I don't know what was wrong, but it seems that Simone fixed the problem promptly.

In the eighteenth century, Alessandro Grandi's palace was rebuilt and given the name of its new owners, the Cerasi family. Then, in 1877, Babuino disappeared while street repairs were being done in the neighborhood. There was, of course, great consternation among the residents. H.V. Morton, writing in the 1960s, compared the event to Nelson disappearing from his column in Trafalgar Square.[4] The beloved eyesore did not reappear until the 1920s, when he was found in the courtyard of Palazzo Cerasi and promptly shut up in a city warehouse.

Babuino languished in storage for decades, but in 1957 the city installed him on his eponymous street, albeit in a new location, in front of the Caffè Canova Tadolini. Sometime after 2002, the wall behind him, which was usually covered in rather mindless graffiti—not at all the clever *pasquinades* of the sixteenth century that had

Top: The Baboon Fountain: Babuino surveys his street. The Caffè Canova Tadolini was once the workshop of the great sculptor, Antonio Canova. He left it to Adamo Tadolini, who carved the lions on the Fountain of Moses. It's now a restaurant. *Bottom:* The ancient statue was originally a figure of Silenus, a particularly drunken follower of the god Dionysus. In fact, in some tales he was Dionysus' foster father.

once adorned him in the days of the "Congress of Wits"—was given a special coating that so far has defeated the witless spray painters of today.

After admiring Babuino, and perhaps enjoying a coffee at the café, it's just a short stroll to our last fountain. Turn right 50 feet or so past Babuino into Vicolo dell Orto di Napoli and then right again into via Margutta. Continue until you see the fountain mounted on a wall to your left. This lovely little street is only three blocks long, sheltered beneath the flank of the Pincian Hill, and you might find it interesting to stroll the whole length.

The Artists' Fountain—La Fontana degli Artisti (1927)
ARCHITECT: PIETRO LOMBARDI

If you are a fan of classic Hollywood movies, via Margutta may sound familiar. Perhaps you'll recall Gregory Peck, in that laconic baritone voice, telling an impatient cab driver to take him (and a sleepy Audrey Hepburn) to "via Margutta, 51," in the 1953 romantic comedy *Roman Holiday*. The flat that Peck's character, the not-so-cynical reporter Joe Bradley, rented is still there, up that little flight of stairs from the building's courtyard, or so I've heard. But the gate was always locked

The Artists' Fountain: Little via Margutta was once a low-rent haven for artists, which is why the neighborhood fountain has an artistic theme. Nowadays it's an attractive, rather posh residential and shopping street.

whenever I was there. Federico Fellini and his wife, Giulietta Masina, lived at number 110. Today their home is marked by a plaque. One of Fellini's favorite hangouts, Bar Canova, is nearby, around the corner in Piazza del Popolo. Among other famous people who have lived on via Margutta is Truman Capote, who wrote the script for John Huston's movie *Beat the Devil* while living at number 33. But the street has historically been known for more than movies.

In medieval times, artists began to congregate on the little street below the Pincian Hill. It was a low-rent area then; waste from the homes above tended to be carried down the hill when heavy rains created runoff. In fact, the name "Margutta" is a contraction of "Marisgutta," or "Sea Drop," an ironic euphemism for the streams of dirty water flowing from the Pincio villas above. But the low-cost studios for sculptors and painters flourished, and for centuries the street was known for its artists.

Nowadays the street is gentrified—rather exclusive, in fact. It is lined with small "boutique" hotels, B&Bs, restaurants and cafés—and, lest anyone forget the tradition, even a few galleries selling art! From time to time a juried arts festival, called the "100 Pittori di via Margutta" (https://www.centopittoriviamargutta.it), is held on—where else?—via Margutta, but the dates vary.

Finally, of course, there is the fountain, halfway between Vicolo dell Orto di Napoli and via Alibert. It's one of Pietro Lombardi's *rione* fountains, and, like the rest, it reflects the traditions of the historic neighborhood for which it was built. On via Margutta, of course, the artists of the district are honored. (In 1927, Lombardi—a young architect already well known for having designed the Amphorae Fountain, which we'll visit in Chapter 15—won a competition to supply small, accessible fountains for ten of Rome's historic districts, or *rioni*. The fountains were to incorporate images reflecting each *rione*'s unique qualities.)

At the top of the triangular composition, Lombardi carved a bucket or pail containing a fine selection of painters' brushes. The bucket sits on two stone easels, their edges meeting in front at a 90-degree angle. Water flows from a spout where the easels meet. On each easel, a mask is carved—one joyful, one sorrowful—representing, I suppose, the varying emotions artists experience in the process of creation (or possibly success or failure in selling a piece to pay for dinner). Water spouts from the masks at a level convenient for thirsty passersby, falling into basins just above street level.

Below the easels are artists' stools, of the traditional kind, each with a paint box on the seat—one of them hollowed out to form a basin to catch the water flowing from the spout between the easels. As it is on each of Lombardi's fountains, the legend SPQR is proudly carved on the arch framing the fountain. In this case, it signifies, no doubt, the pride that Rome takes in its long and unparalleled history of artistic creation.

The Artists' Fountain is the last stop on this tour. If you do not want to walk from here to the beginning of our next chapter's tour, the Spagna Metro stop is the nearest to your current location if you want to return to your lodgings; there are also normally plenty of taxis in Piazza di Spagna. To get to the next tour by public transport, I recommend that you take the Metro to Flaminio (line A) and follow the directions in Chapter 4.

The Artists' Fountain: All the tools of the trade are featured on Pietro Lombardi's *Fontana degli Artisti*—paintboxes, stools, easels, compass, a bucket of paintbrushes, and the masks of comedy and tragedy for inspiration.

To walk from the Artists' Fountain to the next tour, return to via del Babuino by way of Vicolo dell Orto di Napoli. Turn right on via del Babuino and continue for about 500 yards into Piazza del Popolo. Then follow the right-hand curving wall of the huge piazza until the wall ends; to the right, you'll see stone steps ascending the Pincian Hill. Climb the steps, and follow the directions in Chapter 4 from "at the top of the steps." (As you no doubt recall, the maps in this book do not cover the walking routes between chapters, but don't let that stop you!)

~ 4 ~

Nero's Bones, Pharaohs, and Roman Gods

Piazza del Popolo Area

THE WALK BEGINS AT THE TERRAZA DEL PINCIO, OVERLOOKING PIAZZA DEL POPOLO.

The nearest Metro stop for this itinerary is Flaminio (line A). If you are starting from the Flaminio Metro stop, find via Flaminia, which runs between the two exits

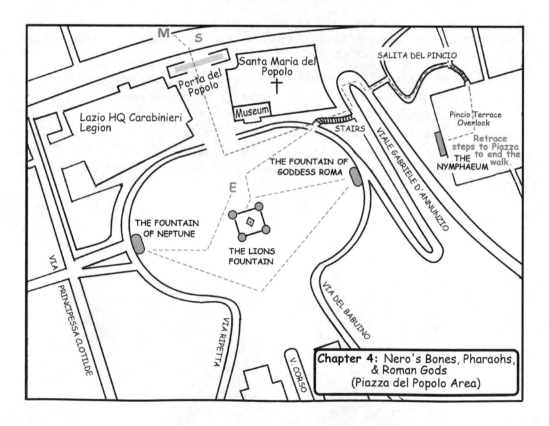

from the Metro. Go toward the great Renaissance Porta del Popolo gate, crossing three busy streets on the way. Once through the gate and in Piazza del Popolo, past the Santa Maria del Popolo *church and the Leonardo Museum, look left and take the stone steps up the Pincian Hill.*

At the top of the steps, turn left on viale Gabriele d'Annunzio, and continue as the road makes a hairpin turn to the right. Immediately after the turn, look for a path winding uphill on your left—it's known as the Salita del Pincio, though it's not well designated; you'll see a sculpture of a lion beside the path—and continue to the top, turning right at a stone wall and up some shallow steps called viale Valadier. You are now in the westernmost part of Villa Borghese, called the Terraza del Pincio, and you'll see a paved terrace with stone balustrades overlooking Piazza del Popolo.

Enjoy the view! When you're ready, we'll head back down the hill into the piazza for a closer look at the fountains—and perhaps a spritz from the lions if it's a hot day. I'm not referring to the Aperol kind of spritz, though you can get one of those at Bar Canova, right where via del Babuino enters the piazza.

First a little about Piazza del Popolo:

From the terrace at the western edge of the Pincian Hill, behind the balustrades built in the 1820s by Giuseppe Valadier, you have a dramatic, sweeping view of Rome, toward the great dome of Saint Peter's Basilica. In the foreground is the elegant oval shape of Piazza del Popolo, paved in black *sanpietrini* cobbles, with its ancient Egyptian obelisk in the center surrounded by charming marble lionesses spouting water into basins. There are two other fountains on the perimeter, facing

Piazza del Popolo, seen here from the Pincio Terrace at dusk, contains three major fountain ensembles.

each other across the piazza, surmounted by grand neoclassical statuary. It's a busy space; in fine weather, the ever-present tourists have been, in the past, joined by local families whose children delighted in climbing onto the backs of the friendly lions while Mom and Dad picnicked on the fountain steps.

(As I have mentioned elsewhere, recently revised regulations regarding the protection of fountains forbid climbing, sitting, or eating on them, and the *Leoni* fountain is among several famous fountains specifically mentioned, including the Trevi, *La Barcaccia*, and the *Fontanone dell'Acqua Paola*. Time will tell how long such a prohibition will persist for the *Leoni*, a fountain that has seemed, for generations of kids, to have been designed for climbing.)

To your right (though obscured by trees) is the Porta del Popolo, Rome's northern gate through the Aurelian Walls, where the ancient via Flaminia enters Rome, all the way from Rimini on the Adriatic coast. (If you started from the Flaminio Metro station, you entered the piazza through that gate.) Just inside the gate, there is a church ten centuries old, though it's still young compared to the walls. To your left, past the obelisk, two newer churches, nearly identical to each other, stand where three roads branch out like a trident. One street, once called via Lata but now called via del Corso, runs straight south between the churches into the heart of Rome, ending at Piazza Venezia. The leftmost street is via del Babuino, and its southeasterly course ends at Piazza di Spagna, as you know. The right-hand street strikes southwest, passing the Mausoleum of Augustus, toward the old river port, Porto Ripetta, from which the street takes its name, via Ripetta.

Long ago, though, when the old church beside the gate was built, before there was a comfortable, level terrace from which to view the city, you'd have to teeter on the slope of a steep, wooded hill if you wanted to enjoy the scene. And you would see no obelisk, no lions, no grand fountains, no twin churches, no cobbled surface; though you might see Saint Peter's Basilica in the distance, it would be much smaller, and there would be no dome, because you would be looking at the *first* Saint Peter's, the one built by Constantine in 319 AD. The Porta del Popolo would be there, but it would look very different—it's been remodeled frequently over the centuries. It was called *Porta Fiumentana* (*fiume* means "river") in those days, because it was often flooded when the Tiber backed up behind the northern bridge, Ponte Milvio.

There was a huge walnut tree at the bottom of the hill, or so an old legend says[1]; this tree was inhabited by demons in the shape of crows, because the evil emperor Nero, who burned thousands of Christians at the stake, was buried beneath the tree. Pilgrims entering Rome from the north were frequently attacked by these demons, so in 1099, during Lent, Pope Paschal II led a procession of Romans to the site, had the tree dug up, found Nero's bones, and ordered them thrown into the Tiber. Then, having disposed of the evil, the pope laid the first stone of a small chapel that, in time, became the church of *Santa Maria del Popolo*.

It may be that, over time, some of the facts of the story have gotten a bit confused: Nero was buried in his family's crypt on top of the hill, not at the bottom; the demons who tormented (and robbed) the pilgrims were probably bandits who frequented the wooded area below the Pincian Hill; and the only documented time

Pope Paschal had a corpse tossed into the river was after the anti-pope Clement III died, when Paschal ordered him exhumed from his family crypt and disposed of in the Tiber. But never mind—the church that the pope founded ten centuries ago, *Santa Maria del Popolo*, is undeniably there and well worth a visit for many reasons, especially the wealth of art it contains, including two sculptures by Gian Lorenzo Bernini and the *Conversion of Saint Paul* and the *Crucifixion of Saint Peter*, two masterpieces by Caravaggio.

The Lions Fountain or the Obelisk Fountain— La Fontana dei Leoni, aka La Fontana dell' Obelisco (1823)
ARCHITECT: GIUSEPPE VALADIER

Giacomo della Porta installed a handsome fountain in the center of what is now Piazza del Popolo in 1572. Its large octagonal lower basin (originally in Aurelian's Temple of the Sun in the Forum) had been carved in antiquity from a single piece of marble. Seventeen years after the fountain was inaugurated, Pope Sixtus V ordered that a great obelisk be moved from the Circus Maximus (where it had lain in three pieces since the fall of the Western Empire) and erected next to della Porta's fountain. The obelisk was Egyptian, part of Augustus' spoils from his conquest of Egypt in 30 BC. It, too, came from a temple of the sun, in Heliopolis, an ancient city now buried beneath modern Cairo. The obelisk bears hieroglyphs in praise of pharaohs Seti I and his son Ramses II. In Rome, it had served as part of the *spina*, the middle dividing structure of the Circus, around which chariots used to race.

The Lions Fountain (also known as the Obelisk Fountain) dominates the center of Piazza del Popolo.

For more than two centuries, most people coming to Rome from the north found welcome refreshment in the *Acqua Vergine* water flowing into Giacomo's marble basin, and they were no doubt suitably impressed with the towering obelisk. Still, though the (nearly) twin churches of *Santa Maria dei Miracoli* and *Santa Maria di Montesanto* were built during the 1660s and the 1670s, the area between them and the Porta del Popolo remained unfinished.

In 1811, the great Italian architect Giuseppe Valadier developed a plan to make a grand public space of the whole area from the city gate to the three streets that enter the city between and beside the twin churches. He began by dismantling della Porta's old fountain and replacing it with four stepped fountains surrounding the base of the obelisk. On top of each series of steps he placed a crouching lioness, carved from white marble, spouting a broad fan of water that landed in a marble basin at the foot of the steps. The lions, far from being fearsome, seem to express a serene sense of amused *noblesse oblige*, especially on a hot day as perspiring sightseers enjoy a cooling spray of mist.

Giacomo della Porta's sixteenth-century fountain, after Valadier removed it from Piazza del Popolo, was reassembled, first in front of the church of San Pietro in

The Lions Fountain: With a little help, a young visitor climbs aboard one of the four lionesses.

Montorio and then later (1950) in the Piazza Nicosia, where it imparts a bit of nobility to the dozens of cars parked in the square.

The Nymphaeum on the Pincian Hill (1937)
Architects: Giuseppe Valadier and Raffaele di Vico

Part of Valadier's renovation plans included connecting the piazza with the top of the Pincian Hill, where he created the terrace overlooking Rome. He designed a switch-backed carriage drive for vehicles and a flight of steps up the hill from the piazza for pedestrians. A path at the top of the stairs leads past the supporting structure for the terrace: a triple-arched nymphaeum, made of pale marble, where water from one branch of a new aqueduct, the *Nuovo Acquedotto Vergine Elevato*, makes its first appearance in Rome as a waterfall behind the arches. The nymphaeum was not completed until 1937, after the new aqueduct was put into service, but its design was inspired by Valadier's plans. So the nymphaeum, which is easy to overlook, is actually the *mostra* for an important water source, because the *Acqua Vergine Nuova*

Here the friendly felines of the Lions Fountain spray their fans of water, while in the background the goddess Roma looks on above her fountain; beyond her, the triple arches of the Nymphaeum on the Pincian Hill loom.

(its shorter name) gave a badly needed boost to the city's supply. The water comes from the same source as the ancient *Aqua Virgo*, but the new aqueduct uses an elevated tower, a pumping station, and cast-iron piping to deliver three times the volume of the old *Virgo*.

From the piazza, looking eastward, the nymphaeum acts as a backdrop for another notable fountain.

The Fountain of the Goddess Roma between the Tiber and the Aniene—La Fontana della dea Roma (1824)
ARCHITECTS: GIUSEPPE VALADIER AND GIOVANNI CECCARINI

Here, Rome is presented as a rather imperious and warlike goddess, wearing a plumed helmet and leaning on a shield. Bearded allegorical figures on either side represent two rivers, the Tiber and the Aniene. The Tiber (on the right as you face the fountain) holds an overflowing cornucopia, while the figure of the Aniene carries a rudder on his shoulder, evidently suggesting that his namesake stream is navigable. At Roma's feet is a version of the Capitoline Wolf, suckling Romulus and Remus. Water falls from a small pedestal fountain into a larger, shell-shaped basin,

Surrounding the Fountain of the Goddess Roma—*La Fontana della dea Roma*—a large number of people gather to enjoy the piazza.

which in turn overflows into a large, semi-circular basin at ground level. Giovanni Ceccarini designed and executed this fountain, according to the overall plans of Giuseppe Valadier; he also created the group across the piazza, facing the goddess Roma.

The Fountain of Neptune between Two Tritons— La Fontana del Nettuno (1824)
ARCHITECTS: GIUSEPPE VALADIER AND GIOVANNI CECCARINI

Neptune stands commandingly atop a rocky mound, his cape draped across his shoulder and his raised right hand grasping his trident. One of the young Tritons flanking him kneels, grasping the jaw of a giant fish whose open mouth displays an impressive set of teeth. In his free hand, the Triton grasps a knobbed stick, for all the world as if he intends to prop the creature's mouth open to perform some dental work. The other Triton, on Neptune's left, clasps another giant fish affectionately with one arm and, twisting sideways, raises a conch shell to his lips as if to blow a fanfare. This fountain mirrors the Fountain of the Goddess Roma with its triple-tiered water flow and large basin at ground level.

The Neptune Fountain: Across the piazza from the Fountain of the Goddess Roma, *La Fontana del Nettuno* typically draws a smaller crowd than the goddess.

The Neptune Fountain: The young Triton on Neptune's right appears to be planning some dental work for his fishy friend.

The Flaminio Metro Station is handy just across three busy streets outside the Porta del Popolo if you're calling it a day and want to return to your lodgings. Or you can check www.atac.roma.it for a bus ride; taxis also line up on via del Babuino between the Saint Mary in Montesanto church and Café Canova. The next itinerary starts from here in Piazza del Popolo, so go right on to Chapter 5.

❧ 5 ❧

Pax Romana
to the Porter's Water Barrel
via Ripetta and via del Corso Area

The walk begins in the Piazza del Popolo.

As I mentioned in the last chapter, there are two "twin" seventeenth-century churches that welcome travelers to Rome; in fact, that was their original purpose. Pope Alexander VII wanted a splendid backdrop for the great piazza that greeted pilgrims entering Rome on the via Flaminia. *Santa Maria dei Miracoli* and *Santa Maria di Montesanto* are actually not quite identical, but they make a satisfyingly symmetrical picture, dividing access to the ancient city into a trident of streets: one to the left of the two churches, one to the right, and a central one between them. The central route is known today as via del Corso, and it runs straight into the heart of Rome, from Piazza del Popolo to Piazza Venezia, passing historic churches, historic hotels, historic palazzi, and lots of not-so-historic shopping venues. The street to the left is via del Babuino—"Baboon Street"—and its story is told in Chapter 3. The street to the right is via Ripetta, which ends at Piazza Nicosia. The area bounded by via del Corso and via Ripetta boasts five important fountains, each with a unique story to tell.

To begin the tour, face the two churches and then take the rightmost of the three streets, via Ripetta. After about a third of a mile, you will find yourself between two ancient monuments, both built during the reign of Augustus. One of them, on your left, is the Mausoleum of Augustus, which I remember as always having been a giant, circular, weed-covered mound of earth and broken stone, hidden behind trees and protected by a chain-link fence. Through the centuries, besides being the burial place for Augustus and his kin, it served as a fortress, a bullfight arena, a concert hall, and, from the 1930s until recently, an abandoned ruin. However, the city began restoration work in 2016, and in March 2021 it opened to the public for tours, though I believe it's necessary to book well ahead at www.mausoleodiaugusto.it.

On your right is an extremely modernistic building, the Museo dell'Ara Pacis, which contains something very ancient and very special, and, oh yes, there's a fountain, too. We'll get to the fountain soon, but first I must set the stage with a little history about the unique and ancient treasure inside this very modern museum.

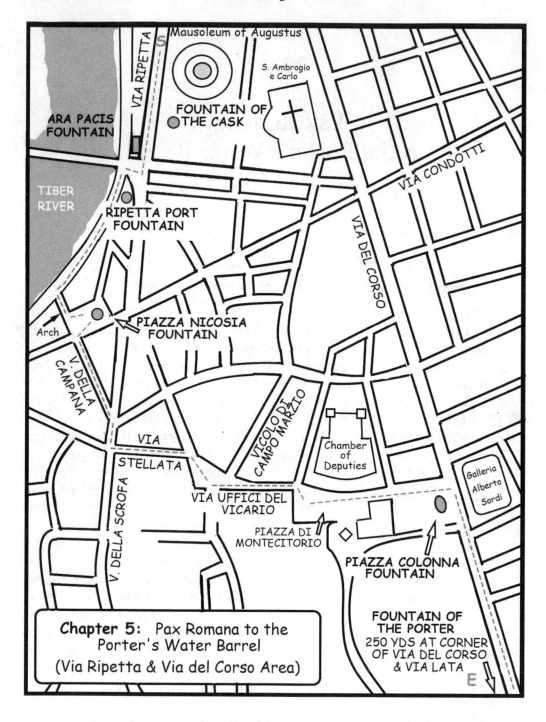

Chapter 5: Pax Romana to the Porter's Water Barrel
(Via Ripetta & Via del Corso Area)

Gaius Octavius, the young, adopted son of Julius Caesar, outwitted, outma-
neuvered, and defeated a gaggle of the most ambitious power seekers of antiquity
(including Brutus, Cassius, half the Roman Senate, Lepidus, Mark Anthony, and
Cleopatra) to finally emerge as the undisputed ruler of the Roman Empire. With
the help of his childhood friend Marcus Agrippa, he defeated Mark Anthony and

The Fountain of Ara Pacis: Richard Meier's ultra-modern museum structure, which shelters the ancient Altar of Augustan Peace, includes a fountain with leaping jets and gentle water-flows down travertine walls.

Cleopatra at the Battle of Actium in 31 BC and was given absolute power by the Senate in 27 BC, when he was awarded the name *Augustus*, meaning "majestic" or "venerable." Augustus is the name by which he is remembered today.

Augustus was a brilliant leader, an administrator of genius. He governed autocratically but successfully maintained the pretense that he was merely the *princeps*, the "first among equals"; in addition, he managed to give the Roman Empire a period of stability and relative peace—the *Pax Romana*, which lasted until the death of Marcus Aurelius in 180 AD.

Just before he died in 14 AD, Augustus composed his official political autobiography. It's called the *Res Gestae Augustae*—"Deeds of the Divine Augustus"—and it lists the great accomplishments of his life, including an accounting of all the money he spent keeping the Romans entertained. Inscribed on two bronze plates, it was mounted beside the doors of his mausoleum, and copies were sent out all over the empire.

In 13 BC, the Senate ordered that a monument of white marble should be built in the Field of Mars. *Ara Pacis Augustae*, it was called: the Altar of Augustan Peace. The actual altar was enclosed inside a rectangle of marble walls, sculpted on the lower half with an elaborate relief design of curving acanthus leaves, flowers, frogs, lizards, and swans, signifying nature at peace. On the upper half, there were portraits of the imperial family, with friends, officials and priests, in a solemn procession around the walls. Augustus himself was there, with his wife

Livia, her sons Tiberius and Drusus, and Marcus Agrippa, Augustus' best friend and son-in-law. Other panels portrayed mythological scenes, such as Tellus (the Roman Mother Earth) holding two babies in her lap, symbolizing fertility and plenty.

After the Roman Empire fell, the Ara Pacis slowly deteriorated, undermined by a rising water table. Covered by mud and debris, it was forgotten for a thousand years. When parts of Ara Pacis were found during building excavations in 1568, no one knew what they were, and the pieces were dispersed. Some became part of the Villa Medici garden wall in Rome; some went to the Vatican or to the Louvre in Paris, and some even ended up in museums in Vienna.

During the Fascist rule in the 1930s, archaeologists identified most of the scattered pieces of Ara Pacis, and it was partially reconstructed between the Mausoleum of Augustus and the banks of the Tiber. A protective structure was built, enclosing the entire monument, and the text of the *Res Gestae* was engraved on one wall. Since then, most missing pieces of the monument have been recovered. In 2006, the old protective enclosure was replaced by a modernistic, glass-walled building by the architect Richard Meier, who nevertheless retained the *Res Gestae* wall, in memory of the first emperor of Rome, who insisted he was merely "first among equals." The modern building is now the *Museo dell'Ara Pacis* (www.arapacis.it), and the beautifully restored Altar of Augustan Peace, protected from the elements but gleaming in natural light through the glass walls, can be enjoyed by visitors.

The Fountain of the Altar of Augustan Peace—
La Fontana dell'Ara Pacis Augustae (2006)
ARCHITECT: RICHARD MEIER

Richard Meier's ultra-modern building unquestionably provides a good home for the altar, but the design has many critics who take issue with its stark modernity. Besides the skylights and glass curtain walls housing the monument, the building contains an auditorium, a café, and a roof terrace. There is an extensive forecourt of concrete steps leading up to the main entrance, and at the street level there is a large fountain consisting of sixteen powerful jets within a rectangular pool bordered by low concrete benches and, on the Tiber side, a tall travertine block wall down which water cascades.

If you decide to have a seat on the stepped forecourt of Meier's building, between the main structure and the fountain, look across the street into Largo San Rocco. You'll see an enclosed bridge, or corridor, carried on two arches between the churches on either side. Embedded in the pillar between the arches is an interesting and attractive niche fountain.

Top: The Fountain of Ara Pacis: The museum structure has been widely criticized for its severe minimalism, but the subtle textural differences make the fountain an interesting creation. *Bottom:* Though Meier's work does contrast starkly with the sober and dignified architecture of the neighborhood, people are still drawn to the fountain.

The Fountain of the Cask—La Fontana della Botticella di Ripetta (1774)
ARCHITECT: UNKNOWN

Pope Clement XIV, near the end of his life, granted an allocation of *Acqua Vergine* water to the Ospedale di San Rocco, but he required the hospital to use some of the water for a public fountain mounted in the wall of nearby Palazzo Valdambrini. The resulting fountain, made of travertine and marble, portrays a large barrel lying on its side in a wall niche, with a small, shallow, rectangular basin atop it. The basin may be intended to suggest a receptacle usually placed below the barrel's spigot to capture spillage when filling wine containers. The barrel and basin seem to be covered by tumbled rocks. Above the rocks, on the back wall of the niche, is the smiling face of a winemaker or vineyard worker, with a traditional *berretto* cap on his head and a kerchief round his neck, spitting an arc of water into a semi-circular basin below his torso. The nearby Porto di Ripetta was where wine was offloaded from barges in the eighteenth and nineteenth centuries.

In 1934, when Palazzo Valdambrini was demolished, the fountain was removed from its original location; in 1940, it was reinstalled in one of the pillars supporting the arched bridge that connects the churches of Saint Rocco and Saint Girolamo degli Schiavoni.

The Fountain of the Cask—*La Fontana della Botticella*—honors the winemakers who shipped their product by barge on the Tiber, to be offloaded at the Porto di Ripetta.

Just past the Ara Pacis fountain, via Ripetta crosses via Tomacelli. To your right, the Ponte Cavour bridge crosses the Tiber, but we won't. Just across via Tomacelli on via Ripetta, there is a small square called Piazza del Porto di Ripetta. Part of the square is elevated and not accessible on the left side. Enter the piazza at the traffic island and the crosswalks, and circle the elevated area to the right until you see a ruined, dry fountain and a couple of stone columns. This fountain is not much to look at, but it has an interesting history.

The Ripetta Port Fountain, aka the Navigators' Fountain— La Fontana del Porto di Ripetta, aka La Fontana dei Navigatori (1704)
Architects: Alessandro Specchi and Carlo Fontana

By an old tradition, when people speak of the "left" or "right" sides of a river, they refer to the river as viewed looking downstream, and this is true in Rome. So

The Navigators' Fountain used to be topped with a lantern to guide the vessels landing at the Porto di Ripetta; the accompanying marble columns measured the periodic floods.

Trastevere is on the "right" bank of the river, and all of the fountains we've visited so far are on the "left," even though on a standard map, oriented north-south, the opposite appears to be true. Most river ports in Rome were on the left bank, to serve the more heavily populated side of the river.

So it's on the left bank of the Tiber that you find the Piazza del Porto di Ripetta,

The Navigators' Fountain: Also called the Ripetta Port Fountain, the Navigators' Fountain was once a landmark. But it was left high and dry when the river was walled with embankments and the port was closed.

in which stands a rather forlorn-looking fountain that for many years has been dry. It was built to accompany and symbolize the important Porto di Ripetta, created in 1704 to handle barge traffic to and from the northern reaches of the Tiber. Material for construction of the port and the fountain came from a unique source: travertine stones from three collapsed arches of the Coliseum that had been dislodged by a recent earthquake.

The fountain originally was near the banks of the river, where the port facilities were located, and its design was unusual. It stood in its own riverside terrace, flanked by two travertine columns that were used to measure floodwaters. On a single-stepped base, an oval, nearly circular lower basin with a rounded rim, unornamented, contains another basin with a scalloped edge. But the inner basin's shape is incomplete: a mound of tumbled boulders, artfully arranged as if collapsing over one side of the basin, obscures one side. Two dolphins cling to the rocks, flanking a large carved shell, from which water presumably flowed into the empty part of the basin. This reservoir probably held water for pack animals working in the port. On the other side of the boulders is carved Pope Clement XI's coat-of-arms, containing an eight-pointed star and the stylized three-mountain symbol of his family, the Albani. The boulders rise to a peak (once the three Albani mountains, but now hardly recognizable), surmounted by a cast-iron tripod that originally supported a streetlamp. It's said that on foggy nights the lamp was a "lighthouse" for bargemen trying to locate the wharves.

The port facility was demolished in the early twentieth century, after the riverbank was altered to accommodate both the new Ponte Cavour bridge and the embankment walls that control Rome's periodic floods. The fountain was dismantled and put into storage. In 1930, however, the fountain and its terrace were reassembled nearby in Piazza del Porto di Ripetta, complete with the two flood-measuring columns, though they are now high above the river and its protective embankments. Neither they nor the fountain will likely get wet again, except when it rains, because in the 1990s the water supply to the fountain was disconnected, apparently for good.

On the way to the next fountain, why not take a stroll along the Tiber? To the right of the Piazza del Porto di Ripetta is a street called Lungotevere Marzio. Most streets following the riverbank in Rome are called "Lungotevere" followed by an indication of their neighborhood or history. Anyway, head left on Lungotevere Marzio. Walking along the right-hand sidewalk, you can see a curve of the river over the low wall, and ahead the Ponte Umberto I bridge, with the rear façade of the huge Palace of Justice at the opposite end across the river, where the Italians keep their Supreme Court. But after only a few hundred feet, well before the bridge, you'll turn left, crossing the street, at via dei Somaschi and pass under an arch connecting two halves of an apartment block. You're now in Piazza Nicosia, and you'll see a fountain at the far end of the piazza, surrounded by parked cars and motorcycles. Do you remember the fountain I told you about that used to be in Piazza del Popolo, whose lower basin was carved from a single piece of marble from Aurelian's Temple of the Sun ...?

The Fountain in Piazza Nicosia—La Fontana di Piazza Nicosia (1572)
ARCHITECT: GIACOMO DELLA PORTA

Pope Gregory XIII commissioned a fountain from Giacomo della Porta in 1570, which the great fountain builder completed in 1572. It was the first of eighteen fountains that were built in Rome after the reactivation of the ancient *Aqua Virgo* (renamed *Acqua Vergine*). It can fairly be called the first "modern" fountain in Rome, since the *Acqua Vergine* terminal outlets in Piazza dei Crociferi and later in Piazza di Trevi were at first rather modest, wall-mounted efforts. The grand *mostra* that later made Piazza di Trevi famous wasn't finished until almost two centuries later, in 1762.

The fountain della Porta made for Pope Gregory was in the center of Piazza del Popolo. Its lower basin was octagonal and made from a single piece of Carrara marble. Old texts and engravings describe a baluster (pillar) in the center of the basin, decorated with dolphins, on which a smaller basin sat, decorated with griffins; rising still higher was the third and smallest basin.

Only seventeen years later, Pope Sixtus V decided that the huge Piazza del Popolo needed something grander than the fairly modest (though very handsome)

The Fountain of Piazza Nicosia: This fountain, once the center of attention in Piazza del Popolo, was replaced by four marble lions in the nineteenth century. Moved to Piazza Nicosia, a busy parking lot, it's still a handsome work of art.

fountain, so a great Egyptian obelisk was moved from the Circus Maximus and erected next to the fountain. For the next two centuries, the fountain and the obelisk welcomed travelers arriving on the via Flaminia through the northern gate of Rome, but in the early nineteenth century the fountain was dismantled, hauled away, and then reassembled in front of the church of San Pietro in Montorio, on the Janiculum Hill. The architect Giuseppe Valadier replaced it with the four marble lionesses that still surround the obelisk today, spraying fans of water for the delight of visiting children (see Chapter 4).

At some point, della Porta's fountain was removed from the Janiculum and put into storage, where it remained until 1950, when it was installed in its present home, Piazza di Nicosia, where it is usually surrounded by a sea of parked cars and motorcycles. The original Carrara marble lower basin remains, but the two original smaller basins and their carved decorations have been lost. Who knows whether they are still in service as a small fountain in some interior courtyard somewhere in Rome? At any rate, they have been replaced with beautifully sculpted replicas based on an etching by Giovanni Battista Falda from the 1670s.[1] Despite its difficult location, when I last saw the fountain it had recently been cleaned, and even with a bit of residual lichen, it certainly dressed up the parking lot.

The route to our next fountain in Piazza Colonna takes us across what was once a Tiber floodplain called the Campo Marzio (Field of Mars), where citizen

The Fountain of Piazza Nicosia was designed by the great Giacomo della Porta, but when it was moved, the upper basins and the central baluster disappeared. In the 1950s, they were reconstructed from a sixteenth-century engraving.

soldiers of the Roman Republic trained for battle. To begin, go to the end of Piazza Nicosia opposite the fountain. Notice the arch under which you first entered the piazza, turn your back to it, and leave the piazza in the opposite direction on Vicolo della Campana. After a couple of blocks, Vicolo della Campana will merge with via della Scrofa. Continue on via della Scrofa about 100 feet and take the second left onto via della Stellata. Two blocks later, via della Stellata ends, and you should bear right into the small, irregularly shaped piazza in Campo Marzio. Continue through this piazza, bearing left into via degli Uffici del Vicario. You'll soon see Giolitti's gelato emporium—one of Rome's most famous ice cream parlors. Stay on via degli Uffici del Vicario until it ends in about 200 yards. Bear right into the grand Piazza di Monte Citorio, with the Palazzo Montecitorio, where the Italian Chamber of Deputies meets, on your left. The Chamber of Deputies is the lower house of the Italian Parliament; the upper house is the Senate. You'll also notice an Egyptian obelisk in the piazza.

This obelisk once was used as the gnomon of a gigantic sundial next to the Ara Pacis in ancient times, before the Ara Pacis, the sundial, and the obelisk collapsed after Rome fell and were buried in the mud, forgotten until the sixteenth century.

But onward! Pass through the Piazza di Monte Citorio in front of the Palazzo Montecitorio, and you'll see the wide opening into Piazza Colonna.

The Fountain in Piazza Colonna—La Fontana di Piazza Colonna (1577)
Architect: Giacomo della Porta

Piazza Colonna is on the west side of via del Corso, a half-mile north of Piazza Venezia. It's in an important location both historically and politically. The piazza's north side is formed by the façade of Palazzo Chigi, which nowadays is the official residence of the prime minister of Italy, and, as we've seen, just a few steps away is Palazzo Montecitorio, home to the Italian Parliament's Chamber of Deputies. Across the street to the east is Galleria Alberto Sordi, renamed in 2003 for the beloved Italian actor—previously, the nineteenth-century shopping mall was called Galleria Colonna. The piazza itself is named for something you can't miss: a tall stone column (*colonna*) honoring Emperor Marcus Aurelius. It's 97 feet high, sits on a marble base 33 feet high, and is carved in ascending spiral reliefs celebrating Marcus' victories over various Germanic tribes in the northern part of the Roman Empire. And, luckily for us, there is a fountain.

Commissioned by Pope Gregory XIII, it is one of several fountains constructed to bring the *Acqua Vergine* water to some of the most important squares in Rome, including the original fountain in Piazza del Popolo (now located, as I've described, in Piazza di Nicosia) and the two fountains—Moor and Neptune—at either end of Piazza Navona. Piazza Colonna is rather elevated in relation to the *castello* (distribution tank) that feeds the *Vergine* water to the fountain, so della Porta didn't have

The Fountain in Piazza Colonna: Giacomo della Porta created an elegantly undulating basin with a low baluster and basin in the center, because of weak water pressure. The dolphins and shells were added later.

enough water pressure to create strong sprays of water jetting upward from the fountain to impress the piazza's neighbors. Instead, he made what amounts to an elegant pool of gently shimmering water contained in a large, gracefully undulating basin made of subtly multicolored *portasanta* marble.

The outer sides of the basin are decorated by small lion heads from which bands of contrasting white marble descend to ground level, emphasizing the curving shapes that form the basin. In the center of the pool, a small, table-shaped marble basin and baluster rise a few feet above the water, emitting a gentle plume of water that flows over the edges of the "tabletop," with just enough force to slightly agitate the pool's surface and create spreading ripples. In the 1830s, two sculptural groups by Achille Stocchi were added, one at each end of the pool. They each depict two dolphins—or fish, or some other fanciful sea creatures—curled, with their tails entwined within a large seashell. From the creatures' mouths, gentle fans of water fall into the fountain.

It's not far to our next fountain. Exit from Piazza Colonna onto via del Corso, and turn right, staying on the right side of the street. After less than 400 yards, you'll come to via Lata. Around the corner to the right, looking out from a niche in the wall of the Banca di Roma building, you'll see the marble figure of a little man with a floppy hat and a battered face. He's carrying a wooden cask from which a stream of water flows. If you're thirsty, have a drink; it's Acqua Vergine *water, acclaimed since antiquity as the sweetest water in Rome.*

The Fountain in Piazza Colonna: The gentle fall of water from the small central basin contrasts well with the busy via del Corso and the tall, martial column of Marcus Aurelius in the piazza.

The Fountain of the Porter—La Fontana del Facchino (1580)
ARCHITECT: JACOPINO DEL CONTE?

La Fontana del Facchino is also called "The Fountain of the Porter," though it is likely that the little man holding a barrel from which water flows was actually an *acquaerolo*, or "water carrier." You can find him waiting patiently in a wall niche in via Lata, just a few feet from via del Corso, offering a refreshing drink to all passersby.

Rome's aqueducts ceased reliably bringing water into the city in the sixth century, partly because, in the collapsing Roman Empire, the engineering skill needed to repair them had been lost, and partly because many aqueducts were destroyed by invading German tribes. Nearly a thousand years passed before they began to be restored or built during the Renaissance. During that millennium, the city's water distribution was performed by the water carriers. They delivered water to homes, shops, and even construction sites, carrying their barrels on oxcarts.

No one knows Facchino's name, though the sculpture may represent a real person. One possibility is that he was a well-known porter named Abbondio Rizzio. It's said by some that there was originally a plaque beside the fountain that memorialized Rizzio with this inscription: "He carried as much weight as he wanted, lived as long as he could but died one day carrying a barrel on his shoulder."[2] Another version of the epitaph is "He carried as much weight as he wanted, lived as long as he

The Fountain of the Porter: Facchino the water carrier still offers refreshing water from the *Acqua Vergine,* **even after four centuries on the job.**

could, but died one day carrying two barrels of wine: one on his shoulder and one inside." However, the plaque is long gone, and the reference to a barrel of wine is probably apocryphal. In any case, the fountain is not in its original location—or even its second. It is likely the fountain was installed around 1580 by a successful Mannerist painter named Jacopino del Conte, on the façade of his house on via del Corso. He may also have designed the sculpture. The house was demolished in 1724, and the fountain was moved to the façade of Palazzo de Carolis-Simonetti; then, to make it more accessible to the public, it was moved again, a few steps away, to its present location in 1872.

Facchino is one of six famous sculptures in Rome collectively called the "Talking Statues" or the "Congress of Wits."[3] It was a popular custom to paste or hang critical (well, actually insulting) messages about public and church officials on these statues, and often the statues would have satirical "dialogues" with each other. (See the entry in Chapter 7 about the Marforio Fountain for an example.) "Talking statue" he may have been, but what Facchino whispers to you now is that of all the *acquaeroli* who quenched the city's thirst until the aqueducts returned, only he remains.

To return to your lodging, I'm afraid there's no handy Metro stop nearby, but there are bus stops on via del Corso and plenty of bus routes to all parts of town from Piazza Venezia, just a bit farther down via del Corso. You can also find one end of

The Fountain of the Porter: For reasons that are not clear, it seems that Facchino's face has been battered by hooligans throwing cobblestones at him. One theory is that his cap reminded people of one worn by Martin Luther.

Tram Line 8 roughly 200 feet west of Piazza Venezia on Piazza San Marco. Check in with www.atac.roma.it to find your route. Taxis line up in Piazza della Madonna di Loreto, on the east side of Piazza Venezia (head toward Trajan's Column). Our next itinerary starts right here at Facchino's fountain, so when you're ready to start, turn to Chapter 6.

6

The Altar of the Fatherland to the Altar of Heaven

Piazza Venezia Area

THE WALK BEGINS AT IL FACCHINO,
THE FOUNTAIN OF THE PORTER,
CORNER OF VIA DEL CORSO AND VIA LATA.

Our last walk ended with the little water carrier, Facchino, so, just for fun, let's begin from the same place. Fill up your water bottle, return to via del Corso, and turn right. The second building you'll see on the right-hand side of the street is Palazzo Doria Pamphilj, the great palace of the noble and ancient Doria Pamphilj family, who still own it. In the cloister-like courtyard of the palace, there is a fine fountain. Consider it a bonus fountain. You can see it for free, but you might like to buy a ticket and visit one of Rome's finest private art collections.

Inside the palace is the Doria Pamphilj Gallery, where works by Titian, Velasquez, Filippo Lippi and Caravaggio (and many other fine artists) compete with the seventeenth-century splendor of the palace.

The two Caravaggios are *Penitent Magdalene* and *The Rest on the Flight to Egypt*. The star of the collection is Diego Velasquez's portrait of Pope Innocent X (Giovanni Battista Pamphilj), the man who commissioned the Fountain of the Four Rivers in Piazza Navona (see Chapter 10). It shows a man with a ruddy face, a bulbous nose, big ears, a wispy beard and moustache, and rather menacing eyes. Not exactly a flattering likeness, but the pope's reaction when he saw it (if the story is to be believed) was "*troppo vero!*"—too true! The rueful exclamation is widely quoted but difficult to verify.

There is another portrait of Pope Innocent X in the gallery, a bust in Carrara marble by Gian Lorenzo Bernini. It contrasts greatly with the painting. The pope is shown as a much more thoughtful, sensitive man. Some writers argue that Innocent was terrorized by his widowed sister-in-law, Donna Olimpia Maidalchini.[1] You can also see her portrait bust, by Alessandro Algardi, before leaving and decide for yourself whether she seems like someone who could intimidate the pope. If you

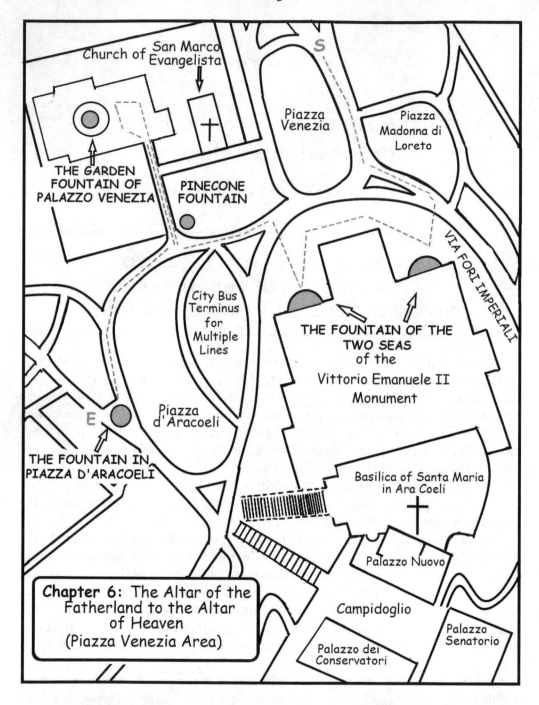

Church of San Marco Evangelista

S

Piazza Venezia

Piazza Madonna di Loreto

THE GARDEN FOUNTAIN OF PALAZZO VENEZIA

PINECONE FOUNTAIN

VIA FORI IMPERIALI

City Bus Terminus for Multiple Lines

THE FOUNTAIN OF THE TWO SEAS
of the
Vittorio Emanuele II Monument

E

Piazza d'Aracoeli

THE FOUNTAIN IN PIAZZA D'ARACOELI

Basilica of Santa Maria in Ara Coeli

Palazzo Nuovo

Chapter 6: The Altar of the Fatherland to the Altar of Heaven (Piazza Venezia Area)

Campidoglio

Palazzo Senatorio

Palazzo dei Conservatori

visit the gallery (it's usually open daily from 10:00 a.m. to 8:00 p.m., but check www. doriapamphilj.it), take the free audio guide. Most of the commentary is by the present owner, Prince Jonathan Doria Pamphilj, and he does a great job, though I still don't know why Pamphilj is spelled with a "j."

As you continue along via del Corso, you can't miss the enormous façade of the Vittoriano facing you beyond the end of the street. That's your objective, the grand pile of white marble with its columns and statues and Victor Emmanuel II on his gargantuan bronze horse. Actually, your first objective is the lower left-hand corner of the building's base. So continue until the Corso spits you out into Piazza Venezia, and stay left of the grassy center of the traffic circle. Keep as far left as you can, out of the street and the traffic flow, until you can safely cross at a crosswalk in front of Piazza Madonna di Loreto, toward the Vittoriano. As I write, Piazza Madonna di Loreto is really just a large archeological dig surrounded by concrete barriers, so be careful. Take a look at Trajan's Column on your left, with spiral reliefs telling the history of his conquest of the Dacians (today's Romanians). At the end of the crosswalk, turn left on the sidewalk and notice our next fountain to your right, forming a corner of the Vittoriano's base. It features a muscular marble chap wearing nothing but a giant seashell on his head, sitting above a waterfall.

The Fountain of the Two Seas—
La Fontana dei Due Marione (1906)
ARCHITECTS: GIUSEPPE SACCONI, PIETRO CANONICA, AND EMILIO QUADRELLI

The Vittoriano, also known as the Altare della Patria (Altar of the Fatherland), and in English as the Victor Emmanuel II Monument, is an enormous neoclassical structure made of white Brescian marble. Located between the Capitoline Hill and Piazza Venezia, it is a symbol of the unification of Italy under King Victor Emmanuel II, which was accomplished in 1870 when the forces of the Risorgimento wrested control of Rome from the papacy. The monument, whose dominating presence is unpopular with many Romans, has been the object of ridicule, with nicknames such as "The Wedding Cake" and "The Typewriter." Nevertheless, for many others, it is a powerful symbol of national unity and pride, especially since 1921, when the unidentified remains of an Italian soldier were interred in an altar on the first terrace of the monument. This "Tomb of the Unknown Italian Soldier" (along with its eternal flame) is guarded 24 hours a day, every day, by members of the Italian military.

Whether you like the aesthetics of the monument or not, it's a lot of fun to explore. There's an old-fashioned Museum of the Risorgimento inside, where you can see somewhat dusty but fascinating relics of that great movement, and, rather sadly, you'll likely have it to yourself, because the hordes of tourists outside rarely seem to visit. In season, you can have lunch on one of the terraces. There are sensational views of Rome from all the terraces, especially the very top one, which you reach by taking a glass-walled elevator. Someone who disliked the Vittoriano once remarked that the best thing about the views is that they're the only panoramas of Rome that don't include the Vittoriano.

The monument was designed by architect Giuseppe Sacconi and required thousands of workers, artisans, and artists to complete. Two well-known sculptors were commissioned to create fountains at the base of the structure, at either end of the façade. The two works are now considered one composition known as "The Fountain

The Fountain of the Adriatic Sea: This cascade and the muscular showoff above are part of the Fountain of the Two Seas. Located at one corner of the Altar of the Fatherland (the Vittoriano), this half represents the Adriatic Sea.

of the Two Seas." As we often see, the classical device of personifying bodies of water through powerful, semi-reclining male figures was used. The fountain on the left as you face the monument, sculpted by Emilio Quatrelli, represents the Adriatic Sea. The sea god seems to shade his eyes from the rising sun as he scans the eastern sea.

Now, you must circle around the front of the Vittoriano, to the opposite corner of the monument, and visit the second half of our fountain.

On the right, the spirit of the Tyrrhenian Sea, created by Pietro Canonica, seems to sit more upright on his rocky perch, as if listening for an approaching storm from the west. Both fountains—or, rather, both halves of the fountain—consist of the sculpted figure on a ledge, and from underneath the ledge a forceful waterfall fills a semi-circular basin, which overflows in a curtain of tumbling water into a large pool. Both fountains are satisfyingly noisy and a treat for kids. Pietro Canonica, by the way, was a very important sculptor in the early twentieth century. Many of his works can be seen in the Villa Borghese park at a museum dedicated to him: the *Museo Pietro Canonica* (www.museocanonica.it).

Now, with your back to the Tyrrhenian Sea sculpture, look ahead, across the busy streets in front of you. Just to the left of Piazza Venezia's big traffic circle, there's a small grassy park with a few umbrella pines. Through the trees, beyond the park and sandwiched between buildings, you'll see the white façade of a church, with three

The Fountain of the Tyrrhenian Sea: At the opposite corner of the Vittoriano, you'll find the allegorical depiction of the Tyrrhenian Sea, sitting on a rock, with a cascade below him, similar to the one for the Adriatic.

arched doors on the ground level and a three-arched loggia above. The church is San Marco Evangelista, and the park is Piazza San Marco. Find the long crosswalk and carefully cross the tangle of streets between you and the park. Once on the sidewalk in front of the park, turn left. At the next corner, you'll find a little fountain in the form of a pinecone.

The Pinecone Fountain of Piazza San Marco— La Fontana della Pigna di Piazza San Marco (1927)
Architect: Pietro Lombardi

This little fountain in the southwest corner of Piazza San Marco, in front of the Church of San Marco Evangelista, was designed by Pietro Lombardi as one of ten *rioni* fountains commissioned by the Rome municipality. They were intended to honor the traditional symbols of each ancient district, or *rione*. *Pigna* means pinecone, and the Pigna *rione* was named for a famous sculpture of the first century AD that stood near the Pantheon until the eighth century, when it was moved to the courtyard of the old Saint Peter's Basilica. It was a bronze pinecone, 12 feet high, and it now occupies its own courtyard in the Vatican Museums. (You can read all about it in Chapter 13, which deals with Vatican fountains.)

The Pinecone Fountain of Piazza San Marco—*La Fontana della Pigna di Piazza San Marco.* **This little fountain honors the Pigna district of Rome and provides a welcome drink of pure water to those visiting the busy Piazza Venezia area.**

Lombardi's little Pigna Fountain evokes the giant pinecone, but on a much more human scale. It's made of travertine and depicts a pinecone resting on what may be two flower petals. On either side of the fountain, there is a small basin between the petals, which catches the flow from a nozzle at just the right height for pedestrians to use. It is much appreciated by the crowds of sightseers drawn by the Vittoriano and nearby Piazza Venezia.

Now, standing just to the left the Pinecone Fountain, with your back to the Vittoriano, go straight ahead for about 100 feet, toward an inside corner formed by two wings of the huge palazzo that frames the little park. Sitting massively where the walls meet, you'll see a giant marble sculpture of a woman—just her head and upper torso, very eroded by time. This is "Madame Lucrezia," a very important icon of Rome.

Madame Lucrezia is one of the six sculptures known as the "Congress of Wits" or "Talking Statues," who were surreptitiously adorned, centuries ago, with satirical and often scurrilous messages about Rome's rulers. We've met Facchino and Babuino already, and we'll meet some other members of the group along the way. I'll tell you more about them when we meet another, up on the Capitoline Hill.

For now, though, just to the right of Madame Lucrezia, there's an arched doorway, which should be invitingly open if it's between 8:15 a.m. and 7:30 p.m. It leads into the Giardino di Palazzo Venezia. Farther to the right of the doorway is the façade and entrance of the San Marco Evangelista church, very ancient but Baroqued in the eighteenth century. Let's step into the church for a quick look.

Luckily, the Byzantine-style ninth-century apse mosaic survives. Among other scenes, you'll see Saint Mark introducing Pope Gregory IV (who commissioned the mosaic) to Christ. Gregory has a square halo, meaning that when the mosaic was made, he was still alive—and, obviously, optimistic.

But you came here to enjoy a fountain, so return to the arched doorway beside Madame Lucrezia and step through it, into the garden.

The Garden Fountain of Palazzo Venezia—La Fontana del Giardino di Palazzo Venezia (1730)
ARCHITECT: CARLO MONALDI

Also called *Venezia Sposa il Mare* (Venice Marries the Sea), this fountain is in the courtyard garden of Palazzo Venezia. The palace was built for Cardinal Pietro

The Garden Fountain of Palazzo Venezia: This lovely but strange fountain in the courtyard garden of Palazzo Venezia portrays a female doge of Venice "marrying" the Adriatic Sea by dropping a golden ring in the water.

Barbo in 1455, and when Barbo became Pope Paul II in 1464, he set about enlarg-
ing the palace substantially, so that it became one of the most imposing private resi-
dences in Rome. It remained a papal summer residence until 1564, when it was given
to the Republic of Venice by Pope Pius IV and used by *La Serenissima* as the Venetian Embassy. In 1797, when the Venetian republic fell to Napoleon and was subse-
quently traded by him to Austria, the palace became the Austrian Embassy to the
Vatican. Palazzo Venezia was acquired by the Italian state in 1915. During the Fascist era, Benito Mussolini had his office in the palace and used to address the public
gathered in Piazza Venezia from the balcony. Palazzo Venezia now houses the *Museo
Nazionale del Palazzo di Venezia*, featuring art, ceramics, and statuary (http://
museopalazzovenezia.beniculturali.it).

The fountain is within a circle of palm trees in the peaceful *cortile*, and it shows
a young female doge holding a ring between her thumb and index finger, about to
cast it into the sea. I probably shouldn't call her a doge, because I suppose Carlo
Monaldi simply meant her to symbolize Venice—historically, all the doges of Venice
have been male. In hundreds of artworks, though, the city of Venice is represented
as a woman, and no doubt Monaldi put the ducal *corno* on her head to emphasize
her role as *La Serenissima*. She stands on an open bivalve seashell with a ridged surface. Water flows down the ridges into a pool below. At her feet, the lion of Venice
crouches, holding the traditional open book, on which is written *Pax tibi, Marce,*

The Garden Fountain of Palazzo Venezia: The doge has been hesitating about dropping the
ring since 1730.

Evangelista meus—"Peace be unto you, Mark, my Evangelist." Opposite the lion, a cherub displays a scroll with tributes to Popes Alexander VIII and Benedict XIII. The shell is supported by three muscular Tritons, while dolphins sport in the pool beneath the fountain and putti play on the rim.

This is an interestingly different depiction of an actual ceremony performed by the doges of Venice each Ascension Day, when Venice symbolically "married" the sea, the traditional source of the city's wealth and power. The ritual involved a procession of boats, including the doge's state barge *Bucintoro*, to the northwest end of the Lido opposite the Isola Sant'Andrea, where the Venice Lagoon meets the Adriatic. Here the doge would drop a gold ring into the water, saying (in Latin), "We marry thee, sea, as a sign of true and perpetual domination."

After you exit from the Giardino di Palazzo Venezia through the arched doorway, go past the Pigna Fountain, carefully crossing the street toward the stone steps ahead of you. The steps lead into the graveled, tree-shaded center of Piazza d'Aracoeli. You can, if you prefer, skirt the park on the sidewalk on the right, or continue about half-way through the park, less than 100 yards. Find the exit from the park with a crosswalk across via di San Venanzio, and, after crossing, you'll find yourself next to a grand (if somewhat bedraggled) fountain.

The Fountain in Piazza d'Aracoeli—La Fontana di Piazza d'Aracoeli (1589)
ARCHITECT: GIACOMO DELLA PORTA

A little background about the area around Piazza d'Aracoeli: On the highest point of the Capitoline Hill, at the top of a steep flight of 134 steps called the *Scalinata dell'Ara Coeli*, is the *Basilica di Santa Maria in Ara Coeli* (Basilica of Saint Mary in the Altar of Heaven). It's the official church of Rome's city council and home to relics of Saint Helena—Constantine the Great's mother—and the *Santo Bambino*, a carved wooden image of the infant Jesus, which is credited with miraculous healing powers. In fact, during the nineteenth century, the *Santo Bambino* was frequently brought to the bedsides of people who were too ill to get to the church.

The church and its convent are wedged tightly between the Campidoglio to the south and the Vittoriano monument to the north. At the bottom of the *Scalinata* and a few steps north, encircled by busy streets, is a large oval area, which contains both the outdoor bus terminal and the graveled park you just crossed. This is the Piazza d'Aracoeli. And the fountain here, on the grimy triangle of pavement you've reached, is a grizzled veteran of many years in one of the busiest, noisiest, most historic, and most changeable parts of Rome.

Piazza d'Aracoeli once hosted two important markets: one, known simply as the *Mercato*, was on the western slope of the Capitoline Hill, and the second, the *Mercatello* ("Little Market"), was in the northern part of the piazza. Two medieval towers rose beside the square, close to the *Mercato*. By the time Giacomo della Porta began construction of the fountain, the towers had been long demolished, the markets were gone, and stately sixteenth-century palazzi lined the square, proving

The Fountain in Piazza d'Aracoeli: I hope someday to drop by the piazza and find that the thick mineral coating disfiguring this venerable fountain has been removed. Someday ...

that gentrification is nothing new. Some of the palazzi are still there, on the west side, though most houses on the entire eastern side of the piazza were razed in 1885 to make way for the Vittoriano. Then, in 1930, Mussolini had a large street built, running from Piazza Venezia past the Theatre of Marcellus southward to support expansion of the city toward the sea. Construction of this "via del Teatro di Marcello" demolished even more buildings in the neighborhood, and a very busy feeder street now separates the fountain from the actual Piazza d'Aracoeli. However, the fountain is very well known to the Romans, who seat themselves precariously on the iron railing surrounding the lower basin while waiting for one of the many buses that stop there.

Della Porta's design features an irregularly oval marble basin, decorated with carved masks. In the center of the basin, a marble baluster supports a smaller, circular basin whose underside is also adorned with masks. On the baluster, two small escutcheons bear the SPQR emblem of the Roman people, and two larger shields are carved with the coat-of-arms of the Chigi family, honoring Pope Alexander VII (born Fabio Chigi). A triangular arrangement of six small mounds representing mountains is one of the heraldic symbols of the family; it can be faintly seen on the shields, but the "mountains" are prominently displayed in the middle of the upper circular basin. It is from the topmost of these mounds that a plume of water issues, filling the basin and starting a cascade of water over the rims of the two basins and into a large, circular pool at ground level. Surrounding and supporting the six terracotta-colored mounds at the top are four marble putti.

The Fountain in Piazza d'Aracoeli: As you can see, Piazza d'Aracoeli is just a few steps from the Campidoglio, the most beautiful piazza in Rome. Beyond the fountain, one of the *Dioscuri* **waits with his horse at the top of the Cordonata Stairs.**

The putti were placed there by della Porta to preserve the memory of a famous fountain, in the old Saint Peter's Square, that was destroyed when construction of the new Saint Peter's church and square began.[2] The old fountain had featured identical putti. The memory, alas, is gone once more. When I last saw this fountain, the putti were nearly unrecognizable, almost completely covered by accumulated limestone deposits, and the rims of both basins were invisible under their own plump mineral coats, left by the water that has washed over them since … well … who knows when they were last cleaned?

By now you know that Piazza Venezia is replete with city buses, so if you want to return to your lodgings rather than continuing on to the next chapter and you aren't within walking distance of your hotel or B&B, you can catch a ride. Check the www. atac.roma.it *site. Or there is a taxi stand in Piazza Madonna di Loreto on the east side of Piazza Venezia, almost at the foot of Trajan's Column.*

If you are ready to soldier on immediately, stand by the Fountain in Piazza d'Aracoeli with the Vittoriano to your left and look straight up the street. Where the street curves right, you'll see two great staircases. One leads steeply up from the street to the left, and another rides a gentler slope almost straight ahead. It is the gentler slope you want to climb. The stairs are called the "Cordonata Staircase," and that is where we begin Chapter 7.

⋙ 7 ⋘

Caput Mundi

Capitoline Area

THE WALK BEGINS FROM THE BOTTOM OF THE CORDONATA STAIRS BELOW THE CAMPIDOGLIO.

Cordonata simply means an inclined path with shallow steps. They were designed by Michelangelo, and they are such a pleasure to climb that you'd think you were on an escalator—500 years old, but the only one in Rome that never fails. Actually, the steps are shallow and wide so that, long ago, people could ride their horses up the hill.

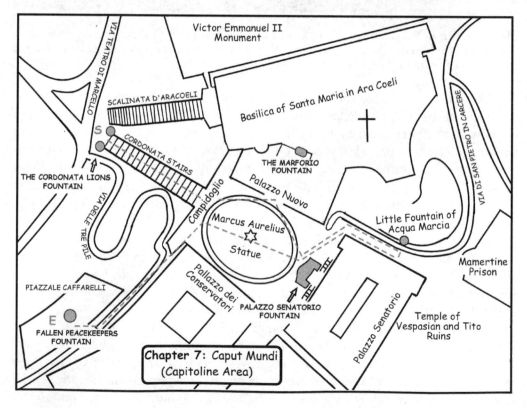

Chapter 7: Caput Mundi
(Capitoline Area)

Our next group of fountains begins at the bottom of the steps and continues above them. But first, a bit of history about the piazza at the top:

In the fourth century BC, the Romans built a defensive wall surrounding seven hills: the Aventine, Caelian, Capitoline, Esquiline, Palatine, Quirinal and Viminal. The Servian Wall, it was called, after King Tullius Servius. Ever after, Rome has been "the City on Seven Hills," despite the fact that Servius' wall crumbled and was replaced seven centuries later by the Aurelian Walls, which were much longer and encircled numerous other hills. Yet even today Rome's heart is still defined by those seven famous hills.

On one of the hills there was a temple, completed in 509 BC, dedicated to Jupiter Optimus Maximus, also known as Jupiter Capitolinus. The temple was called the Capitolium, and so the hill soon bore the same name, keeping it throughout the centuries in which Latin was the language of the Republic and the Empire. In English, we call it the Capitoline Hill, but in later medieval times, as the Italian language evolved from Latin, the word *Capitolium* morphed into *Campidoglio*, and that is what Italians call the hill today. The English word *capitol* is derived from the same root, and *capital* (meaning "money") also dates back to the Capitoline Hill: the goddess Juno, in her identity as *Juno Moneta*, had a temple in her honor on the hill, where, it seems, Roman coins were minted.

The Egyptian Lions Fountain: The two lions guarding the entrance to the Cordonata staircase are, collectively, also called the Cordonata Lions Fountain. On a good day, they spit arcs of water into the basins before them. In this photograph, the water is turned off.

In antiquity, the Capitolium was the site of another important building: the Tabularium. It was a grand, multi-story structure near the southeast edge of the hilltop, and it was used as office space for government officials; more importantly, it contained all the official records of the ancient Roman Republic. Amazingly, part of it still remains on the Capitoline, from which point there are thrilling views of the Forum and the Coliseum. You can visit it, where it forms part of the architectural ensemble of the hill.

It's almost time to climb that wonderful staircase, which will gently deposit you in the most beautiful piazza in Rome. But first notice the two Egyptian lions, carved from dark grey (almost black) granite, or perhaps basalt, resting on the balusters flanking the bottom of the stairs.

The Egyptian Lions Fountain, aka the Cordonata Lions— La Fontana dei Leoni Egizi (1562)
Architects: Unknown sculptor of antiquity and Michelangelo Buonarotti, completed by Giacomo della Porta

The two lions were actually installed on Michelangelo's balustrade in 1562 by Giacomo della Porta, on the orders of Pope Pius IV. They're much older than

The Egyptian Lions Fountain: Here, the Cordonata Lions are in full expectoration. The stairs lead to the Capitol Hill, known as the Campidoglio.

the stairs. They were part of the décor of the first-century BC Temple of Isis, in the *Campus Martius* (the ancient "Field of Mars"), not far from the Pantheon. Both the Temple of Isis and its next-door neighbor, the Temple of Serapis, were built for an Egyptian religious cult that had become popular in Rome, in a century that saw the crumbling of the Republic and the beginning of the Empire. I don't know whether the lions were carved in Rome in the Egyptian style or whether they were imported from Egypt. Most early descriptions appear to assume an Egyptian origin, and the stone does appear to be Egyptian basalt.

Sometimes the lions are allowed to eject streams of water from the little pipes they hold in their mouths. They have calmly spouted water, off and on, since 1588, when the *Acqua Felice* was extended to the Capitoline Hill. There is a persistent legend that the lions have even been used to celebrate the election of some popes—specifically, Clement X in 1670—by dispensing wine, both *rosso* and *bianco*, instead of water, and the story is briefly mentioned in at least one source, though I can't confirm it. I hope it's true![1]

Anyway, let's go up the Cordonata steps. At the top of the stairs, you'll be welcomed by the marble statues of Castor and Pollux, each standing beside his horse.

These young gentlemen were the twin sons of Leda, who, you may recall, was visited by Zeus in the form of a swan—which may be why both brothers wear odd

The Egyptian Lions Fountain: From this angle, the lion is framed by a corner of the Vittori-ano on the left and the church of *Santa Maria in Ara Coeli* on the right. The church's name means "Saint Mary of the Altar of Heaven."

conical hats, perhaps meant to recall the shells of the eggs from which they hatched. (We met these two young men before, and their horses, at the Fountain of Monte Cavallo!)

Beyond the twins, there is another statue, a monumental equestrian bronze of a bearded man, bareback, astride a powerful, prancing warhorse. The rider's right arm is raised, as if to bestow a blessing or command attention. The bronze rider is dark, but long ago the statue in the piazza was covered with pure gold and glistened in the sunlight. What you see now is a copy of the original statue; in 1981, the genuine ancient work was moved inside the great building on the right side of the square. It is the only complete monumental equestrian bronze statue of a pagan Roman emperor to have survived from antiquity, and some of the ancient gold still clings to the bronze. It escaped being melted down for cannons or coins during the Middle Ages because it was believed to represent the Christian emperor Constantine. In fact, the bearded rider is Marcus Aurelius, a second-century AD warrior emperor, enlightened ruler, and author of the *Meditations of Marcus Aurelius* (an important work of Stoic philosophy).

On either side of the ersatz Marcus are noble buildings with nearly identical façades, each decorated with statues along the roofline. On the right, the building that houses the original mounted statue of the emperor is one wing of an important museum containing many famous ancient Roman sculptures and artifacts, as well

The Campidoglio: In the center of the piazza, Marcus Aurelius, astride his horse, welcomes visitors. Behind him is the Palazzo Senatorio (Rome's City Hall).

as medieval and Renaissance art. It's called the Palazzo dei Conservatori. The other half of the museum is on the left, and it's called the Palazzo Nuovo, since it was built much later to match its older sibling across the square.

When you visit the Palazzo dei Conservatori, you can cross the square to the Palazzo Nuovo via an underground passage that connects them, called the *Galleria di Congiunzione*; on the way, there is a branch tunnel to an arcaded part of the old Tabularium, from whose great arched openings there is an unsurpassed view of the Forum and, in the distance, the Coliseum. The whole museum complex is known as the *Musei Capitolini*—that is, the "Capitoline Museums" (www.museicapitolini.org).

Beyond the great statue there is another splendid palace, with a double staircase across its façade. This is the Palazzo Senatorio, seat of Rome's government, and it was built on top of the surviving structure of the Tabularium, still standing after twenty-one centuries.

You'll notice that the dark cobbled surface of the piazza is embellished with an elaborate rosette pattern in white marble, centered on a twelve-pointed star surrounding the Aurelius statue; this design was the invention of Michelangelo Buonarotti, who redesigned the piazza in 1536. Interestingly, the marble pattern he drew for the pavement in 1536 wasn't completely installed until 1940, four centuries later, replacing a design installed by Giacomo della Porta.

But Michelangelo's revamping of the hill was a huge project that took shape slowly over many years. It included the construction of the Palazzo Nuovo, the redesign of both the Palazzo Senatorio and the Palazzo dei Conservatori, the design of the staircase to the piazza, and much else, including placing two ancient sculptures on the Senatorio façade that later became fountains—though Michelangelo didn't necessarily know that there would actually be fountains, because there was no water laid on to the hill until after the great artist's death. But then, in 1588, the fountains began to flow.

About halfway along Palazzo Nuovo's façade, there is an opening through which you can see a huge fountain—or at least part of it. You can peek through the opening, but there's usually a guard posted who'll cough meaningfully if you get too close. I hate to mention it, but if you want a closeup look at the fountain (which is named for the giant figure, Marforio, who dominates it), you'll have to buy a ticket to the Capitoline Museums. Believe me, it's worth it, and not just to see Marforio. Both palazzi are part of the museum system. You'll probably spend the whole day there, but don't worry—you won't starve. In the Palazzo dei Conservatori there's a café with both indoor and outdoor dining in season, as well as wonderful views.

The Marforio Fountain—*La Fontana di Marforio* (first century AD, assembled 1734)
ARCHITECTS: UNKNOWN SCULPTOR (CA. FIRST CENTURY AD), GIACOMO DELLA PORTA, AND FILIPPO BARIGIONI

Marforio is another huge reclining river god (or perhaps an ocean god, since an inscription on the granite basin that was discovered with him reads "*mare in foro*,"

The Marforio Fountain: In the time of the Caesars, Marforio poured water to refresh the crowds in the Roman Forum. Now he presides grandly over the Capitoline Museums on the Campidoglio.

which could account for his name). He's a big fellow, about 20 feet long, but he seems an amiable giant, with a relaxed and peaceful expression; his full moustache and curly beard, if they were white, would look perfect on a mall Santa.

He apparently was part of an operating fountain in antiquity, located in the Forum between the Mamertine Prison (where Saint Peter was imprisoned) and the Arch of Septimius Severus—just a few hundred feet east of the Campidoglio. Lost from sight in the early Middle Ages, he was rediscovered in the thirteenth century, along with the great granite basin into which he had politely poured water in the glory days of ancient Rome.

In 1588, Marforio was moved to Piazza San Marco in order to decorate that small square near Palazzo Venezia, but the granite basin, his long-time companion, was moved to the middle of the unexcavated part of the Forum (then called Campo Vaccino, or, as we would say, the "Field of Cows"), where it served as a drinking trough for the cattle that browsed there. It was during this time that Marforio was adopted by the people of Rome as part of the "Congress of Wits," a group I've mentioned before, also known as the "Talking Statues": six statues on which disgruntled citizens pasted or hung satirical notes lampooning the ruling clergy or government figures, including the pope.

The Marforio Fountain: Now that he's an old man, Marforio no longer has to pour water—two angry-looking little dolphins and what looks like a lion-headed octopus fill up the pool.

Marforio was partnered with the most famous of the "Talking Statues," Pasquino (from whom the word *pasquinade* comes), as a couple of wisecracking comedians. Pasquino still inhabits the small square named for him near Piazza Navona. During Napoleon Bonaparte's occupation of Rome, Marforio exclaimed, "*Pasquino, tutti I francesi sono ladri!*" ("Pasquino, all the French are thieves!"). Pasquino replied, "*Non tutti, Marforio, ma buona parte*" ("Not all, Marforio, but a good part"—a pun on Napoleon's surname).

We've previously encountered three other members of the "Congress of Wits": Facchino, Babuino, and Madame Lucrezia. Marforio brings the total to four. I've told you a bit about Pasquino, though we won't actually meet him until Chapter 10. There is another, Abbot Luigi, whom we'll encounter in Chapter 9. Of the six "Talking Statues," Facchino, Babuino, and Marforio are also fountains.

In 1594, Giacomo della Porta brought Marforio to the top of the Campidoglio and installed him on the north side of the piazza (where Michelangelo's Palazzo Nuovo would eventually be completed), with a new basin. Here Marforio served *Acqua Felice* water for a number of years, until the Palazzo Nuovo was built and the fountain was demolished, though the statue was spared. Marforio finally found a comfortable home in 1734, when Filippo Barigioni created a courtyard within the Palazzo Nuovo with a splendid setting for Marforio, where he rests placidly, in front

The Fountain of Palazzo Senatorio: Under a double staircase designed by Michelangelo, beneath a porphyry image of Minerva, and flanked by gigantic stone river gods, the fountain is also called *La Fontana della Dea Roma*.

of a backdrop of Egyptian granite columns, in a marble, semi-circular basin. He doesn't even have to pour water nowadays—the water flows into the basin through the mouths of a couple of grumpy dolphin heads and from the lips of a creature that seems to be half lion and half octopus.

Marforio's original granite basin, once humiliated as a drinking trough for cattle, was rescued in 1818 and now is the functional centerpiece of the great fountain on Monte Cavallo.

Palazzo Senatorio is the building at the back of the square, past Marcus Aurelius, facing the Cordonata Stairs. It's not part of the Capitoline Museums—it's actually Rome's City Hall. Its façade is the setting for our next fountain.

The Fountain of Palazzo Senatorio—La Fontana di Palazzo Senatorio (1588), aka La Fontana della Dea Roma
ARCHITECTS: UNKNOWN SCULPTOR OF ANTIQUITY AND MICHELANGELO BUONAROTTI, COMPLETED BY GIACOMO DELLA PORTA

When Michelangelo designed the new façade of the Palazzo Senatorio and built the impressive double staircase there, he placed two huge first-century statues of river gods beneath the steps. Under the left flight of stairs (as you face the building) is a reclining marble giant resting on a sphinx. He represents the Nile, of course.

The Fountain of Palazzo Senatorio: What river does this gigantic river god represent? The little sphinx on whom the statue leans might give us a clue, if he's into riddles.

On the right, another colossal figure rests his elbow on a stony niche containing the infant twins Romulus and Remus. The boys are playing with the Capitoline Wolf, their adoptive mother. This statue represents Rome's Tiber River, although in fact the statue has been altered. Originally, there was a tiger where the twins and the wolf are now, because the statue once honored the Tigris River in ancient Mesopotamia.

Both of the statues were moved from the Quirinal Hill, where they may have been part of the Baths of Constantine—though they date stylistically to a period three centuries earlier than Constantine's fourth-century AD complex. Above the two river god statues, in a huge niche in the palazzo's façade, a rather smallish statue of the goddess Roma stands on a triple plinth, holding a globe and a spear. She was originally meant to be Minerva, but, like the Tigris River god, she was repurposed. Her face, arms and toes are of white marble, but her dress is a deep purple porphyry.

When the *Acqua Felice* water arrived on the hill, Giacomo della Porta added two marble basins to the Senatorio's façade, a smaller one within and above the larger. Water wells up within the small basin and overflows in sparkling drops into the larger, whose rim is between waist and chest height for most visitors—handy for dabbling your fingers.

To the left of the Palazzo Senatorio (as you face the building), there is a column supporting one of the most famous sculptures in Rome, one that is duplicated, even today, in far-flung outposts of the ancient Roman Empire. I'm speaking of the Etruscan

Top: The Fountain of Palazzo Senatorio: Here's a riddle from the fountain's other river god: Someone reworked the tiger under the god's right elbow into Romulus and Remus and the she-wolf. Which river is represented? (Hint: It's not the Tigris.) *Bottom:* The rim of the lower basin serves as a desktop for these visiting French students as they make notes about the Campidoglio. The Palazzo dei Conservatori, part of the Capitoline Museums, is in the background.

carving of the Capitoline Wolf, the foster mother of Romulus and Remus, the mythical founders of Rome. After you pass the sculpture of the wolf and the suckling babes, you'll be on via San Pietro in Carcere. Ahead, looming beyond the crest of the hill, you can see the top of the Arch of Septimius Severus, sitting in the Forum, looking like you could almost reach out and touch it. However, if it's a warm day, you may be more interested in a small, rather humble fountain mounted on a garden wall to your left.

The Little Drinking Fountain of Acqua Marcia—La Fontanella dell'Acqua Marcia (late nineteenth or early twentieth century?)
ARCHITECT: UNKNOWN

There is a curved spout dispensing a clear stream of water into a travertine basin with a graceful pedestal beneath. After you've had a drink, you'll notice the inscription SPQR on the arched surface above the spout, and below it, the words *Acqua Marcia*.

The Little Drinking Fountain of *Acqua Marcia*: The convenient, attractive, and historic little drinking fountain on the Campidoglio, *La Fontanella dell'Acqua Marcia*, offers you refreshment on your way to the Forum Overlook.

The *Aqua Marcia* was one of the four greatest aqueducts of ancient Rome, and drinking from so distinguished a source would certainly be an honor. Alas, the inscription has slightly misled you. Like a similar small fountain, *La Fontana di Borgo Pio* (which you'll meet in Chapter 13, which describes the Vatican and Borgo), the inscription claims *Aqua Marcia* as the water source. This is not *exactly* true. In the 1860s, during the papacy of Pius IX, a part of the old *Aqua Marcia* was restored and given a new channel; the restored aqueduct was given the name *Acqua Pia Antica Marcia*, in honor of the pope. Thus, it is water from a fairly modern offspring of the *Aqua Marcia*, and not the original aqueduct, that flows from the modest little fountain.

Exactly when the fountain was installed is a bit of a mystery. No one seems to know. It cannot have been before 1860, because the new *Acqua Pia Antica Marcia* aqueduct didn't yet exist. Actually, it couldn't have been before 1870, because during the papal rule in Rome the letters SPQR had rarely been used since antiquity on public structures in Rome—rather, the coat-of-arms or other insignia of the current pope was used. Since papal rule in Rome ended with Italian unification in 1870 (when poor Pius became "a prisoner in the Vatican"), that is the earliest possible date the fountain could have been installed. It was a tumultuous time, as the Kingdom of Italy and the papacy struggled for control of Rome, and perhaps the records regarding this fountain's creation were lost. My guess is that it was installed in the late nineteenth century.

The Little Drinking Fountain of *Acqua Marcia*: From the overlook, it almost seems that you can touch the Arch of Septimius Severus. The ever-flowing stream from the little fountain is on the left of this picture, behind the tourist in the red jacket.

Before leaving the Campidoglio, turn left just before the Cordonata steps and proceed along the side of the Palazzo dei Conservatori on via delle Tre Pile. You will soon see a small, graveled piazza to your right, shaded by deciduous trees. The far side of the piazza forms a terrace, with a fine northwest view of the rooftops and domes of Rome, over the Theatre of Marcellus and then sweeping north toward the Pantheon and Piazza Navona. Here you'll find a rather mysterious fountain.

The Fountain in Piazzale Caffarelli—La Fontana di Piazzale Caffarelli (2010)
ARCHITECT: UNKNOWN

In the center of the square, in a sunken basin, is a cone-shaped fountain of copper, from the top of which water bubbles and flows down the sides of the cone. Atop

The Fountain in Piazzale Caffarelli: Two well-dressed gentlemen take a break in front of the Fountain of the Fallen Peacekeepers, a modern fountain honoring Italian peacekeeping forces killed in a terrorist attack in Iraq.

the cone is an upright stone, bearing a carved relief of an ancient warrior, and on one sloping side of the fountain there is a bronze plaque that reads, *"Ai Caduti militari e civili nelle missioni internazionali per la pace, 12 novembre 2010"* ("To the military and civilian casualties of international peacekeeping missions, 12 November 2010").

I call this memorial "The Fountain of the Fallen Peacekeepers." There is no other information about the fountain at the site, and after much research I still do not know who designed, constructed, or paid for the fountain. However, the fountain appears to memorialize a tragedy that took place in Nasiriyah, Iraq, seven years before the fountain was dedicated, when, on November 12, 2003, a suicide bomber drove a tanker truck at high speed toward the headquarters of the Italian *Carabinieri* unit charged with peacekeeping in the area. When the truck struck the building, it exploded in a huge fireball, killing twelve *Carabinieri*, six other Italian soldiers, one Italian civilian, and nine Iraqi civilians. Many other residents of the area, which is near the Euphrates River in southern Iraq, were injured. Every year on November 12, there are memorial events around Italy, honoring the victims of the attack, usually in venues larger than this tiny piazza. Often the events are organized by the Italian Ministry of Defense, so it's possible the fountain was sponsored by that agency.

And now, some useful information: Directly across via delle Tre Pile from the Fallen Peacekeepers fountain, a door in the wall of the museum (it has a plaque reading "Piazzale Caffarelli" next to it) is usually open during museum hours. You can

The Fountain in Piazzale Caffarelli: The Fallen Peacekeepers fountain is a mixture of ancient and modern, just like the vista of Rome behind it.

enter here without paying, and up the stairs are public toilets. Farther up the stairs, you can get into the museum's café, also without paying for a museum visit. All perfectly legal, though you can't go from the café into the exhibits.

Our walk ends here. If you want to get back to where you're staying, and it's too far to walk, the area below the Campidoglio is served by a multitude of buses; check with www.atac.roma.it for a bus ride. There is also a taxi stand near Trajan's Column, in Piazza Madonna di Loreto. To proceed to our next group of fountains, return to the Campidoglio, go down the Cordonata Stairs, and turn to Chapter 8.

~ 8 ~

Walls, Gates, Fountains, and Memories

Roman Ghetto Area

THIS WALK, LIKE THE PREVIOUS ONE, BEGINS AT THE BOTTOM OF THE CORDONATA STAIRS.

Say goodbye to the Cordonata Lions and turn left into via del Teatro di Marcello. On your way, you'll see ahead something resembling a smallish version of the

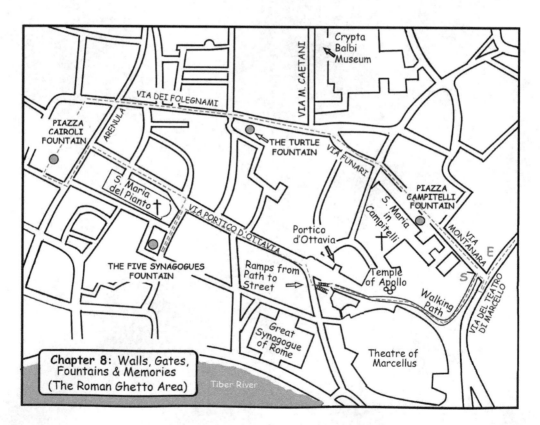

Chapter 8: Walls, Gates, Fountains & Memories (The Roman Ghetto Area)

110

Coliseum. It's actually the Theatre of Marcellus, which was built during the reign of Augustus and named after his nephew. Marcellus probably would have followed Augustus as emperor had he not died young.

After about 200 yards, before you reach Marcellus' theater, cross via del Teatro di Marcello at the crosswalk. Just to the right of the crosswalk is via Montanara, and five or six feet into via Montanara, on the left, is a gate in a tall metal fence. The fence protects the Area Archeologica del Teatro di Marcello e del Portico di Ottavia. The gate should be open every day between 9:00 a.m. and 7:00 p.m. in summer and 9:00 a.m. and 6:00 p.m. in winter (so plan this walk accordingly). We'll step through the gate soon and take an ancient path into the old Roman ghetto, through a famous portico. But first let me briefly introduce the area through which we'll travel, meeting four fountains and lots of history.

There were Jewish residents in Rome as far back as the second century BC. Many of them were slaves (particularly after Rome captured Jerusalem in 70 AD), but others were merchants and traders who had migrated from the Roman province of Judea in more peaceful times. They were a familiar presence and part of the economic and cultural fabric of the city for many centuries, until in 1556 Pope Paul IV decreed that the Jews should be segregated into a low-lying area near the Tiber, often subject to flooding, just west of the Campidoglio. From north to south the ghetto extended approximately from today's via delle Botteghe Oscure to the Tiber River, and east to west from via del Teatro di Marcello to near via Arenula.

Various cruel restrictions and requirements were placed on the Jewish population. They were forbidden to be outside the ghetto when the gates were closed, from two hours after sunset until sunrise. They were excluded from many occupations and generally lived in extreme poverty and crowded conditions, though they were allowed to operate pawn shops (a profession forbidden to Christians). The men were required to wear blue scarves outside the ghetto, and the women wore blue veils. They could not own real property, even within the ghetto—though one small protection was that the Christian owners from whom ghetto residents rented their dwellings could not evict them without cause, nor raise their rents. William Hazlitt, recounting a visit to Rome in 1826, said that on every Good Friday, Jewish residents were forced to attend Catholic church for a sermon on the truth of Christianity and then run races on the Corso "for the entertainment of the rabble."[1]

The requirement for Jews to live in the Roman ghetto ended in 1870, when the Kingdom of Italy wrested control of the city from the papacy. The walls were demolished in 1888.

Until 1453, when the ancient *Aqua Virgo* aqueduct was restored by Pope Nicholas V and renamed *Acqua Vergine*, most Romans got their water from the Tiber River or from wells. The repaired aqueduct fed an early, modest Trevi Fountain, where city dwellers could get plenty of fresh water. But it was a long trek, to collect water in buckets, from the ghetto to the Trevi and back.

Pope Sixtus V commissioned a new aqueduct, the *Acqua Felice*, completed in 1586, which eventually fed twenty-seven new fountains, large and small, in Rome. There are four large fountains in or very near the ghetto; two of them were among those created for (and watered by) *Acqua Felice*. All of them are graceful, elegantly designed fountains, and one of them is world famous.

Now, let's go through the gate, heading down a slight slope toward the Theatre of Marcellus. At the bottom of the slope, the path turns right, skirting the perimeter of the theater. On the right are three tall, fluted columns on a broken plinth, topped with remnants of a pediment. Below, huge sections of broken columns and other marble pieces lie scattered along the side of the path. The three columns and the fallen bits are all that's left of the Temple of Apollo Sosianus. Behind Apollo's ruined temple are the remains of another temple, dedicated to the warrior goddess Bellona, the sister (or perhaps wife) of Mars. Both temples date to pre-imperial times, though the standing columns of Apollo were erected by Augustus. Where the path divides ahead, keep right.

About 100 yards past Apollo's temple, just after passing a row of four broken columns on the right, the path will pass beneath an elevated walkway. Almost immediately beyond the walkway, the path will end. On your left, a series of modern ramps, in a switchback arrangement, will take you from the path to the street a dozen or so feet above.

At the top of the ramp, you will emerge into Largo 16 Ottobre 1943, named for the date when over a thousand people were deported from here to Auschwitz. Only sixteen of the deportees survived. There is a chill here, in any weather.

If you'd like to visit the historic main synagogue of Rome, the Tempio Maggiore, which also contains the Museo Ebraico *of Rome, its entrance is to your left, at the*

Pathway to the Porto d'Ottavia: This path passes between the Theatre of Marcellus and the three columns of the ruined Temple of Apollo Sosianus on its way to the historic Roman ghetto.

corner of Largo 16 Ottobre 1943 and via Catalana, but I suggest that you check open-
ing times and tour arrangements at www.museoebraico.it/en/ before visiting.

For now, turn right from the top of the ramp, where the largo narrows into via del
Porto d'Ottavia.

The street is named for an ancient, arched structure of brick, with marble columns, to your right. It was once an entrance to the Circo Flaminio, a chariot race-
track of imperial times. The Porto d'Ottavia was built by Augustus around 27 BC and
dedicated to his sister, Ottavia. No doubt she was an ardent fan of chariot racing.

Via del Porto d'Ottavia is "Main Street" for the ghetto, and the street, as well as
the surrounding area, is well worth exploring, and not only for the array of restaurants, most offering traditional Roman Jewish fare. (One famous dish I recommend
is *carciofi alla Giudia*, crisp deep-fried artichokes—it looks like vegetable roadkill
but tastes like heaven, if done right!)

Continue on via del Porto d'Ottavia about 200 yards, until, at a wide intersec-
tion, you see a large, four-lobed shape outlined in white marble in the road surface.

Stop and look around. There was once a great square here, Piazza Giudia. It has
vanished, filled with the buildings and businesses of our modern world. There was a
fountain here, too, long ago, just outside the ghetto gate. It was the main fresh water
supply for the people who lived behind the walls. The fountain was removed when

Restaurant menu on via del Porto d'Ottavia: A gastronomic specialty of the ghetto—deep-
fried artichokes Jewish style (*carciofi alla Giudia*).

the ghetto walls came down, but the place where it stood from 1593 until 1888 is
marked, for remembrance, in the pavement.

*Turn left now, into a short street that leads, after about 100 feet, into Piazza delle
Cinque Scole. Here you'll find a fountain with a familiar shape.*

The Five Synagogues Fountain—La Fontana del Pianto, aka La Fontana di Piazza delle Cinque Scole (1593)
ARCHITECT: GIACOMO DELLA PORTA

Piazza Giudia was once the main square of the Roman ghetto, and its fountain
was a fine example of Giacomo della Porta's work. It still is. Pope Gregory XIII commissioned it from della Porta in 1591, and it was installed two years later, providing a reliable, nearby water source for many ghetto residents. There are two elevated
marble basins, a small circular one above a larger, four-lobed vessel. The upper basin
emits water from four *mascheroni* (carved masks) into the vessel below. Beneath
both, water collects in a travertine pool.

When the ghetto walls were demolished in 1888, Piazza Giudia was demolished
and built over, and the fountain was dismantled and put into storage. Half a century
later, in the 1930s, the fountain was reinstalled here in Piazza delle Cinque Scole,

The Five Synagogues Fountain: *La Fontana delle Cinque Scole* was, historically, one of the
few sources of water for Ghetto residents. The fountain was moved when the Ghetto closed.
Its historic location, about a hundred yards away, is marked by a white marble outline in the
modern street.

not far from the church of *Santa Maria del Pianto*—hence the two names by which it is known today. Piazza delle Cinque Scole is named for the five *scole* (synagogues) of the historical Jewish communities in Rome: the Castilian, Sicilian, Temple, New, and Catalan.

Return to via del Porto d'Ottavia, at the white fountain outline, and turn left. At this point the street becomes via Santa Maria del Pianto and, after about 100 yards, ends at via Arenula. You will see a small park across via Arenula, called Piazza Cairoli, enclosed by a low metal fence. Turn left. After one block, at the left end of the park, you'll find a crosswalk. Cross via Arenula here. You'll see a sizable fountain within the park near the left end. There is an entrance to the piazza just behind the fountain.

The Fountain in Piazza Cairoli—La Fontana di Piazza Cairoli (1888)
ARCHITECT: EDOUARD ANDRÉ

Baron Guglielmo Huffer must have been a very wealthy man, as well as a generous one, because in 1888 he financed the creation of a public garden in central Rome, just outside the Roman ghetto, about a five-minute walk from Sant'Andrea

The Fountain in Piazza Cairoli: A simple, pleasant fountain in what should be a pretty park, Piazza Cairoli, if they ever finish working on it.

della Valle. It happened that the city planners were demolishing the ghetto walls and rerouting a street at the time, and they were only too happy to put the empty space they'd created to use. Except for his garden, which is now called Piazza Cairoli, the good baron doesn't seem to have left much of a mark on history.

A French designer, Edouard André, was hired to create the garden. He wanted a fountain in his design, and luckily an ancient granite basin had just been unearthed in the forum. So his fountain consisted of that giant basin, sitting on a square marble pedestal with volutes at the corners, and a smaller basin above on a fluted marble stem. The smaller basin's "stem" (technically called a baluster) was originally decorated with carved dolphins, but they have been lost.

The garden is named for Benedetto Cairoli, who was a hero of the Risorgimento and briefly prime minister of Italy. There is a bronze statue on a marble plinth in a corner of the garden, depicting a gentleman deep in thought. Curiously, the statue is not of Benedetto Cairoli. The thoughtful chap is actually Federico Seismit-Doda, another patriot in Italy's struggle for freedom. Although he was born in Dalmatia—now Croatia—he was part of Venice's struggle with Austria in the heady days of the 1848 insurrection against Austrian rule.

I would not be surprised if, whenever you visit, you find Piazza Cairoli overgrown, unkempt, or undergoing renovation. I always have. It's a mystery.

You can leave Piazza Cairoli at the opening in the fence just past Seismit-Doda's statue. Turn right and cross via Arenula at the crosswalk, and then go left and quickly right into via Falegnami. After about 150 yards, you'll see a small piazza on your right, with a fountain in the center. You'll find this famous fountain in all the guidebooks and travelogues.

The Turtle Fountain—La Fontana delle Tartarughe (1588)
Architects: Giacomo della Porta, Taddeo Landini, and Gian Lorenzo Bernini

The "Turtle Fountain," in Piazza Mattei, gets its water from the *Acqua Vergine*, which was renovated and expanded in the 1560s. Originally, it was to have been installed in Piazza Giudia, the main square of the Roman ghetto, but a local nobleman, Muzio Mattei, petitioned the pope to allow the fountain to be built next to his property in a small square named for his family. In return, he agreed to pave the square and maintain both the piazza and the fountain.

Unlike most municipal fountains of the time, the Turtle Fountain prominently features realistic bronze sculptures contrasting spectacularly with several varieties of marble. The fountain is composed of a basin of grey African marble atop a white marble baluster, at the bottom of which are four colorful *portasanta* marble basins in the form of seashells. The whole composition, on a base of porphyry and white marble, stands in the center of a wide travertine pool.

There are bronze figures of four naked youths (*ephebes*, meaning "adolescents") leaning negligently above the "seashell" basins, facing outward from the baluster. Each holds the tail of a bronze dolphin in one hand and rests his opposite foot on the

The Turtle Fountain—*La Fontana delle Tartarughe*—is one of the most famous in Rome, partly because it is composed of four distinct types of marble, plus porphyry. (And the little turtles, of course!)

dolphin's head. There are four bronze turtles poised on the upper basin's rim, seemingly reluctant to dive into the water; each youth extends one arm upward, as if gently encouraging the little turtles to take a swim.

The upper basin is filled by a water nozzle in its center, and the water is released to fill the seashells through the mouths of putti masks on the basin's sides and from the open mouths of the four dolphins.

The fountain's marble structure was designed by Giacomo della Porta, and both the dolphins and the bronze *ephebes* were cast by Taddeo Landini. Originally there were eight dolphins, but only four were used on this fountain. It's thought that the extra four were planned for the upper basin rim, to help fill it, but there was not enough water pressure to use them. It's probable that they were eventually used on the Soup Bowl Fountain in front of the *Chiesa Nuova* but ultimately lost. The upper basin rim remained empty until, in 1658, during a renovation commissioned by Pope Alexander VII, the little turtles were added. Gian Lorenzo Bernini is said to have created them, thus providing a visual reason for the youths' raised arms. A word to the wise: Don't drink the water; it's treated chemically to protect the bronze figures.

There is a rather odd legend that Duke Muzio Mattei hoped to marry a young

Top: The Turtle Fountain: Gian Lorenzo Bernini added the namesake turtles to the fountain's upper rim in 1658. *Bottom:* The Turtle Fountain is also much admired for the four bronze *ephebes* (adolescent boys), cast by Taddeo Landini in 1587.

woman whose father considered the duke a layabout and refused to consent to the marriage. The duke (so goes the story) invited the father and daughter to a party in his palazzo and kept the father up until dawn. In the morning he flung open a window overlooking the piazza, exclaiming, "See what a Mattei can do in one night!" There was the fountain, complete and flowing with water! The girl's father was astonished and consented to the marriage. The duke had the window walled up, to remember the great event, and they all lived happily ever after.

In retrospect, Muzio's all-night blowout must have been pretty rowdy. Construction of an elaborate marble and bronze fountain outside your house, especially in an era before modern double glazing, cannot have been easy to ignore. (Actually, construction of the fountain, even without the turtles, took about seven years.)

At Piazza Mattei, via Falegnami changes to via dei Funari. Turn right out of Piazza Mattei into via dei Funari, and follow it until it ends in about 200 yards. Be careful to remain on via dei Funari: At a point where the street passes an old, apparently abandoned church, the Chiesa di Santa Catarina dei Funari, *there is an alleyway called via dei Delfini. Don't take it—bear right on via dei Funari. Shortly thereafter, via dei Funari ends. Here, there are three streets to choose from; take the middle one, which bears slightly to the right. It quickly becomes Piazza Campitelli. After about 50 yards, you'll see the grand façade of* Santa Maria in Campitelli *on your right, with a distinctive "broken" pediment above the door; just beyond the church, you'll see the fountain.*

The Fountain in Piazza Campitelli—La Fontana di Piazza Campitelli (1589)
ARCHITECTS: GIACOMO DELLA PORTA AND POMPILIO DE BENEDETTI

Another fine fountain created by the indefatigable Giacomo della Porta's workshops, it was presumably commissioned by four noble families who lived in the adjacent streets. (The imposing palazzo of the Capizucchi family is just across the street from the fountain.) The families' coats of arms are carved on four sides of the octagonal main basin of the fountain. Two of the remaining sides have the insignia of the city of Rome, and the two other sides are decorated with grotesque masks, traditional *mascheroni*.

In the center of the octagonal basin is a marble baluster, supporting a small circular basin of polychrome marble, filled by a plume of water that overflows into the octagonal basin below.

The water empties, finally, through pipes in the mouths of the *mascheroni*, into a square pool just above street level. The eight bollards in the street that support an iron railing around the fountain are actually short sections of ancient columns recovered from the area around the Theatre of Marcellus.

You'll see the Baroque façade of the *Chiesa di Santa Maria in Campitelli* nearby on the square. The fountain is nearly a century older than the church, and it once occupied pride of place in the center of the piazza. However, when the church was built, beginning in 1679, the fountain was moved to the southwest corner of the piazza.

Top: The Fountain in Piazza Campitelli: No doubt you've noticed by now that most of the major fountains in Rome were commissioned by popes. However, this fountain was commissioned by four noble families in the neighborhood. *Bottom:* The splendid façades surrounding Piazza Campitelli make a fine background for the graceful curves of the fountain.

Looking at the fountain with your back to Palazzo Capizucchi, you'll see, just to the left of the fountain, an arch in the set-back portion of the building ahead of you. There's a glass door in the arch, and if it is unlocked, you can pass through it onto a terrace. The terrace and the area below it make up the *Cortile del Tempio di Apollo in Circo*. This is an archeological site that contains many of the giant scattered and broken stones that made up the southern half of the Circus Flaminia. From the terrace you can also see the Theatre of Marcellus, the remaining columns of the Temple of Apollo, and part of the path you took when you began this itinerary.

Our visit to the fountains of the Roman ghetto ends here. The beginning of the next chapter's tour is about 1,000 yards away. If you don't want to walk there immediately, continue past the fountain, where Piazza Campitelli becomes via Montanara. This will lead you, after just one block, to via del Teatro di Marcello. You may recognize the gate at the corner! To find public transport back to your lodgings, turn left on via del Teatro di Marcello; there will be lots of bus stops near the Cordonata Lions or Piazza d'Aracoeli. As usual, consult www.atac.roma.it to find your route. There are taxis near Piazza Venezia next to Trajan's Column.

To continue to our next group of fountains: From the Fountain in Piazza Campitelli, head back up the street with the façade of Santa Maria in Campitelli *church on your left. After about 50 yards, when you get to the intersection of three streets,*

A view of the Theatre of Marcellus from the terrace of the *Cortile del Tempio di Apollo in Circo*. Below is an archeological area littered with the stony remains of the Circus Flaminia, from the time of Augustus.

the smaller, middle street will be the same via dei Funari you took from the Turtle Fountain to Piazza Campitelli in the last tour. Take via dei Funari, but before you get to the Turtle Fountain, just past Chiesa di Santa Catarina dei Funari, *turn right on via Michelangelo Caetani and continue for one long block, about 150 yards. As you approach the next corner, you'll pass (on your right) the flank of a building that shelters the Crypta Balbi, part of the National Roman Museum, with remnants of an ancient Roman theater's portico, as well as medieval structures and exhibits of once-buried artifacts from a thousand years of daily life in this city block. If you want to visit, the entrance is just around the corner to the right on the next street, via delle Botteghe Oscure. (But check https://museonazionaleromano.it/en/crypta-balbi first, because visiting days and hours may be limited.)*

However, to continue on to our next fountain group, cross via delle Botteghe Oscure at the crosswalk in front of the Crypta Balbi, and turn left. Continue on via delle Botteghe Oscure about 200 yards. Turn right on via di Torre Argentina. You'll walk about 100 yards, beside the Largo di Torre Argentina archeological ruins on your right. The remains of four very early Roman temples are there, as well as the Theatre and Curia of Pompey. The curia is where Julius Caesar was murdered, or so it's said. Down among the ruins there is a cat sanctuary, where volunteers feed and tend feral cats.

When you get to the end of Largo di Torre Argentina, cross to the left side of via di Torre Argentina, turn right, and cross via del Sudario. Then bear left into Corso Vittorio Emanuele II. After about 350 yards, you'll see the façade of the church of Sant'Andrea della Valle on your left and the Piazza di Sant'Andrea della Valle across the Corso on your right. Our next fountain is in the piazza.

9

Tosca's Church to Agrippa's Temple
Pantheon Area

Across the Corso Vittorio Emanuele II from the fountain is the elegant Baroque façade of the Basilica of Sant'Andrea della Valle. Facing the church, take a look along the building's left flank, to where the wall forms a corner with an adjacent church building. You'll see a marble statue of a man in a Roman toga. He probably was a senator back in the days of the Republic. Today, however, he is Abbot Luigi, so named by neighborhood people in the fifteenth century, who made him one of the "Talking Statues" and routinely hung satirical notes on him mocking the ruling classes. We discussed the "Talking Statues" at some length in Chapter 7, when visiting the Marforio Fountain.

You may find that Abbot Luigi is missing his head. I've never seen his head, actually, but originally he had one. Stealing it and then waiting for the authorities to replace it with a plaster copy was great fun, I'm sure. At one point someone hung a sign around his headless neck: "Whoever stole my head better return it quick or they'll put me in the government." Apparently, the authorities got tired of the game and stopped supplying the abbot with a new noggin. However, Abbot Luigi, the last time I saw him, was just a headless statue, not a fountain, so we'd better press on. Cross the street to the piazza (carefully, it's a busy intersection), and I'll tell you a bit about the fountain's past life.

The Fountain of Sant'Andrea della Valle—La Fontana di Sant'Andrea della Valle (1614)
ARCHITECT: CARLO MADERNO

When the Kingdom of Italy wrested control of Rome from the papacy in 1870, Pope Pius IX declared himself "a prisoner in the Vatican," and for 59 years the popes of Rome refused to set foot outside of the Vatican's small territory, because

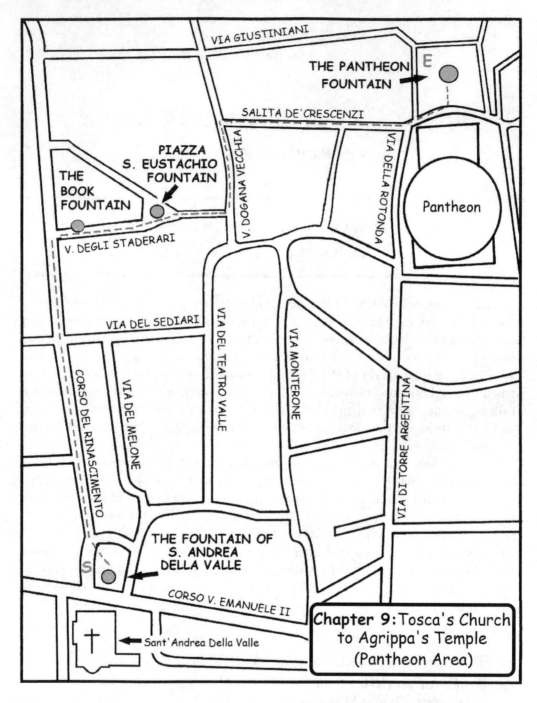

VIA GIUSTINIANI

THE PANTHEON FOUNTAIN

E

SALITA DE'CRESCENZI

PIAZZA S. EUSTACHIO FOUNTAIN

THE BOOK FOUNTAIN

Pantheon

V. DOGANA VECCHIA

VIA DELLA ROTONDA

V. DEGLI STADERARI

VIA DEL SEDIARI

CORSO DEL RINASCIMENTO

VIA DEL MELONE

VIA DEL TEATRO VALLE

VIA MONTERONE

VIA DI TORRE ARGENTINA

THE FOUNTAIN OF S. ANDREA DELLA VALLE

S

CORSO V. EMANUELE II

Sant'Andrea Della Valle

Chapter 9: Tosca's Church to Agrippa's Temple (Pantheon Area)

doing so would be tacit acknowledgment of the Italian state's authority over Rome. Eventually, a compromise was reached in 1929, and *Il Duce* (Benito Mussolini) decided to celebrate by constructing a grand boulevard, stretching all the way from Castel Sant'Angelo to Saint Peter's Square; part of it plowed right through the medieval labyrinth of the Borgo district, bordering the Vatican. In Piazza Scossacavalli, directly in the path of the new via della Conciliazione, there was a fine fountain

The Fountain of Sant'Andrea della Valle stands across the street from the famous church, which, opera fans will recall, is the setting for the first act of *Tosca*.

that Carlo Maderno had made for Pope Paul V in 1614. Construction of via della Conciliazione took many years to complete, so it was not until the late 1930s that Piazza Scossacavalli was demolished and the fountain was dismantled and placed in storage. There was an ill-fated attempt to place it in Piazza della Pilotta on the Quirinal Hill, but that project was abandoned. In 1958, though, the fountain finally found a new home, just 100 yards or so south of the *Fontana della Sapienza*, facing the Basilica of Sant'Andrea della Valle. The fountain is now wholly identified with the church.

The church is deservedly famous for its sophisticated Baroque façade and its lavishly frescoed nave and interior dome, but it is perhaps most famous as the setting for the first act of Giacomo Puccini's opera *Tosca*. However, although there are many intriguing chapels in the church, the Cappella Attavanti (where, in the opera, the painter Cavaradossi hides the fugitive political prisoner Angelotti) is fictional, and you won't find Cavaradossi's painting of the Holy Virgin, either, because Cavaradossi is also fictional.

For the fountain, Maderno relied on a tried-and-true formula: a basin formed from a marble square with semi-circular lobes extending from each side, plus an ornamental pedestal in the middle (this one has griffins and eagles clinging to double scrollwork volutes) supporting a smaller basin, into which water spills from a mound of marble acanthus leaves. Piazza Sant'Andrea della Valle is next to the heavily traveled Corso Vittorio Emanuele II, and both trucks and buses use the piazza to

The Fountain of Sant'Andrea della Valle: For more than 300 years, the fountain was the pride of quiet Piazza Scossacavalli, in the Borgo. Then, in 1930, Mussolini bulldozed the piazza to make way for via della Conciliazione, and the fountain was moved here.

turn into via del Melone and out of Corso Rinascimento, so beware when admiring the fountain close up!

Now, for the next fountain, begin with your back to the church, and, passing left of the fountain, take the street straight ahead, Corso del Rinascimento. Stay on the right side of the street. After about 200 yards, you'll see a large stone portal topped with a pediment on your right.

If the door is open, you can step through and enter a roomy courtyard, which, since the fifteenth century, has graced a great palazzo belonging to the University of Rome. At the opposite end of the courtyard is the unique curved façade of Francesco Borromini's seventeenth-century church, *Sant'Ivo alla Sapienza*. Notice the strange corkscrew design of the spire-like lantern of the dome. If you happen to be there on a Sunday morning, you may be able to peek inside the church. The rest of the palazzo now contains the Italian State Archives.

However, let us return to Corso del Rinascimento, continue to the next corner, and turn right on via degli Staderari. About 20 feet from the corner is an interesting wall-mounted fountain.

The Fountain of Wisdom, aka the Book Fountain— La Fontana della Sapienza, aka La Fontana dei Libri (1931)
ARCHITECT: PIETRO LOMBARDI

This small fountain is the last of the ten neighborhood fountains that the Municipality of Rome commissioned from Pietro Lombardi in 1925. We've seen other fountains from this commission. Their purpose, besides providing a convenient source of drinking water, was to celebrate the historical *rioni* (districts) of Rome by memorializing important aspects of each district in the design of the fountain. This fountain is in the Sant'Eustachio district.

Sapienza, in Italian, means "wisdom," and *La Sapienza* is the popular name of the University of Rome. The fifteenth-century building that borders almost the entire length of via degli Staderari's south side was once the university's home. *La Fontana della Sapienza*, which is embedded in the building's wall, still bears the university's name, although it is also known as the *La Fontana dei Libri*—the "Fountain of the Books"—because the sculptural composition features four large books,

The Book Fountain (*La Fontana della Sapienza*): Obviously a popular rendezvous for thirsty people, it is named for the building in whose wall it is embedded. Once the home of the University of Rome—*La Sapienza*—the building now houses the Italian State Archives.

flanking the Sant'Eustachio district's symbol (a deer head below a cross). There are bookmarks depicted as hanging from the pages of the books, terminating in hemispherical water nozzles. There are two other streams of water arcing from the center of the upper books.

Originally, carved *fasces* (bundles of rods that symbolize authority) decorated the ends of the bookmarks. During the 1920s and 1930s, they also represented the Fascist regime, both as a symbol and as the source of Fascism's name; the *fasces* were chiseled out of the fountain after Mussolini fell from power.

The fountain underwent a thorough restoration in the winter of 2018, thanks partly to a gang of Dutch hooligans who, after a football match in 2015, damaged the *Barcaccia* fountain in Piazza di Spagna. An association of Dutch students, calling themselves *Wij Zijn Romeinen*—"We are also Romans"—started a crowdfunding drive to pay for the restoration of *La Barcaccia*, but by the time they had raised a substantial amount to donate to the repairs, the Little Boat Fountain had already been restored. So, the money was diverted to the repair of other fountains in Rome, including Bernini's Fountain of the Bees in the via Veneto and the Book Fountain. When I last saw the fountain, in February 2018, repairs and restoration work had just been completed, and the fountain was sparkling clean, but the water supply had not yet been turned on.

The Book Fountain: For obvious reasons, the fountain is popularly known as the Book Fountain (*La Fontana dei Libri*).

The Book Fountain: A group of football hooligans unwittingly helped pay for the cleaning and restoration of the fountain. This is how it looked immediately afterward: sort of naked.

Now, continue on via degli Staderari, and within a block you'll come to a small piazza. There are often soldiers or police around this area, because the Italian Senate buildings border the piazza. Here you'll find our next fountain.

The Fountain in Piazza S. Eustachio—La Fontana di Piazza S. Eustachio, aka La Fontana del Senato (ca. 62 AD)
Architect: Unknown

Palazzo Madama is the home of the Italian Senate, and that is why this fountain, near the palazzo, is often called the Fountain of the Senate. But the palazzo was originally a Medici palace. It is named for Madama Margherita of Austria, an illegitimate daughter of Emperor Charles V, who lived there after her husband Alessandro de' Medici, Duke of Florence, was assassinated in 1537 by his cousin Lorenzino de' Medici. (Sorry, I don't have space to tell you that story here, but it's worth a little digging if scandal, sex, betrayal, political intrigue and murder interest you.)

Palazzo Madama sits over part of the Neronian Baths, which date from around 62 AD, so it isn't too surprising that twentieth-century excavations nearby turned up a large basin made of Egyptian granite from Aswan. Although the great vessel was in eight pieces, it was such a fine example of first-century workmanship that it was carefully repaired and erected where via degli Staderari widens toward Piazza Sant'Eustachio. It is set atop a pedestal of Carrara marble, within a wide octagonal pool made of volcanic peperino stone. Water wells up from the center of the basin

The Fountain in Piazza S. Eustachio, also known as *La Fontana di Piazza S. Eustachio* or *La Fontana del Senato*. This ancient granite basin once spent time as a hot tub in Nero's baths. Oh, what tales it could tell!

and overflows into the pool below. The fountain was inaugurated on the fortieth anniversary of the Italian Constitution, December 22, 1987. (After World War II, the Italian monarchy was ended by referendum, and the constitution was written and adopted soon afterward.)

Continue on via degli Staderari for 100 feet or so, and turn left into via della Dogana Vecchia. After a long block, turn right on Salita de' Crescenzi. Ahead you'll see the columns of the Pantheon's porch, at the end of the Salita. This is where you'll enter the Piazza della Rotonda, the square in front of the Pantheon, where you can admire the historic building (and the fountain in front of it). This piazza and this building are history incarnate, so we'd better talk about it a little before considering the fountain:

Marcus Vipsanius Agrippa was a man of many talents. He could command Roman legions on land or a fleet of warships at sea. He could plan and construct miles of aqueducts. He managed Rome's water supply and built hundreds of fountains, bringing fresh water to every part of the city. He built the earliest public baths in Rome. He served as consul three times. Shortly after he led Octavian's naval forces to victory against Mark Anthony and Cleopatra in 31 BC, he began construction of a temple celebrating this event. He may or may not have called it the "Pantheon" or dedicated it to "all the gods," as the name suggests. The building was completed around 27 BC, only to be damaged by fire in 80 AD and again in 110 AD.

Until recently, it was almost universally believed that the damaged remains of the original building were demolished during the reign of Emperor Hadrian, who built the present Pantheon building (perhaps to his own plans), finishing it around 125 AD, and that, as a noble and generous tribute to the great Agrippa, Hadrian repeated an inscription from the earlier building—*M Agrippa L F Cos Tertium Fecit* ("Marcus Agrippa, son of Lucius, three times Consul, made this")—on the frieze above the porch of his new building. In addition, it was believed that Agrippa's original Pantheon was a conventional, rectangular temple.

Recent archeological discoveries cast some doubt on this narrative.[1] It now seems that Agrippa's original building may have been about the same size as the present structure and that it, too, had a columned porch and a circular rotunda. What's more, studies of the bricks used to complete the present building date most of them to 110 AD, during the reign of Emperor Trajan, Hadrian's predecessor, though it is still believed that the Pantheon we see today was completed by Hadrian around 125 AD. So, it may be that both Trajan and Hadrian should be credited with rebuilding the temple, and it also may be true that Hadrian considered the building a *reconstruction* of Agrippa's Pantheon, rather than a replacement. He may have thought of the structure as, in fact, Agrippa's—repaired, improved, and modernized, with a breathtaking hemispherical dome—still the largest unreinforced concrete dome in the world—lit with an oculus almost 100 feet in diameter at the top.

After the collapse of the Western Roman Empire, many of the great buildings and monuments of Rome became quarries for building materials, but the Pantheon survived relatively intact, partly because it was such a unique and awe-inspiring structure, but also because in the seventh century Pope Boniface IV consecrated it as a Christian church, Saint Mary and the Martyrs. Ordinary folk swiftly nicknamed it Saint Mary Rotonda and called the large forecourt Piazza della Rotonda, which quickly became choked with small shops, sheds, and market stalls.

In the early fifteenth century, Pope Eugenius IV cleared and paved the area, which of course was soon full, once again, with small shops, sheds, and market stalls. But at least the vendors and their customers didn't have to wade through mud on rainy days. And, in time, the square would have its own splendid fountain.

The Pantheon Fountain—La Fontana del Pantheon (1575)
ARCHITECT: GIACOMO DELLA PORTA

In the 1430s, Pope Eugenius IV had his engineers install a porphyry basin and two basalt Egyptian-style lions in Piazza della Rotonda. The lions were originally from the Temple of Isis, which, in antiquity, was just south of the Pantheon near today's *Basilica di Santa Maria sopra Minerva*. I don't know where the basin originated. For many years, this modest fountain served the fishmongers in the square as a convenient place to keep their wares fresh, but in 1575 Pope Gregory XIII

The Pantheon Fountain shares Piazza della Rotonda with possibly the most unique and admired ancient building in the world, and it is topped with a genuine Egyptian obelisk from the Temple of Ra in Heliopolis. Architectural overload!

commissioned that tireless creator of fountains, Giacomo della Porta, to replace the basin and lions with a grander fountain that could utilize the newly plentiful water from the *Acqua Vergine* aqueduct, whose capacity had been recently increased. In fact, della Porta had been hired to create eighteen new fountains for Rome, and he set up a mass-production workshop that produced enough marble seashells, grotesque masks, and dolphins to decorate new fountains all over town. The fountains at either end of Piazza Navona and the fountain in Piazza Colonna were part of the contract.

For the Pantheon Fountain, he used a traditional design for the basin: a marble square with semi-circular lobes in the center of each side and travertine stairs accessing the basin. Water pours into the basin from a grotesque mask at each lobe. (The lions and the old porphyry basin were shunted off to one side of the square, and during the papacy of Sixtus V the lions were moved to the Fountain of Moses on the Quirinal. Much later, in 1740, Pope Benedict XIV had the porphyry basin taken to the church of Saint John Lateran, where his predecessor, Clement XII, was buried in it.)

In 1711, Pope Clement XI ordered that a red-granite obelisk, originally from the Temple of Ra in Heliopolis (an ancient city in Egypt, now buried beneath the streets of modern Cairo), be brought from Piazza San Macuto, just east of the Pantheon,

The Pantheon Fountain: Giacomo della Porta encrusted the central structure of the fountain with a riot of bizarre sea creatures and grotesque faces. His "dolphins" (as they're usually called) always look ferocious, not a bit like Flipper.

and erected in the center of the Pantheon Fountain. The obelisk, originally created for Pharaoh Ramses II, had been brought to Rome, probably in the first century, to decorate the Temple of Isis. It was rediscovered in 1373 and had stood where it was found ever since. The sculptor Filippo Barigioni moved it to Piazza della Rotonda and successfully raised it above the fountain, atop a new central pedestal decorated with four sinuous dolphins spouting water.

Before leaving the area, take a quick look at the streets behind the Pantheon. To begin, face the porch from the piazza and walk along the left flank of the building on via della Minerva.

You'll notice that in the giant masonry wall of the rotunda, there are brick arch patterns here and there. These aren't decorative—they're functional "relieving" arches that help sustain the enormous weight of the walls.

Just beyond the Pantheon, on your left, you'll see a unique sight: an Egyptian obelisk, sitting on the back of an elephant made of pinkish marble. Gian Lorenzo Bernini made the elephant, of course—can't get away from the guy. It was commissioned by Pope Alexander VII around 1665 and stands in front of the Gothic *Basilica di Santa Maria sopra Minerva*, so called because it was built above the buried ruins of a temple dedicated to Isis, which was mistakenly thought to have been a temple to

The Pantheon Fountain: The inscription below the pediment of the Pantheon's porch is mysterious. It credits Marcus Agrippa, Augustus' great jack-of-all-trades, with the creation of the building, although it was rebuilt during Hadrian's reign, more than a century after Agrippa died.

Minerva. In the church, there's a statue of Christ the Redeemer holding a cross (one of Michelangelo's lesser-known major works), as well as glowing frescoes by Filippino Lippi and a vaulted nave painted as the vault of heaven.

Our walk ends here. If you want to return to your accommodation at this point, there is a taxi stand in Piazza della Minerva, right beside the elephant and obelisk. For buses, there's Largo di Torre Argentina. To get there, return to the fountain, face the Pantheon's porch and take via della Rotonda along the right flank of the Pantheon. Continue straight, as the street name changes to via di Largo Argentina. After less than 400 yards, you'll be at Corso Vittorio Emanuele II. To check for your route, go to www.atac.roma.it. There's a taxi stand here, too, at the near end of the ruins, across the Corso.

Our next walk begins in Piazza San Simeone. As you know, the maps in this book don't cover routes from one chapter to another, but if you're up for it, here's how to get there anyway. It's simple, really, and there are some treats along the way.

To get to Piazza San Simeone from the Pantheon, start from the Pantheon fountain, facing away from the Pantheon's porch. Walk to the leftmost corner of the square, and turn left into via Giustiniani. After one long block, you'll come to a corner with the Baroque façade of the San Luigi dei Francesi church facing you on the right. Turn right into Piazza di San Luigi dei Francesi, in front of the church. If the church is open, you might like to step inside—in the Contarelli Chapel, there are three timeless masterpieces by Caravaggio: The Calling of Saint Matthew, The Martyrdom of Saint Matthew, *and* Saint Matthew and the Angel. *I don't want to be a spoiler by telling you about them, but prepare to be amazed.*

Anyway, continue straight past the church's façade one block, passing through Largo Giuseppe Toniolo into via della Scrofa; continue one more block on via della Scrofa, and then turn left onto via di Sant'Agostino. You'll see an archway at the far end of the block, but before you get there, you'll find a small piazza on your right, and the façade of another church, unsurprisingly called Chiesa di Sant'Agostino. *If you like Caravaggio, and the church is open, this is your lucky day. His* Madonna di Loreto *is here.*

Continuing through the archway, passing straight through Piazza delle Cinque Lune, you'll soon come to Piazza di Tor Sanguigna. There's an archeological museum here, where you can descend beneath a buried corner of Domitian's Circus, but we will return to that shortly. For now, continue straight through the piazza, and at the end, where three streets meet, take the narrow one directly ahead, via dei Coronari. Enjoy this pleasant little street, lined with shops, for about 500 feet; at this point, in a piazza to your right, you'll find a handsome sixteenth-century fountain with an unusual history.

One Ballerina, Two Sea Gods, and Four Rivers

Piazza Navona Area

Here you'll find a fine and venerable fountain, retired peacefully in a quiet, dignified little piazza after a busy career.

The Fountain in Piazza San Simeone—La Fontana di Piazza San Simeone (1589, rebuilt 1696)
ARCHITECT: GIACOMO DELLA PORTA

There was a square in Rome at the foot of the ancient Theatre of Marcellus, known as Piazza Montanara. It was named, some say, after the "mountain dwellers" who met there every day. They were rustic laborers and farmhands who were collected up and contracted by landowners and vineyard owners who needed workers. The piazza was, in fact, a labor exchange. In 1589, the Roman authorities hired Giacomo della Porta to construct a fountain to "supply water for the needs of the poor men." In 1696, the original simple fountain—just a travertine basin with a four-sided water-dispensing shaft in the center—was ornamented with a vase-shaped bowl atop the shaft, and the shaft was provided with carved masks on each side from which the water spouted.

Just off the square, in an alley called Vicolo della Campana, was the *Osteria della Campana* (Tavern of the Bell), which also catered to the thirst of the workers. The tavern was there long before the fountain; in fact, it existed as early as 1549. And it was still there in 1786 when Johann Wolfgang von Goethe, fleeing his life as a German bureaucrat and thirsting for adventure, met the innkeeper's daughter Faustina and furthered his Roman education considerably.

By the twentieth century, Piazza Montanara had become a popular meeting place and market square. Shopkeepers used the spaces under the lower arches of the

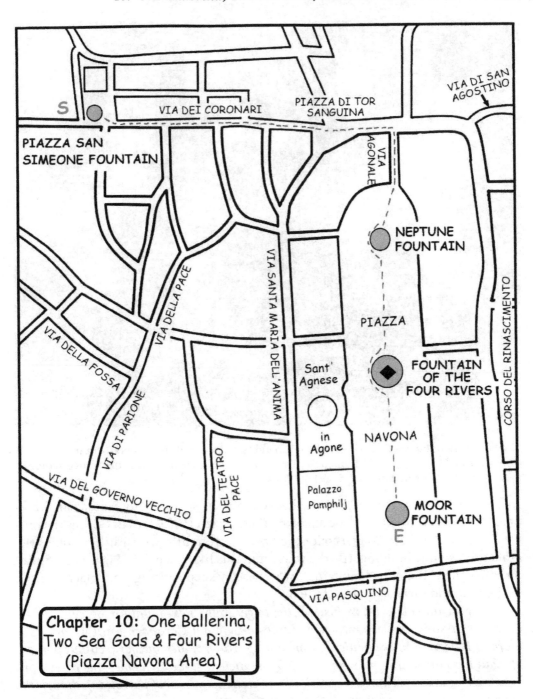

S

VIA DI SAN AGOSTINO

VIA DEI CORONARI

PIAZZA DI TOR SANGUINA

VIA AGONALE

PIAZZA SAN SIMEONE FOUNTAIN

NEPTUNE FOUNTAIN

VIA DELLA PACE

VIA SANTA MARIA DELL'ANIMA

PIAZZA

VIA DELLA FOSSA

CORSO DEL RINASCIMENTO

Sant' Agnese

FOUNTAIN OF THE FOUR RIVERS

VIA DI PARIONE

in Agone

NAVONA

VIA DEL TEATRO PACE

VIA DEL GOVERNO VECCHIO

Palazzo Pamphilj

MOOR FOUNTAIN

E

VIA PASQUINO

Chapter 10: One Ballerina, Two Sea Gods & Four Rivers (Piazza Navona Area)

Theatre of Marcellus to set out their wares, but the whole square disappeared in 1932 when a new street, via del Teatro di Marcello, was driven through the neighborhood. The fountain, luckily, was spared. It was carted off and reassembled in the Giardino degli Aranci (Orange Garden), on the Aventine Hill, next to the ancient church of Santa Sabina; in this most lovely setting, it dispensed water to visitors for over four decades.

The Fountain in Piazza San Simeone is comfortably retired in its quiet piazza after a career as a "ballerina." In the world of Roman fountains, ballerinas are fountains that move around a great deal. This one had two previous locations.

At last, in 1973, the fountain was moved into the small, shady Piazza San Simeone. One side of the piazza is occupied by the Palazzo Lancellotti ai Coronari, completed in 1610 by Carlo Maderno for the Lancellotti family, which still occupies the graceful Baroque building. (By the way, fountains like the one in Piazza San Simeone are called "Ballerina Fountains," because they keep dancing from place to place in the city; and there are many of them.)

Now we must backtrack, just a little, to get to the next fountain. So, leaving the Piazza San Simeone, let's retrace our steps on via dei Coronari, until we are once more in Piazza di Tor Sanguigna. Continuing straight, look out for a cutout portion of a building on your right, with the top of an ancient stone arch emerging from a pit. This is the small Museum of the Stadio Domiziano (Stadium of Domitian), though the entrance is around the building's corner, behind you.

Here, you can (for a fee) descend beneath a section of the curved northern edge of the stadium, where excavations have exposed part of the old structure. It seems to be one of the entrances to the grandstands, which were held up by great stone arches. It allows you a glimpse of what sports fans of long ago might have experienced on their way to their seats.

To reach our destination, though, continue past the cutout and turn right at the end of the building, into via Agonale. There are three famous fountains in a line before you.

The fountains are spectacular, but they benefit from an equally spectacular setting. So I hope you will indulge me, just for a little, while I talk about one of Rome's most beloved meeting places: Piazza Navona.

If you're an English speaker and you translate the word *piazza* in your head, you probably think "square"—like Trafalgar Square or Times Square. But Piazza Navona is definitely not square—it's a very long rectangle, oriented north-south, roughly rounded at its north end and truncated by a street on the south. It's lined by historic palazzi, grand Baroque churches, cafés, and *gelaterie*, and it's usually busy with sightseers, musicians, magicians, jugglers, caricaturists, souvenir stands, Greek statues that come to life for a euro—and perhaps a few pickpockets. But if you could step aboard a time machine in the piazza, and set it for the end of the first century AD, the musicians would quickly unplay their songs, the pickpockets would put the purloined wallets back in the tourists' pockets and exit the piazza backward, the grand buildings would melt away, and you would finally find yourself in a huge stadium—one whose stands might be full of perhaps 20,000 people, watching you try to dodge the thundering horses and chariots heading your way.

Once you reached safety, you would quickly deduce that you were in a Roman *circus*, or stadium, and you might recall that Emperor Domitian built one back in 86 AD, perhaps to provide entertainment to the people of Rome and help them forget their suspicion that he had murdered the previous emperor, his popular brother Titus.[1] And you would be right.

However, since you don't really have a time machine, we must resort to plain history. Domitian's stadium was called the Circus Agonalis after the Greek word *agone*, meaning games or contests; though the stadium was actually too small for chariot racing, the arena was used for other spectacles and sporting events, like footraces, discus or javelin throwing, horse racing, and bull baiting; in the Middle Ages, you might have seen knights jousting there. But eventually the stands were replaced by houses and tenement blocks. By the fifteenth century, the open area had become a fish-and-vegetable marketplace, until in 1869 the market was moved to Campo de' Fiori. Somehow, the name Circus Agonalis morphed into Piazza Navona. But via Agonale still leads to the piazza from the north, and Corsia Agonale enters from the east, showing that the old name is not forgotten.

In the sixteenth century, Pope Gregory VIII ordered the installation of three fountains, two of which were designed by Giacomo della Porta and placed at the north and south ends of the rectangle. The third was little more than a watering trough for horses in the center.

From the middle of the seventeenth century until late in the nineteenth, it was the custom on summer weekends to stop the drains and let the fountains overflow and flood the piazza so Roman citizens, rich and poor, could cool off in the temporary lake. (Of course, the wealthy tended to drive their carriages through the water rather than tucking up their skirts and trousers and wading like the ordinary folks!)

Now, on to the first fountain.

The Neptune Fountain in Piazza Navona—
La Fontana del Nettuno (1574)
Architect: Giacomo della Porta

The northern fountain, installed in 1574, was at first called the *Fontana dei Cal-derari* because a nearby street was occupied by foundries and workshops where copper cauldrons and other metal products of brass or bronze were made. The fountain was a large and handsome marble basin, but it had no decorative sculpture until 1878. (However, there is an engraving by Giovanni Battista Piranesi from 1751 showing the fountain with four large *mascheroni* adorning the sides. Piranesi apparently based his depiction not on the fountain as he found it but on a fountain design by Michelangelo that he believed had been used by Giacomo della Porta. One source says that della Porta himself removed the masks to use them on the Pantheon Fountain instead.[2])

In any case, by 1878 the other two fountains in Piazza Navona—the Fountain of the Moor and the Fountain of the Four Rivers—had been famous landmarks for many years. The new nation of united Italy had just been created, and since Rome was no longer ruled by the Vatican, the city council decided to update the old basin to compete with the two church-built fountains. So they commissioned the sculptor Antonio della Bitta to create a monumental statue of Neptune spearing a giant octopus for the center of the fountain; they also hired Gregorio Zappalà, who added an assortment of water nymphs, cupids, giant fish, crabs, and rearing aquatic horses to the composition. At that point, the fountain's name became *Fontana del Nettuno*—the Fountain of Neptune.

The Neptune Fountain: A lively group of nymphs, horses, dolphins, putti, and nameless other weird creatures sport on the rim of della Porta's basin, while in the center Neptune spears an angry octopus.

Top: The Neptune Fountain: The lights are coming on in the buildings on the square, and some of the vendors are thinking of packing up their wares—but the struggle goes on in the fountain. *Bottom:* Gregorio Zappalà's animated figures seem always on the point of movement. If the little *amorino* (putto) can evade the fish, maybe he'll swat that pesky pigeon away.

Little seems to be known about Antonio della Bitta, although the Neptune figure is an impressive work of sculpture. Gregorio Zappalà, who created the jolly group sporting in the fountain's basin, is better known. He started off working in a foundry (appropriate for one who helped decorate the former *Fontana dei Calderari!*). He had a successful career as a sculptor, creating, among other works, a statue of Saint Peter for the great *San Paolo fuori la Mura* church, and he received the Order of the Crown of Italy from King Victor Emmanuel II. And it is from him I learned that water nymphs have tails like satyrs—take a look!

The central theme of the composition makes an obvious reference to the Moor fountain's muscular sea god, who wrestles a twisting dolphin. It seems the Roman sea gods had a rather contentious relationship with some of their subjects, because the Neptune figure in the center of *this* fountain is attempting to spear a giant octopus, whose tentacles are wrapped tightly around his thighs, and it looks like he'd better hurry before the octopus gets a grip on any … ah … *vital* organs.

Next, we come to Bernini's blockbuster.

The Fountain of the Four Rivers—
La Fontana dei Quattro Fiumi (1651)
ARCHITECT: GIAN LORENZO BERNINI

Bernini had created masterpieces for Cardinal Scipione Borghese early in his career, like *The Rape of Proserpina* and *Apollo and Daphne*, but when his friend Maffeo Barberini became Pope Urban VIII, he gained an even greater patron and made the most of his good fortune. Working as both sculptor and architect, he created palaces like Palazzo Barberini, monumental fountains like the Triton in Piazza Barberini, and adornments for Saint Peter's Basilica, including the *Baldacchino* (a huge, four-story tall bronze rendering of the traditional cloth canopy used to protect a pope), which stands above the grave of Christianity's first pope, Saint Peter. According to tradition, Urban VIII ordered 200 tons of bronze removed from the porch of the Pantheon, to be used for the *Baldacchino*, which inspired this famous *pasquinade*: *Quod non fecerunt barbari, fecerunt Barberini*—"what the barbarians didn't do, the Barberini did." (It's likely that the bronze was actually used to cast 80 cannons for the Castel Sant'Angelo,[3] but the quip is still appropriate.)

However, Bernini encountered a serious setback when, in 1646, as the architect of Saint Peter's, he began to erect the bell towers he had designed, and the structures started cracking under their own weight. They had to be pulled down. Urban VIII had died two years earlier, and the new pope, Innocent X (Giovanni Battista Pamphilj), was an admirer of neither his predecessor nor Bernini. So when Innocent decided, in 1647, to commission a grand new fountain for the center of Piazza Navona, he invited designs from all the leading architects and designers in Rome—except Bernini.

Pope Innocent was particularly interested in this project because his family palace, Palazzo Pamphilj, faced the piazza, and the beautiful Baroque church of *Sant'Agnese in Agone*, whose construction the pope was sponsoring, would also be

Bernini's Fountain of the Four Rivers was planned as an architectural spectacle, and it is indeed spectacular; the four colossal figures grouped dramatically at the base of an obelisk from the Circus of Maxentius certainly catch the eye.

built adjacent to Piazza Navona. So Bernini knew that his chance to once again be the dominant artist in Rome rested on somehow winning the fountain commission. How he managed to wrest the prize away from his bitter rival, Francesco Borromini, was related in 1682 by Filippo Baldinucci in his biography of Bernini:

Prince Niccolo Ludovisi, who was married to a niece of the Pope and who was not only an intimate friend of Bernini but also had influence with him, prevailed on him to make a model of the fountain.... Bernini made the model, and the Prince arranged for it to be transported to Palazzo Pamphili in Piazza Navona. There it was secretly placed in a room through which the Pope, who on a certain day was to dine there, had to pass as he left the table.... Upon seeing such a noble creation ... he was nearly ecstatic. Since he was a prince of the clearest intelligence and of the loftiest thoughts ... he burst out with the following words: "This is a trick of Prince Ludovisi, but it will be necessary to make use of Bernini despite those who do not wish it, since those who do not want his works must not look at them."[4]

The pope wanted to employ a faux-Egyptian obelisk dating from the time of Domitian in the design of the fountain. The obelisk is Roman in origin and may have originally marked the Temple of Isis and Serapis in the Field of Mars. The hieroglyphics, however, are a hymn to Domitian, as well as to his father and brother, Vespasian and Titus. Sometime during the fourth century AD, it was moved to the Circus of Emperor Maxentius near the Appian Way, where it was found during the Renaissance.

Bernini set the obelisk atop a sculpted support of tumbled stones that form a rough, open, arched structure, and he placed muscular male figures on the four sides of the base. Each nude figure represents a god of one of the four main rivers known to Europeans at that time: the Danube, the Nile, the Ganges, and what was thought to be the largest river in the New World, the Rio de la Plata. There are metaphorical objects or attributes for each figure that identify his titular river. The Danube, for

The Fountain of the Four Rivers: The figure in the middle represents the Danube; to the left, lunging backward with his hand in the air, is the Rio de la Plata; the Ganges is on the right.

example, is near Innocent X's coat-of-arms, showing that it is nearest to his dominions; the Nile god's face is covered, because, at that point in history, the river's source was unknown; the Ganges figure holds an oar, symbolizing the navigability of its waters; and the Rio de la Plata giant has a hoard of spilled coins near him, a reference to the potential riches to be gained in the Americas.

In addition to the more obvious attributes, Bernini included other symbolic touches in his composition. The allegorical figure of the Rio de la Plata has his hand raised as if shielding himself from some sort of threat. Tour guides used to tell visitors that Bernini designed the figure to mock his rival Borromini—as if the river god was warding off the imminent collapse of Borromini's Sant'Agnese church at the edge of the piazza. This delightful legend is, I'm sorry to say, not true: construction of the church did not begin until after the fountain was completed. Rather, the raised hand was probably meant to indicate the reaction of the New World to the blinding light of the Catholic Church's teachings. More mundanely, there is a creature that may be meant as an armadillo (which Bernini had obviously never seen) and some cacti, signifying the exotic Americas.

There is a sea serpent beginning to twine itself around the oar held by the Ganges figure, possibly suggesting the sinuous nature of the course of the Ganges or the sinister nature of the mysterious East. There is also a lion emerging from a grotto beneath a palm tree, part of the tableau of the Nile god. A horse likewise appears from another grotto next to the Danube, a noble, domesticated creature embodying the virtues of the civilized world.[5]

The obelisk, of course, symbolizes the same thing for Pope Innocent that Egyptian obelisks did for the pharaohs: dominion. In this case, it refers to the pope's (and, incidentally, the church's) dominion over all four of the known continents of the world. And, to remove any doubt as to which pope we're talking about, there's a bronze dove at the very top of the obelisk holding a bronze olive branch in its beak—a heraldic symbol of the Pamphilj family.

It's generally acknowledged that Bernini executed the smaller decorative and symbolic elements around the base of the fountain. The four huge river god figures, though, were designed by Bernini as miniature clay *bozzetti* (models), which were used by four different sculptors to carve the giant statues: the Ganges by Claude Poussin, the Danube by Antonio Raggi, the Rio de la Plata by Francesco Baratta, and the Nile by Giovanni Fracchi or Giacomo Fancelli.[6]

The fountain was unveiled in 1651 and had a mixed reaction. Some critics worried that the rough, open-arched base would collapse under the weight of the obelisk. But for many common citizens, it was more a wish than a worry: Rome had recently endured several years of food shortages, and some of the *pasquinades* (notes hung on Rome's "Talking Statues") were bitter indeed: "We don't need fountains! Down with obelisks! We want bread!" Over time, however, the *Fontana dei Quattro Fiumi*—Fountain of the Four Rivers—with its imposing obelisk and titanic river gods marking the very center of Rome's busiest major piazza, has become a favorite of people from all over the world.

And finally a splendid della Porta fountain, with some Bernini-style dash added a century later.

The Fountain of the Four Rivers: Here are the Danube and Ganges again, and on the right we get a glimpse of the Nile, covering his head with a cloth—because when the figure was carved, the source of the Nile had not yet been found.

The Fountain of the Moor—La Fontana del Moro (1575)
ARCHITECTS: GIACOMO DELLA PORTA, GIAN LORENZO BERNINI, AND GIANNANTONIO MARI

Soon after installing the basin that became the Neptune Fountain, della Porta turned his attention to the south end of Piazza Navona, designing another fountain similar to the *Fontana dei Calderari* but using pink *portasanta* marble rather than white stone. This time, though, he adorned the basin with carved shells and grotesque mask-like faces embraced by fantastic creatures: snarling griffins, incongruously wicked-looking dolphins, and fierce birds of prey. Completing the composition were four Tritons blowing jets of water through double trumpet-shaped seashells. In the center of the fountain, a tall spray of water issued from an arrangement of stones. This design lasted unchanged until, in 1652, Pope Innocent X ordered Gian Lorenzo Bernini to replace the central rocks with a better arrangement. Bernini designed a group of shells and dolphins, but the pope was unimpressed and gave the sculpture to his sister-in-law, who made a fountain of it in the gardens of her suburban villa.

Bernini then designed the figure of a sea god struggling with another unruly dolphin, and he commissioned a sculptor named Giannantonio Mari to do the actual carving. (Mari worked for Bernini most of his short career, skillfully and

The Fountain of the Moor: As you admire the powerful, skillfully sculpted figure of the Moor, give a thought to Giannantonio Mari, who carved it to a design by Bernini. Mari died young, but his masterpiece lives on.

faithfully executing the master's designs. You can see a couple of them in the church of *Santa Maria del Popolo*—the figures of Saints Cecilia and Ursula.) Sadly, Mari died young, just thirty years old. But he left something for which he will long be remembered: a vigorous, striking figure, with features that reminded viewers of African people, thus giving the fountain its name: *La Fontana del Moro* (the Fountain of the Moor).

If you'd like to go "home" and relax, there are taxi stands at both ends of Piazza Navona. At the north end, it's in Piazza di Tor Sanguigna; at the south end, there's another in Piazza di San Pantaleo—exit Piazza Navona directly behind the Fountain of the Moor on a small street, via Cuccagna, and you'll be in Piazza San Pantaleo in about a minute. There are not a lot of buses nearby, but you can check www.atac. roma.it to find your best bet.

However, if you're itching to get on with it and see what's waiting for us on our way to the next chapter, read on:

From the Fountain of the Moor, it's not far to Piazza di Pasquino, where we'll meet a long-time Roman VIP, though he's not much to look at. Then, if you agree, we'll go a bit out of our way to see an unusual piece of crockery and a couple of other fountains before finally reaching the Campo de' Fiori.

So, to get to Piazza di Pasquino from Piazza Navona, stand in Piazza Navona,

The Fountain of the Moor: Here the Triton in the Moor fountain's pool joins in celebrating both the Feast of Epiphany and the arrival of La Befana in Piazza Navona.

with the great bronze doors of Palazzo Pamphilj on your right and the Moor on your left. Go straight ahead and turn right, in front of the Museum of Rome in Palazzo Braschi (www.museodiroma.it), which contains historical paintings of Rome and other memorabilia. You'll be in via di Pasquino.

One hundred feet will bring us into Piazza di Pasquino, and there, against a wall to our left, three stone blocks are stacked, like an improvised pedestal. They hold the carved marble torso of a man, missing both arms and with his face nearly weathered away. If you can imagine his arms back into existence, he might be carrying something like a tree stump, except it seems to have a belly button.

This is Pasquino. He probably began his existence as a Greek sculpture of Menelaus carrying the dead body of Patroclus, in an episode from the *Iliad*, but by the time he was unearthed in 1501 he was just this unsightly fragment. He was put up in the piazza anyway, and the locals began pasting satiric (or often just scurrilous) poems on him about the papal bureaucrats who governed Rome. They named the sculpture after a local tailor, Pasquino, who had clients in the Vatican and brought back gossipy tales to the neighborhood about his bigwig customers.

Eventually, Pasquino provoked the authorities enough that they posted a guard to prevent such irreverence, but then other statues around town began to be covered with comments. In time, there were six statues (including three of our fountains), called the "Congress of Wits" or the "Talking Statues," which even had conversations among themselves. Pasquino is remembered nowadays by the English word *pasquinade*, which means a short, satirical saying or poem.

The three fountains in the "Congress of Wits" are Facchino, Marforio, and Babuino. We've also met two non-fountain "wits"—Madame Lucrezia and Abbot Luigi—so I didn't want to leave Pasquino out even though he's not a fountain, and ... well ... he was on our way.

Now, let's bear right through Piazza di Pasquino into via del Governo Vecchio, a pleasant, cobbled street of small shops, cafés, and wine bars. After about 250 yards, at the sixth street on the left after leaving Pasquino, turn into via della Chiesa Nuova. (Don't turn into the small alley called Arco della Chiesa Nuova!) There'll be a weathered, ornately framed oval fresco of the Virgin and Child on the truncated corner of a building at the correct turn. A minute's walk will take you along the flank of the "New Church"—actually Santa Maria in Vallicella*—and will bring you to the piazza in front of the church. You'll see a statue of Pietro Metastasio, an eighteenth-century poet and opera librettist, and to his right, across the piazza, a sunken rectangular pool out of which seems to grow the lid of a giant casserole dish. Welcome to the Soup Bowl Fountain! How it got here, and why it looks the way it does, requires some explanation, but the story doesn't begin here—it begins in the Campo de' Fiori. We will soon visit the campo, but I must tell you a little about it now, because the history of our bowl is part of the history of the campo.*

✂ 11 ✂

Veggie Soup and Wine with the Farnese

Campo de' Fiori Area

THIS WALK BEGINS IN PIAZZA DELLA CHIESA NUOVA.

Campo de' Fiori. The name means "Field of Flowers" because it was once a stop on the long-vanished via Papale, from which a wildflower-filled meadow sloped down to the Tiber. The road led from the Vatican to San Giovanni in Laterano. The campo is now paved with cobblestones, and flowers bloom only in the florists' stalls. It has been a famous marketplace since 1869, when Rome's main vegetable and fish market was relocated there from Piazza Navona. But merchandise changed hands in that location long before the market arrived, and a fine fountain was built there in 1590. The streets that intersect the square are named for the traders who sold their goods there for centuries: tailors from via dei Giubbonari, locksmiths who worked along via dei Chiavari, makers of boxes and crates on via dei Baullari, and even craftsmen who fashioned crossbows in via dei Balestrari. The piazza was also used for another purpose: public executions were carried out there.

The most infamous execution occurred on February 17, 1600, when a Dominican monk, mathematician, and philosopher named Giordano Bruno was burned at the stake for preaching against Catholic doctrine. He was a follower of Nicolaus Copernicus and believed that the universe was infinite, that stars were distant suns around which planets circled, and that there were other sentient creatures living on those planets. Charged with heresy by the Inquisition, he refused to recant despite being imprisoned and repeatedly tortured, telling his questioners, "Perchance you who pronounce my sentence are in greater fear than I who receive it."[1] Some scholars dispute the notion that Bruno was condemned solely because of his Copernican beliefs,[2] while others insist that it was precisely those ideas that the inquisitors found unforgiveable.[3]

Today there is a bronze statue of Giordano Bruno in the center of the Campo, a dark, brooding, hooded figure holding a book. The work of sculptor Ettore Ferrari, it was erected there nearly three centuries after Bruno died. At that time, in 1899,

150

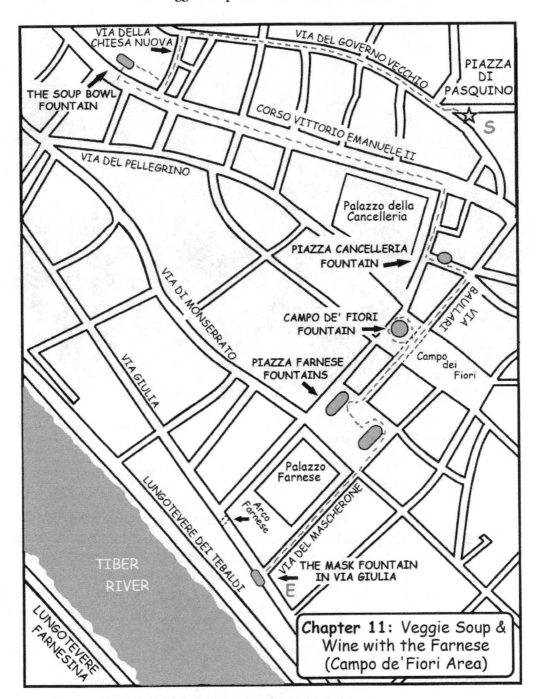

VIA DELLA CHIESA NUOVA

VIA DEL GOVERNO VECCHIO

PIAZZA DI PASQUINO

THE SOUP BOWL FOUNTAIN

CORSO VITTORIO EMANUELE II

S

VIA DEL PELLEGRINO

Palazzo della Cancelleria

PIAZZA CANCELLERIA FOUNTAIN

VIA DI MONSERRATO

VIA BAULLARI

CAMPO DE' FIORI FOUNTAIN

Campo dei Fiori

VIA GIULIA

PIAZZA FARNESE FOUNTAINS

Palazzo Farnese

LUNGOTEVERE DEI TEBALDI

Arco Farnese

VIA DEL MASCHERONE

TIBER RIVER

VIA DEL MASCHERONE

THE MASK FOUNTAIN IN VIA GIULIA

E

LUNGOTEVERE FARNESINA

Chapter 11: Veggie Soup & Wine with the Farnese (Campo de'Fiori Area)

the old fountain from 1590 (which the condemned man surely would have seen as he awaited his fate) had to be removed from the square to make room for his monument. The fountain was an odd-looking creation: on first sight, you might imagine that some giant from mythological times had dropped a Brobdingnagian serving dish, complete with cover, in the middle of the square. The Romans of the time gave it a satiric nickname, of course …

A somber statue of Giordano Bruno stands in the Campo de' Fiori, near where he was burned alive for heresy on February 16, 1600.

The Soup Bowl Fountain—La Fontana della Terrina (1590)
ARCHITECT: GIACOMO DELLA PORTA

Sometime in the 1580s, Pope Gregory VII commissioned a fountain from Giacomo della Porta, to be placed in the Campo de' Fiori. The original design was handsome but conventional: a large, stone basin below ground level (because of low water pressure), in the center of which was another, slightly smaller marble basin on a pedestal, with a flared edge, decorative ring handles, and a large rosette sculpted on each side. Four bronze dolphins on the inner basin's rim spouted water into the lower basin. The dolphins had originally been created to adorn another of Giacomo's fountains (the famous *Fontana delle Tartarughe*) in Piazza Mattei but were not used there.

The fountain in Campo de' Fiori was immediately popular with the vendors in the square, and they used the continually flowing water in the inner basin to cool their fruits and vegetables—and even, it seems, as a place to discard their trimmings. At any rate, after observing for years that the fountain continued to be an eyesore, in 1622 Pope Gregory XV ordered that the open basin be covered with a travertine "lid," complete with an oversized, knob-shaped "handle." There was a small inscription, probably added unofficially by a stone carver, on the base of the knob: *Ama Dio e non fallire, fa del bene e lascia dire*. It's virtually invisible today, but it means

The Soup Bowl Fountain—*La Fontana della Terrina*—which once stood in the Campo de' Fiori, now sits near a bus stop beside Corso Vittorio Emanuele II.

something like "Love God and do not fail, do good and let them talk." Did the carver mean this statement as a tribute to Giordano Bruno? Or was it a rebuke to one who defied the teachings of the church?

When the fountain was removed in 1899 to make way for Bruno's statue, it apparently disappeared into some obscure municipal storage facility and didn't reappear until 1924, when it was reinstalled here, beside via Corso Vittorio Emanuele II, in front of the *Chiesa Nuova* (the "New Church"). Once more, the marble basin (with its lid) was placed in a pool at ground level, but the bronze dolphins that once poured water into the pool were missing. No one seems to know what happened to them. Instead, the water escapes from the "tureen" through holes in the center of the rosettes. It's ironic that the lid was placed on the inner basin because of vegetable refuse when it was in the Campo de' Fiori; now the lower pool is often home to floating—or saturated and sunken—paper rubbish.

It's worth noting that next door to the church is the beautiful Baroque façade of Palazzo Filippini, designed by Francesco Borromini, Gian Lorenzo Bernini's great architectural rival. In 1924, the same year that the Soup Bowl Fountain was planted in the sidewalk here, city planners decided they needed a fountain in Campo de' Fiori after all—and we will visit it in due course.

But first, with your back to the church, cross Corso Vittorio Emanuele II at the crosswalk just to the right of the Soup Bowl Fountain and turn left. Walk about 350 yards on the Corso, and then turn right into Piazza della Cancelleria, just after passing along the enormous flank of the Apostolic Chancery, for which the piazza and its fountain are named. (It's said that the pale, off-white stone from which the building is made was quarried from the Theatre of Pompey.) After you turn into the piazza, you'll walk along the front façade of the chancery building on your right. When you reach the ornamental entrance with its arched doorway framed by two marble columns, turn left into a short street, also named Piazza della Cancelleria, leading directly away from the entrance. On the left, a third of the way along the alley before it meets via dei Baullari, you'll find a small wall-mounted fountain.

The Fountain in Piazza della Cancelleria—
La Fontana di Piazza della Cancelleria (1928)
Architect: Publio Morbiducci

In medieval times, when Rome was divided into districts called *rioni* (somewhat similar to the *contrade* of Siena), each *rione* had its own community fountain. By the early twentieth century, most dwellings in urban Rome had running water,

The Fountain in Piazza della Cancelleria honors the Parione district. The cardinal's hat with all the tassels recalls Cardinal Raffaello Riario, who built the extravagant Palazzo della Cancelleria nearby.

and the medieval neighborhood fountains had been replaced by the simple cast-iron structures with curved nozzles, nicknamed *nasoni* (big noses), that I told you about in the introduction. There are still a couple of thousand *nasoni* in Rome. Anyway, in 1927, the municipality decided to replace ten of the *nasoni* with something a bit more artistic, something that recalled the traditions of the old *rioni*. We've talked about Pietro Lombardi, who designed all ten, when we visited some of his *rioni* fountains. But after he fulfilled his contract, the Parione district was still without a new fountain, and its residents petitioned the city for one. Publio Morbiducci was called on to supply a fountain in keeping with Lombardi's work, and the result is in this alley within Piazza della Cancelleria. It's a small fountain, wall mounted, carved from travertine. Below a globe with three triangular protruding spokes, a cardinal's hat recalls the Parione resident Cardinal Raffaello Riario, who built the Palazzo della Cancelleria. The tassels on the hat fall within a triangular shape, which also contains a carved oval shield. On the shield is a relief of a griffin, symbol of the Parione district, and a rosette shape from which water pours into a small trough, like a miniature sarcophagus. On the front of the trough is the SPQR insignia of the Roman Republic.

Now, continue past the fountain to the end of the alley, and turn right on via dei Baullari, which leads into Campo de' Fiori after one block. As you enter the campo, the fountain will be on your right, usually hidden behind a florist's display.

The Fountain in Campo de' Fiori— La Fontana di Campo de' Fiori (1924)
Architect: Anonymous (after Giacomo Della Porta)

The replacement for the Soup Bowl Fountain was installed in the northern end of Campo de' Fiori. After the original fountain had found a new home in front of the *Chiesa Nuova*, the designers of its replacement in the campo made what is essentially a replica of the first fountain, though without the tureen cover and the four bronze dolphins. The carved decorative ring handles and the rosettes are all there, however. Since the new location isn't in the center of the square, but often hidden behind a large, semi-permanent floral display, it no longer is used for discarded cabbage leaves and such. The florists may use it to cool their bouquets from time to time, and the usual Roman *spazzatura* (litter) often surrounds it, but the fountain doesn't really seem to need the same sort of lid its ancestor wore.

If you got to the campo before noon, you've no doubt browsed the vegetable, flower, and souvenir stalls and perhaps had a coffee at one of the cafés on the square. When you're ready, go back to via dei Baullari and look both ways. When you spot a great building facing you at the end of the street, above whose grand entrance the flags of France and the European Union fly, you'll know which way to go. Our next fountains are there, in the spacious forecourt of Palazzo Farnese.

Top: The Fountain in Campo de' Fiori: In 1924, this fountain replaced the missing Soup Bowl Fountain, which was removed in 1899 to make way for Giordano Bruno's statue (which you can see in the distance, above the fountain's rim). *Bottom:* There *are* flowers in the Campo de' Fiori, in a florist's display usually near the fountain. It's handy for refreshing tired blooms, when necessary.

The Piazza Farnese Fountains—
Le Fontane di Piazza Farnese (1626)
ARCHITECT: GIROLAMO RAINALDI

The splendid façade of Palazzo Farnese, Antonio da Sangallo the Younger's masterpiece (with a little help from Michelangelo), is visible from the Campo de' Fiori, at the end of via dei Baullari. Built for the powerful Farnese family between 1515 and 1517, and expanded in 1534 when Alessandro Farnese became Pope Paul III, the palace now houses the French Embassy to Italy. The building forms the western boundary of a large, cobbled square, Piazza Farnese. Near the southern boundary is an ornamental fountain, with a nearly identical twin at the northern end of the square. Each fountain is formed by a sizeable travertine pool, about waist high, in which a giant Egyptian-granite basin, like a colossal bathtub, sits. Each basin is adorned with two carved ring figures and a lion's head on both sides. In the center of the basin is a marble column holding a scalloped bowl topped by a waterspout in the form of a fleur-de-lis.

The "bathtubs" are, in fact, exactly that, though they certainly accommodated more than one bather and probably were part of the ancient Baths of Caracalla.

The Piazza Farnese Fountains: The "twin" fountains feature two enormous "bathtubs," both probably from the Baths of Caracalla and buried for a thousand years. Excavated half a century apart, they were reunited in the piazza in 1580.

According to most accounts, the first basin was excavated in 1466, during the pontificate of Pope Paul II, who had it placed in Piazza San Marco (near today's Piazza Venezia) to adorn his palace there. The second was discovered during the reign of Paul III and placed in Piazza Farnese sometime in the 1530s. The basin in Piazza San Marco was later acquired by the Farnese family and moved to join its twin in Piazza Farnese in 1580. Neither was used as a fountain, however, since there was no water supply to the area—not until the Borghese pope, Paul V, restored the ancient *Aqua Traiana* aqueduct in 1612 and renamed it *Acqua Paola*, after himself.

The water finally arrived in the Farnese neighborhood in 1626, and the family commissioned Girolamo Rainaldi to design and construct the two fountains. They were strictly for show and were enclosed by gated barriers. But, in return for the right to tap the water supply, the family was required to construct a functional

The Piazza Farnese Fountains: Here, one of the Farnese fountains has attracted a street musician, as Rome's fountains often do.

fountain for the people and animals of the area. That fountain can be found at the southeast corner of Palazzo Farnese's walled gardens, where via Giulia meets via del Mascherone.

So, facing Palazzo Farnese, take the narrow street, via del Mascherone, along the left flank of the palazzo, to where it meets via Giulia. You'll see the fountain before you get there.

The Mask Fountain in via Giulia— La Fontana del Mascherone (ca. 1626)
ARCHITECT: GIROLAMO RAINALDI

Mascherone can be variously translated as "big mask" or "grotesque mask"; in this case, it refers to a giant mask carved from white marble, which has survived from antiquity. It was assembled, presumably at about the same time as the creation of the twin Piazza Farnese fountains, by the same architect. It currently is mounted against a wall of decorative brickwork but originally was freestanding, with a trough for people to use on one side and a second for animals on the other. The surviving trough is made of granite and, like the mask, is a relic of ancient Rome, probably part of a bath complex. The mask itself is embedded in a marble surround of twin spirals (volutes) by Rainaldi, which is topped by a bronze fleur-de-lis, a heraldic symbol of the Farnese clan. Water spouts from the *mascherone*'s mouth into a fluted,

The Mask Fountain in via Giulia: Taking out the trash on a fall day. The Convent of Santa Brigida is located in Piazza Farnese, a minute's walk from *La Fontana del Mascherone*.

shell-shaped marble basin, which overflows into the trough. It's said that on special occasions the *mascherone* spouted wine; the Farnese evidently knew how to throw a block party![4]

Before setting out for Trastevere and its fountains, look right as you face the *mascherone* and you'll see a bridge across via Giulia carried by a picturesque arch draped with vines. Apparently it was built so the Farnese family and friends could observe parades and horse races on the street. If horse racing ever returns to via Giulia, now you know where to get the best view.

Just beyond the bridge, on the left side of the street, is the marble façade of *Santa Maria dell'Orazione e Morte* (Our Lady of Prayer and Death). This church was founded by a confraternity dedicated to burying unidentified corpses found in the countryside and the river back in the sixteenth century. In a period of 300 years, members of the confraternity buried over eight thousand bodies and said prayers for more than eight thousand unknown souls. Fortunately, it's relatively rare for unidentified bodies to turn up nowadays, so the brothers have turned to other charitable work. The church was closed for restoration in 2014 and was still closed when I last saw it in 2019, though the restoration was scheduled to be completed that year. It's said to have a fine altarpiece by a follower of Guido Reni.

If you don't want to begin the next itinerary just now, and your lodging isn't within walking distance, I recommend checking in with www.atac.roma.it to find your

The Mask Fountain in via Giulia: The *mascherone* in springtime. There is some evidence that this fountain has dispensed wine from time to time.

bus route. Alternatively, you can find a taxi stand near Piazza Trilussa, which is where our next walk starts. So, whether you want to start the next group of fountains or you want a taxi ride home, come along to Piazza Trilussa. It's not far.

To reach Piazza Trilussa from the Mask Fountain in via Giulia, face the fountain and turn left. After following via Giulia for less than 100 yards, the street will join Lungotevere dei Tebaldi, and you will see a handsome pedestrian bridge across the Tiber. This is Ponte Sisto, a historic structure built in 1473 and named for Pope Sixtus IV. Cross the bridge and proceed straight on into Piazza Trilussa. If you like, take a seat on the steps of the fountain—everyone else does—and I'll tell you a little about Trastevere.

ᔰ 12 ᔰ

Across the River
and into the Fountains

Trastevere

THIS WALK BEGINS IN PIAZZA TRILUSSA.

(Note: The Trastevere tour is rather long and a little strenuous. You might consider breaking it into two days. If so, stopping the first day's trek at Piazza Mastai, where Tram 8 conveniently stops on Viale Trastevere, just in front of the piazza, might be a good choice.)

A few words about Trastevere before considering our first fountain: You're probably too young to have encountered Lars Porsena in school, but he was the Etruscan ruler of Clusium, back in the days when Rome, having thrown out the last of its Etruscan kings, was struggling to become a republic. This would have been around 508 BC.

> *Lars Porsena of Clusium, by the Nine Gods he swore*
> *That the great house of Tarquin should suffer wrong no more.*[1]

The king who'd been exiled called himself Tarquinius Superbus, which should give you a clue as to why the Romans were glad to be rid of him. Both Lars Porsena and Tarquinius were Etruscans (or Tuscans, as Lord Macaulay, who wrote the poem, called them), and that is why Lars swore to put his fellow Etruscan back on the Roman throne. So he gathered a huge force of soldiers from various Etruscan towns and massed his army on the western bank of the Tiber—*Tevere* in Italian—where the stream wanders eastward, splits in two around Isola Tiberina, and then turns back west toward Porta Portese. In those days there was a wooden bridge called the *Pons Sublicius*, south of the island, which was the only way across the river into Rome. I don't want to spoil the story for you, so if you want to know whether the Roman centurion Horatio was able to hold off the Etruscan hordes long enough for the Romans to destroy the bridge and foil the invasion, you'll just have to read the rest of the poem, about 600 lines. I mention it because it shows the deep historic roots of the area embraced by the river's wide meander, an Etruscan place then, Roman

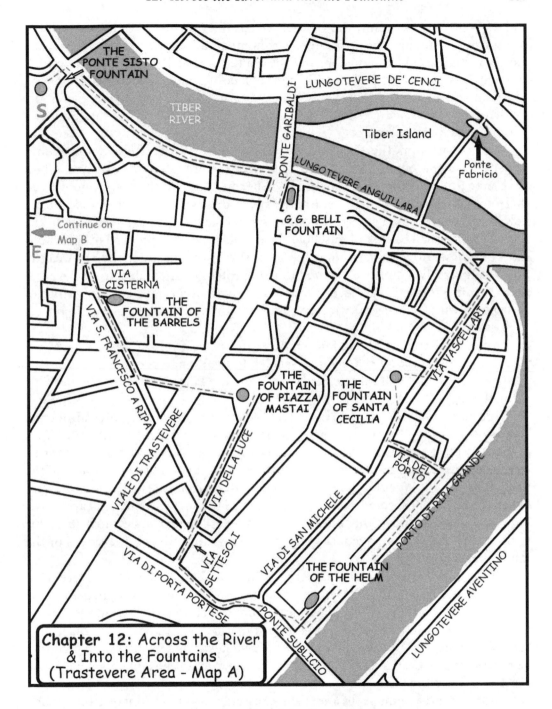

THE PONTE SISTO FOUNTAIN

S

TIBER RIVER

LUNGOTEVERE DE' CENCI

PONTE GARIBALDI

Tiber Island

LUNGOTEVERE ANGUILLARA

Ponte Fabricio

Continue on Map B

E

G.G. BELLI FOUNTAIN

VIA CISTERNA

THE FOUNTAIN OF THE BARRELS

VIA S. FRANCESCO A RIPA

VIA VASCELLARI

THE FOUNTAIN OF PIAZZA MASTAI

THE FOUNTAIN OF SANTA CECILIA

VIALE DI TRASTEVERE

VIA DELLA LUCE

VIA DEL PORTO

PORTO DI RIPA GRANDE

VIA DI SAN MICHELE

VIA SETTESOLI

LUNGOTEVERE AVENTINO

VIA DI PORTA PORTESE

THE FOUNTAIN OF THE HELM

PONTE SUBLICIO

Chapter 12: Across the River & Into the Fountains (Trastevere Area - Map A)

now, but somehow always different from the rest of Rome: the district "across the Tiber"—*Trastevere*.

Today Trastevere is—to paraphrase the usual guidebook description—the Bohemian Quarter of Rome, whose narrow, cobbled streets abound in art galleries, bookstores, restaurants, crowded *trattorie*, bars, and nightlife. There's a youthful feel, partly because of the foreign academic institutions there: John Cabot University and the American Academy in Rome, as well as the Canadian Waterloo School of Architecture, among others. Trastevere is home to a large community of expats, mostly from the United Kingdom and the United States. The guidebooks will tell you that Trastevere is where you will find the "true" Rome as it once was, filled with a lively diversity of free-spirited people enjoying an authentic sojourn far from the well-trodden tourist paths of the *centro storico* across the water. There may even be a grain of truth in this claim.

But, if you think there's exciting diversity in today's Trastevere, you should have been there around the first century BC. Walking the narrow lanes, you might have met Roman sailors and Etruscan fishermen, and vice versa, who'd lived there for generations; or Eastern immigrants from Syria or Judea, looking for a new home; or freedmen and freedwomen, former slaves, starting new lives on the less expensive west bank; or household slaves and servants employed in the elaborate villas of wealthy Romans along the Tiber shore; and, occasionally, the wealthy Romans themselves, borne along on litters to protect their sandals from the mud. And, because some things never change, someone might have cut the strings of your purse while you were distracted by the haughty procession. The pickpockets have never left.

Among the aristocratic landowners in the district was Julius Caesar, whose own villa and gardens, the *Horti Caesaris*, were left to the Roman people in his will. The gardens are thought to have extended south from the Porta Portuensis about a mile along the river.

The early emperors made Trastevere a venue for games and entertainments. Augustus, for example, created a large, shallow lakebed and filled it with water from a specially built aqueduct, so he could stage mock sea battles with ships manned by condemned criminals. Maybe "mock battles" isn't the right phrase—most of the participants died. Wooden stands around the *naumachia* (as such spectacles were called) held 20,000 spectators. The center of the lake may have been near today's Piazza San Cosimato.[2] In the third century AD, after the lake ceased to be used for such deadly shows, the aqueduct's flow powered grain mills on the slopes of the Janiculum Hill.

There are two particularly ancient and famous churches in Trastevere. One was founded around 220 AD by an ex-slave, ex-convict, and ex-gravedigger named Callixtus, who was the pope at the time. At first the church was called the *Titulus Callixti*, but now it is known as *Santa Maria in Trastevere*. Pope Callixtus is now Saint Callixtus, and he is the patron saint of cemetery workers! The second church began as *Titulus Cecilae* in the mid–third century, and it became, in time, *Santa Cecilia in Trastevere*.

More recently, in the 1960s and 1970s, Trastevere was the haunt of artists, musicians, students, and hippies, who made the district a counter-culture enclave. Today, the artists, musicians and students are still there, usually outnumbered by tourists looking for the real, authentic Rome—or at least a relatively cheap meal. The hippies, though, are a rarity, and those who remain have, alas, grown old.

And there are fountains, of course: a particularly diverse group, as might be expected. Here in Piazza Trilussa is the first.

The Fountain of Ponte Sisto—La Fontana di Ponte Sisto (1613)
ARCHITECTS: GIOVANNI VASANZIO, GIOVANNI FONTANA, AND ANGELO VESCOVALI

Ponte Sisto is the first bridge in Rome to be built in "modern times," meaning since the Middle Ages. Commissioned by Pope Sixtus IV in 1473, and named for him, it spanned the Tiber north of Isola Tiberina (Tiber Island). At the time, the only other bridges linking the right bank (Trastevere, the Janiculum Hill, and the Vatican) with the greater city on the left bank were the Ponte Sant'Angelo and the bridges onto and off Isola Tiberina. All these bridges were relics of ancient Rome, and a practical bridge for both foot and wheeled traffic was needed. Another important use for the bridge was found in 1613, during the pontificate of Pope Paul V, after that prelate funded the renovation of the ruined *Aqua Traiana*, originally built by Emperor Trajan in 109 AD. To celebrate the restoration of the aqueduct, which brought water once more from springs around Lake Bracciano, Pope Paul named the aqueduct after himself (*Acqua Paola*) and had a great *mostra* ("show fountain"), the *Fontanone dell'Acqua Paola*, constructed on the slopes of the Janiculum, which you can read about later in this chapter. But after building the fountain, Pope Paul decided to deliver a portion of the water across the Tiber to the left bank, distributing it to several neighborhoods on that side of the river.

The Fountain of Ponte Sisto: Named after the bridge, the fountain has the odd distinction of having been located, at different times, at either end of the bridge.

To do so, he had the water carried across the Ponte Sisto by pipes mounted on the bridge; at the left bank end of the bridge, he built another elegant *mostra*, considerably smaller than the one on the Janiculum. He called it the *Fontana dell'Acqua Paola*, but this name sounded too much like its big brother up the hill, so the Romans called it *La Fontana di Ponte Sisto*.

Giovanni Vasanzio and Giovanni Fontana were given the contract to construct the fountain. But it happened that the area at the left bank end of the bridge was rather crowded. It was just at the southern end of an important street, via Giulia, where there was a large shelter for beggars, the *Ospizio dei Mendicanti*. Moreover, the *Ospizio* had been built 25 years earlier by Giovanni Fontana's brother, Domenico; thus, to minimize damage to Domenico's work, Vasanzio and Fontana decided to mount the fountain on one wall of the hospice building.

However, they didn't skimp on the magnificence of the fountain. They made a great arch of marble and travertine, with a central niche flanked by marble columns. Water pours from an opening in the upper part of the niche into a basin mounted on the wall and, overflowing the basin, cascades into a pool at the bottom of the fountain. Winged dragons decorate the column bases, and eagles nestle between the arch curves and the composite column capitals. Eagles and dragons symbolize Pope Paul V's family, the Borghese. Just to drive home the point, there is a tall attic story above the arch, topped by the Borghese coat-of-arms and a papal tiara resting on the crossed keys of Saint Peter. In addition, on the attic front is an inscription detailing how the pope caused water to be brought from the far-away springs to the Janiculum, and thence across the Ponte Sisto bridge to Rome itself.

The inscription unexpectedly became a problem many years later. In the 1870s, the City of Rome decided to contain, once and for all, the periodic Tiber floods that often devastated much of the city. City leaders undertook the daunting job of protecting the banks of the river with massive stone embankments. In the course of this project, many buildings and structures were destroyed, among them the *Ospizio* and the Ponte Sisto fountain. Happily, the major sculptural elements of the fountain were saved and put into storage.

The fountain was an iconic and popular feature of the city, and in 1889, by popular demand, it was reassembled by the architect Angelo Vescovali, but this time at the *other* end of the bridge, on the opposite bank of the river, in Piazza Trilussa. Now the inscription describing how Pope Paul V had brought the water *across* the river no longer made sense. So, another inscription, explaining what happened, was carved inside the archway, underneath the upper basin from which the water cascades into the lower pool. Like the first inscription, this was written in Latin, so, although the steps leading up to the fountain are a popular hangout area, I doubt very many people can read either message.

Piazza Trilussa, by the way, is named for Carlo Alberto Camilo Mariano Salustri, a famous poet of the early twentieth century who wrote in the Romanesco dialect, spoken by many native Romans. Trilussa, an anagram of his last name, was Salustri's *nom de plume*. It's said that he drank a bit; there is a sculpture of the poet in the square, leaning conspiratorially across a wall, gesturing earnestly, as if he's made friends with us while sharing a bottle of wine and wants to tell us a secret.

The Fountain of Ponte Sisto: Here's a close-up view of the fountain, as well as the inscription explaining the fountain's leap-frog history with the bridge. How's your Latin?

There is a plaque just under the bust of Trilussa, inscribed with the text of his poem *All'Ombra*, written in the Romanesco dialect. *All'Ombra* means "In the Shade" in Italian (and apparently in Romanesco, too). I don't speak Romanesco, but I believe the poem means something like this: "While I'm relaxing in the shade

The Fountain of Ponte Sisto is located in Piazza Trilussa, named for the dialect poet whose bronze sculpture seems intent on talking to us.

and reading my usual newspaper, I see a porker and I say, 'goodbye, pig!' I see a burro and I say, 'goodbye, donkey!' Perhaps the beasts don't understand me, but I take satisfaction that I can talk about things as they are, without fear of finishing up in prison." (Salustri, or rather Trilussa, lived through the years of Fascist rule in Italy.)

With the fountain to your back, exit from Piazza Trilussa to the right, onto Lungotevere Raffaello Sanzio. After about a quarter of a mile, you'll see a large bridge, Ponte Garibaldi, crossing the Tiber to your left, fed by the multi-lane street ahead of you. Make your way carefully across this major street (not the bridge!) and turn right into Piazza Giuseppe Gioachino Belli. Here you'll find a large monument with carved reliefs and a statue of a debonair fellow wearing a top hat.

Monument to G.G. Belli—Monumento a G.G. Belli (1913)
Architect: Michele Tripisciano

As the years have gone by, I suppose the traditional Romanesco dialect has been used more in Trastevere than other areas of Rome, so it's not surprising to find, not far from the piazza named for the Romanesco poet Trilussa, a monument to his most famous predecessor, Giuseppe Gioachino Belli. You'll find it on viale di Trastevere,

The Monument to G.G. Belli: The people of Trastevere paid, by public subscription, for this monument to another dialect poet of the people, Giuseppe Gioachino Belli. It's also a fountain, with a water source and basin at either end.

at the busy bus stop just before the street becomes Ponte Garibaldi and swoops over the Tiber across the upstream prow of Isola Tiberina.

Belli's writings were part of a literary tradition of works, usually poetic, satiric or humorous, in Italian dialects of the common people. Cities other than Rome had their own dialect writers—notably the famous Milanese poet Carlo Porta, who apparently inspired Belli to work in dialect rather than standard Italian.

Although he was of the middle class, and in fact married a wealthy woman whose money allowed him to concentrate on his writing, Belli specialized in poems in which he tried to express the attitudes, stoic or sardonic, of the working people of Rome. He wrote over 2,200 sonnets, none of which were published during his lifetime. Many of the satirical poems targeted the clergy. Some were comically bawdy. So, just before he died in 1863, Belli asked a friend, Monsignor Vincenzo Tizzani, to burn them. Tizzani, however, gave them to Belli's son, who published them to great popular success. Some of Belli's works have been translated into English, by, among others, Anthony Burgess.[3]

The monument, carved from travertine, was financed by popular subscription, which raised 30,000 lire, perhaps equivalent to about 200,000 American dollars today. On a high, rectangular base, the poet stands wearing a top hat and leaning against a wall that is accentuated by an odd, four-faced herm at his elbow. (Herms were, in early civilizations, stone mileposts, boundary markers, or street signs,

The Monument to G.G. Belli: There is a quadruple-headed Janus herm on the monument, referring to an ancient bridge nearby, the Ponte Fabricio, which has two Janus herms on its ramparts. The Roman god of beginnings and endings, Janus gazed forward and backward at the same time.

topped with the head and shoulders of a man.) It is a reference to the ancient Ponte Fabricio, the oldest existing bridge in Rome, also known as the *Ponte dei Quattro Capi* (Bridge of the Four Heads), because there are two Janus herms, each with two faces, on the old bridge's parapets. Janus was the Roman god of beginnings and endings, and so had to look both forward and behind at once. (The bridge, built in 62 BC, connects the Isola Tiberina to the left bank of the Tiber.)

On the front of the fountain's base is an allegory, in shallow relief, of the Tiber River, represented by a reclining male river god, at whose feet is the Capitoline Wolf with the infant twins, Romulus and Remus. Around the back of the base is another scene, in relief, of ordinary Roman citizens, the *cittadini*, gathered around the battered statue of Pasquino, the most famous of the "Talking Statues." The scene seems poetically appropriate.

At either end of the base, a carved mask emits a stream of water into a semi-circular basin. The mask on the end facing the Tiber is the traditional female muse of Poetry; the other end bears the sardonically smiling face of Satire.

If you stand under the statue of Belli, with your back to him and the river to your right, the busy street in front of you, tram tracks and all, is the viale di Trastevere, though at this point it is technically part of Piazza G.G. Belli. Go right, toward the river about 50 feet, and cross Lungotevere degli Anguillara at the crosswalk. Turn right

The Monument to G.G. Belli: On the back side of the Belli monument, the common folk of Rome are shown grouped with their "Talking Statue" spokesman, Pasquino.

along the river. You'll be passing the Isola Tiberina (Tiber Island) on your left. After about 250 yards, you'll see a bridge, Ponte Cestio, to your left.

At this point, you can take a short detour of about 200 yards, if you like, across the river and on across the Isola Tiberina, to see the ancient bridge I told you about— Ponte Fabricio, the oldest bridge in Rome, and the one with the two Janus herms on its parapets. It's a lovely little bridge, its sturdy arches still standing after two thousand years. **But skip the next paragraph if you'd rather continue on immediately to our next fountain.**

For the detour: Go left and cross the Ponte Cestio bridge onto the island, and straight through Piazza San Bartolomeo All'Isola (unless you want to stop for a drink at a café on the square or visit the Basilica di San Bartolomeo All'Isola, *a tenth-century church, rebuilt in the Baroque style but containing a number of original columns and the relics of the Apostle Bartholomew). Continue straight on via di Ponte Quattro Capi (which, you'll remember, is the alternate name of Ponte Fabricio). In just a few steps, you'll be on the old bridge. When you are ready, return to Lungotevere degli Anguillara by retracing your steps back across the island and the Ponte Cestio bridge.*

To continue on to our next fountain: Whether or not you took the detour, take the crosswalk across Lungotevere degli Anguillara and turn left, and we will continue the walk to the next fountain on the right-hand side of the street.

After about 150 yards, keeping to the right side of the road where the roadway splits, you'll see a service station. Just before the station, turn right into via dei Vascellari. Almost immediately, Piazza dei Ponziani will open up to your right, but continue straight on via dei Vascellari on the left edge of the piazza. You may have to avoid café tables or other obstacles at the corner of the square, but the street continues straight ahead, changing its name to via Santa Cecilia after about 100 yards and then, after another 50 yards, entering Piazza di Santa Cecilia. The Basilica di Santa Cecilia in Trastevere *and its fountain are on your right.*

The Fountain in Piazza Santa Cecilia in Trastevere— La Fontana di Piazza Santa Cecilia in Trastevere (1929)
ARCHITECTS: BASIN BY ANTONIUS MUNOZ, VASE BY ANONYMOUS SCULPTOR OF ANTIQUITY

The Fountain in Piazza Santa Cecilia is another *krater* fountain. You can see it through the archway in this picture.

A fine arched gate in a graceful eighteenth-century convent building leads into the atrium of the ancient church of Santa Cecilia in Trastevere. The atrium of many old churches was a space intended for welcoming pilgrims, providing a place to rest and perform some hand and foot washing before entering the porch of the church. Across Santa Cecilia's atrium from the arch is the twelfth-century porch and entrance to the surviving ninth-century church. Pilgrims (as well as tourists) come here to see the remarkably poignant sculpture of the saint, under the altar, showing the position in which her allegedly incorrupt body was found in 1599, when her grave was opened and the sculptor, Stefano Maderno, observed her.

Saint Cecilia's story is highly dramatic: She was born to a wealthy family in the second century AD but became an early Christian convert. Forced to marry although she'd taken a vow of chastity, on her wedding night she converted her husband Valerian to Christianity and persuaded him to live with her in a platonic relationship. Both of them were eventually martyred. Cecilia was shut up in her own sauna-like bath, in an effort to … well … steam her to death, I suppose. It didn't work. She spent the time singing hymns, so the executioner (obviously a severe music critic) cut her throat, but she managed to live three more days, converting several more people through her miraculous survival. I don't know if it was for singing in the caldarium, but she is venerated as the patron saint of music.

The church was built over the house in which Saints Cecilia and Valerian lived.

The Fountain in Piazza Santa Cecilia: The church of Santa Cecilia in Trastevere is famous for the dramatic story of Saint Cecilia and especially for the very poignant sculpture of the saint by Stefano Maderno, located under the altar.

Some remnants of the structure and other Roman artifacts remain and can be visited during the church's open hours. In the middle of the atrium is a large, square pool, in whose center is an enormous vase in the form of a *cantharos*, an ancient wine-mixing vessel, wonderfully carved of white marble, sitting on a tall marble plinth. Water spurts from jets in the pool. The vase, of great antiquity, sat outside the old church throughout the Middle Ages, but it was not made into a fountain until 1929, when the pool was constructed and a water supply provided, by order of the titular cardinal of the church, Bonaventura Cerretti.

Go out of the atrium of the church, through the arched gate where you entered, into Piazza di Santa Cecilia. With your back to the church, find the corner of the piazza (ahead of you and to your right) where you can choose between Piazza dei Mercanti or via di San Michele. Take via di San Michele, and follow it about 200 feet. Take the first street to the left, the narrow via del Porto, but keep to the right side of the road. At the end of via del Porto, there will be a street named via Porto di Ripa Grande, with a crosswalk leading to steps that climb to an elevated section of the street. You'll probably see lots of cars parked there. Climb the stairs, turn right, and walk about 100 yards until you see another set of stairs leading to an elevated walkway with occasional benches dotted along it. From the walkway you can see the Tiber as you walk. This whole riverfront was once an important port for ships and barges. There are ramps left from the old port, which lead down to the river from the walkway, as well as remnants of the port's boat repair facilities.

Just before your elevated walkway ends, about 400 yards from where you entered it, look to your right across the street. You'll see a fountain built into the wall of a building facing the street. At the end of the elevated walkway, take the stairs down and turn right, crossing via Porto di Ripa Grande; once across, you'll find the fountain a few steps to your right. (Around the end of the walkway, you can, if you like, take a stroll on a bike path/walkway along the river, but you'll have to come back here to begin the rest of this itinerary.)

The Fountain of the Helm—La Fontana del Timone (1930)
ARCHITECT: PIETRO LOMBARDI

This fountain is one of two *rione* fountains that Pietro Lombardi designed for Trastevere (the other is the Fountain of the Barrels). Although technically both are in the Trastevere *rione*, the Fountain of the Helm honors the maritime history of the Porto di Ripa Grande, the river port to which seafaring ships (or barges carrying cargo) made their way upriver from the mouth of the Tiber at Fiumicino. The fountain is built onto the river façade of the Cultural Heritage Ministry, which is a rather sad irony, because the building's façade, when I saw it last, was hideously defaced by ugly and mindless graffiti. Across the street from the ministry, beyond the raised walkway you just left, along the river's edge, the once-busy port helped supply the city with merchandise. In 1876, with the construction of the Tiber embankments, the port ceased to exist.

The maritime theme is expressed by a carved helm (wheel) of travertine. Water

The Fountain of the Helm—*La Fontana del Timone*—is another neighborhood *rione* fountain. This one dates from 1930 and honors the memory of the old Porto di Ripa Grande with the image of a ship's wheel—the "helm."

flows from the center of the wheel into a small semi-circular basin. Two sweeping volutes curve outward and down from the bottom of the wheel to encounter stubby stone posts, rather like common bollards, but these bollards have mock mooring rings carved on their front surfaces, and from the center of the rings water flows from small spouts into the street-level drain. The upper part of the composition is flanked by two marble plaques applied to the wall bearing the SPQR legend. Another (illegible) plaque is on the wall above the fountain.

No doubt as you approached the end of the elevated walkway you noticed the bridge crossing the Tiber. It's called the Ponte Sublicio, in honor of one of Rome's first bridges, the same wooden bridge that Horatio defended in the poem I quoted to start this chapter. Ponte Sublicio means "wooden bridge" in an old local dialect from the time of the Republic, so the modern version's name is strictly a historical reference! Via di Porta Portese feeds into the bridge. From the fountain, go to the corner of via Porto di Ripa Grande (the street you're on) and via di Porta Portese, and turn right; after about 250 yards, turn right again into the second street on the right, via Jacopa de'Settesoli. This short street empties into Piazza di San Francesco d'Assisi.

To your right in this piazza you'll see the façade of the church of San Francesco a Ripa Grande, a thirteenth-century building heavily restored in the Baroque style, in which you'll find one of Bernini's most famous and controversial works, the funerary

The Fountain of the Helm: To be frank, the area immediately around the fountain is a bit bleak and uninspiring!

monument to the Blessed Ludovica Albertoni. It is similar in effect to his sculpture of Saint Teresa in the church of Santa Maria della Vittoria. Anyway, when you're ready to leave, exit the piazza on via della Luce, a narrow street to the left of a large building with a four-columned portico. After about 300 yards, you'll enter the large, semi-circular Piazza Mastai, with its stately fountain.

The Fountain in Piazza Mastai, aka the Tobacco Factory Fountain—La Fontana di Piazza Mastai (1865)
Architect: Andrea Busiri Vici

If you are in Rome and you want to buy a lottery ticket or a bus ticket or a pack of gum or cigarettes, usually the most convenient place is a small storefront establishment, whose sign is almost always a large, white letter "T" against a black or blue background. On the same sign, you will read, in smaller letters, "Sali e Tabacchi." *Sali e Tabacchi*—it means "salt and tobacco," as you've no doubt guessed, and the shops were, not too long ago, the only businesses that could sell either of those items. They are still the only outlets for tobacco products in Italy, though salt can now be found in supermarkets—often on a lower shelf, by the way, if you're having trouble finding it.

The Fountain in Piazza Mastai, or the Tobacco Factory Fountain, was built five years before the papacy lost Rome to the Kingdom of Italy.

In the days before refrigeration, salt was one of the few methods available for preserving meat, fish, and poultry and was vastly important for maintaining reliable food supplies; it was one of the most valuable commodities in the world. So, since antiquity, anyone who could monopolize its production and distribution could become very wealthy. Naturally, governments of every kind wanted a piece of that action, and they usually succeeded in getting it. Tobacco, although not exactly a necessity like salt, was perennially in high demand after it was introduced to Europe from the New World, and it, too, was a tempting object for monopolists, whether private or governmental.

For example, as the Risorgimento succeeded in establishing the Kingdom of Italy, one of the kingdom's first financial measures, in 1862, was declaring the production and sale of both salt and tobacco government monopolies. Italy, however, was not yet completely united. Rome, the most important of Italian cities, along with the surrounding region of Lazio, was still ruled by the papacy, in the person of Pius IX (Giovanni Maria Mastai Ferretti).

The pope, who had by this time lost the rest of the former Papal States, was also short of money. So he decided that the papacy would likewise declare the production and sale of salt and tobacco to be state monopolies. Just to ensure that tobacco would be available for sale, he decided to construct a tobacco processing factory in Rome, and by 1865 the building was complete. Ultimately, it didn't produce much profit for him, since the forces of the Kingdom of Italy took Rome in 1870, and the pope went into self-imposed seclusion in the Vatican. But the building is still there, in a large square named Piazza Mastai (after the pope). It has a rather splendid façade of eight engaged columns supporting a large pediment, as well as a Latin inscription explaining that the pope had it built for "processing nicotine leaves." In the piazza, a grand fountain was built to complement the factory—the first monumental fountain built in Trastevere since the *Acqua Paola* fountain rose on the Janiculum Hill in 1612.

Nowadays the government workers in the building, rather than rolling cigars and grinding snuff, very appropriately shuffle papers in the *Agenzia delle Dogane e Monopoli* (Customs and Monopoly Office).

The Fountain in Piazza Mastai: Pope Pius IX built a rather grand tobacco processing factory and ornamented it with this fountain. He hoped, with a monopoly on tobacco, to finance his defense of Rome against the forces of the Risorgimento.

Although the fountain was designed and built in the latter half of the nineteenth century, a casual visitor could easily imagine that it dates back to the sixteenth. It employs the reliable scheme of a lower basin on a supporting base, with upper basins on balusters above the lower vessel. In this case, an octagonal stepped base supports a large octagonal basin of travertine, whose sides are alternately decorated with the pope's coat-of-arms and scrolls displaying his name. Above this basin is a baluster of entwined dolphins, supporting a circular marble basin with four carved lion heads on the rim, from which streams of water issue (when the water is turned on!).

Another smaller, inverted basin rises on a baluster formed of what seem to be four infant Tritons. Water shoots from the center of the inverted basin, falls on the scaled surface of the upended cup, and cascades in broken sheets into the middle basin below—with the same effect, in miniature, as the "twin" fountains by Maderno and Bernini in Saint Peter's Square.

Starting with your back to the tobacco factory, with the fountain on your right, exit Piazza Mastai straight ahead. The large street with tram tracks is viale di Trastevere. Locate the crosswalk and traffic lights to your left, and cross viale di Trastevere at the crosswalk straight into via Cardinale Merry del Val. After perhaps 100 yards, turn right into the first street on the right, via di San Francesco a Ripa. (I hope, by the time you visit, that the city will have cleaned up some of the disgracefully stupid graffiti that lately has defaced this otherwise dignified street.) The second street on the right will be via della Cisterna, and just after you turn the corner you will see a small wall fountain on your right.

The Fountain of the Barrels—La Fontana delle Botte (1927)
Architect: Pietro Lombardi

This is one of two fountains in Trastevere built by Lombardi as part of his contract to provide appropriately decorated drinking fountains in ten of Rome's historic *rioni*. This fountain, representing Trastevere's old *rione* designation, celebrates the wine sellers of the district. It's partially embedded in a stucco wall in via della Cisterna, just east of the Basilica of Santa Maria in Trastevere. In an arched niche is a carved cask, or *caratello*, of the kind in which wine was shipped to the wine shops. A large carafe stands on each side of the cask, and, from spouts in the carafes, water flows into the drain at street level. There's a spout in the center of the cask, too, from which a stream of water pours into a "must vat" below, which, when full, overflows into the street drain. ("Must" is the juice from the first press of wine grapes; it contains skins, seeds, and stems. When the winemaker decides the juice has remained "on the must" for an appropriate time, the liquid is drained off, leaving a mass of solids called pomace, also called *marc* in French and *vinaccia* in Italian. Grappa is made from vinaccia.)

Now exit from via della Cisterna the way you came, but turn right. Via di San Francesco a Ripa ends at this corner, so when you turn right, you will enter into Piazza San Calisto. Cross this small piazza, exiting with the little church of San Calisto on your left, by way of a short alley, into Piazza Santa Maria in Trastevere.

The Fountain of the Barrels: This fountain celebrates Trastevere's history of wine production with a *caratello* (wine cask) and a couple of handy carafes. This photograph also shows that you park in Rome at your own risk.

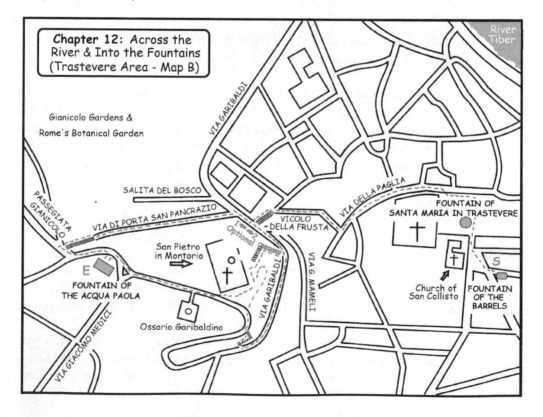

The Fountain of Piazza Santa Maria in Trastevere— La Fontana di Piazza Santa Maria in Trastevere (ca. 1471)
ARCHITECTS: ANONYMOUS; DONATO BRAMANTE; GIOVANNI AND CARLO FONTANA; GIAN LORENZO BERNINI

The church of Santa Maria in Trastevere is very old, having started life as a *titulus*, or parish church, in the middle of the fourth century. There is some historical confusion and dispute about this church; it may have been named, at first, after its founder, Pope Julius I, or perhaps after Pope Calixtus, who was martyred nearby. It seems to have acquired its current name, honoring the Virgin Mary, in the eighth century.

One striking feature of the church, just below the triangular pediment on the façade, is a mosaic illustrating the parable of the wise and foolish virgins from the Book of Matthew. Ten young women bring lamps to welcome the bridegroom to a wedding, but he's running late, and while they wait for him, five of the lamps burn out because their bearers neglected to bring enough oil for them. They scurry away to find more oil, at which point, of course, he arrives. Thus, the five absent women miss the wedding feast. Only the wise virgins with lighted lamps get a seat at the table. The moral, of course, is to be prepared for Judgment Day, because you don't know when Christ will show up and you don't want to miss your chance at the Beatific Vision. Just to drive home the point, Mary is seated among the virgins.

The Fountain in Piazza Santa Maria in Trastevere is a venerable and quite elaborate fountain, and it hosts plenty of backsides.

The Fountain in Piazza Santa Maria in Trastevere: Santa Maria in Trastevere is a very old church, first established in the fourth century AD. Some of the finest early Christian mosaics in Rome are inside.

Another unique aspect of the church is that, if you look closely, you'll see a bell mounted on the very tip-top of the campanile instead of inside the bell chamber. I don't know why it was banished to that unprotected perch, but it still works and is used to ring the hours.

Some of the most famous early Christian mosaics in all of Rome are inside this church. The great apse mosaic, with Christ and Mary enthroned, surrounded by saints, gleams with golden tesserae (bring a euro or two to turn on the lights!). Six mosaic scenes from the life of Mary, by Pietro Cavallini, are depicted below the half-dome in a later, more naturalistic style, though still with plenty of Byzantine gold. If you visit, note the granite columns that line the nave—they are very ancient and came from the Baths of Caracalla.

There was a fountain in front of the Basilica of Santa Maria as far back as the papacy of Adrian I, who reigned from 772 to 779 AD, though no one knows what that fountain looked like. It was used as a *cantharos* in which pilgrims could wash their hands, faces, and feet before entering the church. The first documented fountain was pictured on a map of Rome in 1471, but it probably existed earlier, perhaps even during the time of Pope Adrian. It consisted of two basins, a large one with a

smaller basin above, but other details are not clear. This same fountain was decorated with carved wolf's heads around the rim of the upper basin in the 1490s, and
then it was extensively restored and remodeled by Donato Bramante early in the sixteenth century. In 1592, Giovanni Fontana took his turn repairing and modifying
the lower basin; decades later, in the 1660s, Gian Lorenzo Bernini moved the whole
thing closer to the center of the square, elevated the fountain on a stepped base, and
placed carved seashells (from which water flowed into shell-shaped bowls) around
the octagonal lower basin. The fountain's penultimate form is from 1692, when Carlo
Fontana increased the capacity of the lower basin and replaced Bernini's seashells
and bowls with larger versions.

In 1872, the Municipality of Rome modified Fontana's seashells by adding large
escutcheons marked with the acronym SPQR—the ancient symbol of the Roman
Republic. Adding the symbol was the municipality's way of celebrating the end of
papal rule in the city, which happened in 1870 when the forces of the Risorgimento
seized Rome from the pope.

*Our next destination will take us up the slopes of the Janiculum Hill, so get ready
for some Roman cardio work. I'll suggest two routes, and you can take your pick.
Option 1 takes you on a fairly direct route to the next fountain, La Fontanone dell'Acqua Paola; option 2 is a bit steeper in places, though somewhat more scenic, and, on
the way to the fountain, takes you to the interesting church of San Pietro in Montorio, where Bramante's famous Tempietto can be found. Both options follow the same
route at first and then diverge, so let's start now, and I'll let you know when you have
to make your choice.*

*Facing the church, exit from Piazza Santa Maria in Trastevere into the narrow
street to the right of the church, via della Paglia; after about 200 yards, at the third
street on the right, turn into Vicolo della Frusta. After a few minutes' walk, at a hairpin turn, Vicolo della Frusta will end at a flight of stone steps. Climb the steps, and
when you reach the top, you'll be on via Garibaldi. Here is where the routes diverge.*

*Option 1: Turn right on via Garibaldi, and after about 100 feet, at the first street,
turn left (and uphill) onto via di Porta San Pancrazio. After about 300 yards, you'll
come to another flight of steps. At the top, turn left, and quickly left again, onto via
Garibaldi. Walk another 50 feet or so, and you'll be in front of an enormous fountain.
You have reached the Fountain of the Acqua Paola. You can skip the following instruc-
tions, and go on to the entry for the fountain.*

*Option 2: Turn left on via Garibaldi. Via Garibaldi will lead uphill; don't take via
Goffredo Mameli, which leads downhill. After about 120 feet, you'll see an iron gate in
the concrete wall to your right, with a flight of steps behind it. Go through the gate and
climb the steps, which will bend sharply to the left before reaching another gate that
leads into Piazza di San Pietro in Montorio.*

*(If either gate is locked, continue past the first gate on via Garibaldi, uphill and
around the church property. Keep an eye on the stone wall bordering the street to your
right. After about 175 yards, the wall will end, and you'll see some stairs curving right,
up a small grassy incline topped with trees. Take the stairs, which will put you on
another road surface at the top of the stairs—actually, it's via Garibaldi again, which
has made a long loop ahead of you and doubled back almost on itself; you've taken*

a shortcut between the sides of the loop. Turn right, and you'll see the Church of San Pietro in Montorio about 200 feet ahead of you, with its piazza to the right of the church. There is a small column topped with a cross in the piazza. Enter the piazza.)

Once in the piazza, either from the gates and stairs or from via Garibaldi, you'll see a low building at one end of the piazza, with "Real Academia de Espana" in large letters above the door. (Much of the former monastery of San Pietro in Montorio is occupied by the Spanish Royal Academy in Rome.) In between, and connecting this "Academia" building and the church (which you'll recognize by its double staircase), is the façade of a monastery building with a modest arched doorway. Beyond the arch is a courtyard in which you'll find one of the most iconic (and smallest) buildings of the Renaissance—the Tempietto of Bramante.

This miniature temple was erected around 1510 on the supposed site of Saint Peter's martyrdom, and it embodies the Renaissance ideal of perfect proportion. In the church itself, the first chapel on the right contains a famous *Flagellation of Christ*, painted by Sebastiano del Piombo with help from his good friend Michelangelo.

After you've visited the Tempietto and the church, exit the piazza with the church's double staircase to your right. Turn right on via Garibaldi. You'll pass, on your left, a small white-limestone structure, composed of arches on four sides within an enclosure of low stone balustrades. This is the Mausoleo Ossario Garibaldino, where the remains of more than 1,600 Italian soldiers are buried. These are men who died in the battles for Italian unification between 1849 (when Garibaldi led an unsuccessful defense of the young Italian Republic against the French) and 1870 (when Rome was finally captured by the forces of the Risorgimento). A hundred yards or so farther on, you'll reach the great mostra *of the Acqua Paola.*

The Fountain of the Acqua Paola—La Fontanone dell'Acqua Paola (1612)
ARCHITECTS: FLAMINIO PONZIO AND GIOVANNI FONTANA

I mentioned earlier that Augustus had entertained the Romans with mock sea battles in an artificial lake, called a *naumachia*, in Trastevere. The aqueduct that supplied Augustus' *naumachia* was called the *Aqua Alsietina*. After the taste for naval battles waned, *Aqua Alsietina* powered grain mills and provided irrigation water for farms in the area. When, in the Middle Ages, this watercourse (and another called the *Aqua Traiana*) failed, the people living in the area were left without a reliable water source, either for domestic use or to run the mills that ground their wheat.

In 1608, Pope Paul V decided to resurrect an ancient aqueduct to supply water to the parched citizens of Trastevere. He purchased a tract of land about 30 miles northwest of Rome, near Lake Bracciano, that included a number of natural springs that had supplied water in antiquity to both *Aqua Alsietina* and *Aqua Traiana*. He and his architects restored and reused ancient underground channels as well as some partly buried elevated stretches to bring the water to the slopes of the Janiculum

The Fountain of the *Acqua Paola*: Pope Paul V had his engineers restore the ancient *Aqua Traiana* aqueduct from the time of Trajan and renamed it *Acqua Paola. La Fontanone dell'Acqua Paola* was the terminus of the aqueduct.

Hill. There they built what was then the most majestic of Roman fountains, using marble from various ancient sites in Rome.

Inspired by the Fountain of Moses, the *Fontanone dell'Acqua Paola* features five triumphal arches across the front of the structure—though the two on the ends of the façade are smaller than the middle three. Instead of statues, there are windows in the middle arches, giving a hint of the small garden behind them. The columns framing the arches came from the old Saint Peter's that Constantine built in the fourth century: four are of red Egyptian granite. And from this imposing structure, the waters of the renewed aqueduct—which the pope named *Acqua Paola*, after himself—were introduced to Rome after a journey of about 30 miles.

Fontanone, in Italian, means "big fountain"; in theory, the word might be applied to any large fountain. But in Rome, *Il Fontanone* means *the* big one, the *Acqua Paola* fountain, which, behind the façade, was also designed to manage the outflow of water from its tanks to the rest of its dependent fountains and other, private users; like the Fountain of Moses, it had an apartment to accommodate a company of watermen who operated and maintained the necessary valves and stopcocks.

The watermen were severely tested early in the fountain's existence. In the original design, there was no spacious pool in front, and the water spilled from the five arches into five small basins. One of the reasons Pope Paul had chosen the

The Fountain of the *Acqua Paola*: From this *mostra* high on the Janiculum Hill, the water was distributed to a host of fountains on both sides of the river.

Janiculum for the repaired aqueduct's terminus was that, from such a height, the gravity-fed fountains below the *mostra* would have plenty of water pressure to produce high, soaring plumes of water (for the glory of God, of course). But, when the system was first tested in 1610, the pressure broke one of the marble basins, which continued to release water for several days, causing flooding below the fountain. In fact, for years the fountain intermittently leaked enough to cause mudslides and property damage at the bottom of the hill, in Trastevere. The large pool we admire today was added by Carlo Fontana in 1690, in hopes that its larger capacity would hold enough water to ease the flooding problem; it was partly successful. But the problem eventually was solved by diverting part of the upstream flow into a series of water-powered grain mills high on the Janiculum, which also benefited the area economically.[4]

Though much of the water piped from the newly repaired aqueduct went to the Vatican area and the villas and gardens of the pope's high-placed church colleagues, the Fountain of the *Acqua Paola* also distributed water to civic fountains in all the neighborhoods west of the Tiber, and across the river as well, giving new life to previously impoverished and neglected parts of Rome.

The elegantly carved Latin inscription above the arches says, "Paul V, Pontifex Maximus, brought water from the Bracciano region, collected from the most healthy sources, by restoring ancient channels of the Alsietina Aqueduct and adding new ones, from 35 milestones away, in the year of Our Lord 1612, and the seventh of his pontificate."

The inscription states that the pope's engineers repaired and used the *Aqua Alsietina*, Augustus' channel used to supply his giant *Naumachia Augusti*. However, the water for the *Acqua Paola* fountain actually flowed down the repaired path of the *Aqua Traiana*, which Emperor Trajan built in 109 AD, more than a century after Augustus presented his mock sea battles. But it's obviously hard to tell one aqueduct from another after a millennium and a half.

Alas, the taste of the *Acqua Paola* water never became popular with most Romans, especially after 1672 when Lake Bracciano water was added to the supply. However, the fountains served by the aqueduct are visually some of the finest in Rome. Before leaving, be sure to take advantage of the panoramic view over Rome's rooftops from the Belvedere in front of the fountain.

Our next group of fountains is in and around the Vatican, and it's about a two-mile walk (although a very scenic one) to the starting point, Saint Peter's Square. So if you want to return to your lodgings instead, you can get down the hill using bus number 115, which follows a circular route.

It stops on via Garibaldi. Stand with your back to the fountain, and go right. Follow via Garibaldi (which will bear left, downhill) until you see the bus stop sign,

The Fountain of the *Acqua Paola*: The heraldic symbols on the fountain express Pope Paul's pride in his accomplishment, though he didn't know that it was Trajan's aqueduct he was restoring. He thought it was the *Alsietina*, which dated from Augustus' time.

perhaps 50 yards. It's marked "Garibaldi/Iacobucci." Take bus 115 from this stop and get off at the Trastevere/Ministero Pubblica Istruzione stop. You'll find the stop for Tram 8 nearby; take the tram in the direction "Venezia." Piazza Venezia is the end of the line. Or, if you like, you can get off the tram before it crosses the river, at Piazza G.G. Belli, and find a taxi stand behind the Belli fountain.

You can also take bus numbers 115 or 870 down the Janiculum Hill from a different nearby bus stop. To find it, face the Fountain of the Acqua Paola, go right on via Garibaldi about 200 feet and turn right through a gate, flanked by squared columns, into Passeggiata del Gianicolo. The bus stop, marked "Gianicolo—Villa Corsini," is another 150 feet farther ahead, on the right. From this stop, both the 115 and the 870 buses will take you along the Passeggiata del Gianicolo toward the Vatican. If you get off at the Piazza della Rovere stop (at the bottom of the hill, just after the bus turns right at the river), you'll be quite close to Vatican City, and you can go on to Saint Peter's Square if you like.

From the bus stop, with the river to your right, look for the great corner bastion in the massive stone walls beyond the multi-lane streets ahead of you. Carefully cross the busy streets using the crosswalks, and then turn left. Just before you reach the walls, turn right into via di Porta Santo Spirito.

Continue through the grand marble arch ahead, where the street name changes to via dei Penitenzieri, and, after about 200 yards, cross Borgo Santo Spirito into via dei Cavalieri del Santo Sepolcro, which, after about 40 yards, will meet via della Conciliazione. Turn left, and you will see Saint Peter's Basilica and Saint Peter's Square straight ahead.

However, if you want to experience the entire Passeggiata del Gianicolo up to the start of our tour of the Vatican area, I salute you. Here are the directions. As noted before, walks between chapter itineraries are not covered by the book's maps, but that won't deter you!

Let's begin the journey by facing the Fountain of the Acqua Paola and then following via Garibaldi around the fountain to the right. Very soon you'll see a gate, guarded on either side by a pair of squared columns topped with stone urns. Through the gate you'll begin the Passeggiata del Gianicolo, a famous route that you'll follow for the first three-fourths of a mile of the journey. Lined with plane trees and oaks, the road follows the contours of the Janiculum Hill (or Gianicolo) and, on the right, overlooks Rome. Much of the green area below is the Botanical Garden of Rome, but the famous domes and monuments are spread out before you as well. After about 400 yards, you'll find yourself staring at an enormous monument to Giuseppe Garibaldi, who, along with Cavour, Giuseppe Mazzini, and Victor Emmanuel II, brought the nation of Italy into existence.

High atop the monument, the great general surveys the battle while, clinging to the pedestal, dramatic bronze sculptural groups enact history. "Roma o Morte" is inscribed on the structure. There is a grand view of Rome from the "Belvedere" in front of the statue, while around the back, from a graveled terrace, the Dome of Saint Peter's can be glimpsed through the trees.

You may have noticed a number of marble busts of military-looking gentlemen lining the road, perched on short columns, rather like the herms of ancient Greece.

Old Soldiers Never Die: There are more than eighty marble busts of men who fought for the unification of Italy along the Passeggiata del Gianicolo. These images in stone are a poignant reminder of their courage and sacrifice.

They are portraits of Italian and foreign heroes of the Risorgimento, Italy's struggle for independence. There are eighty-four busts in all, and you'll see more of them as we continue. You'll also see, a little past the Garibaldi monument, on the right, a wide graveled area bordered by a low wall of tan-colored stone, with a text in old-fashioned Italian incised on it. The text is the Constitution of a short-lived "Roman Republic" declared in 1849, which was crushed after five months when the French army restored Pope Pius IX to power. The unification and liberation of Italy was not completely achieved until 1870, at which time it became a kingdom, not a republic. Beyond the wall is a superb view of Rome.

Now look out for a handsome, pale-pink mansion on the right. It's the Embassy of Finland. A few steps farther on, to the left, you'll see a dramatic equestrian statue of a woman on a rearing horse, holding a baby in one hand and brandishing a pistol in the other. This is Giuseppe Garibaldi's Brazilian firebrand wife, Anita Garibaldi. (She fought beside him in several battles. An excellent horsewoman, she taught Giuseppe how to ride gaucho style. She died of a fever at age 27 and is buried in a sarcophagus built into the base of her monument. You can read the bronze plaque there: Qui sono i resti mortali di Anita Garibaldi—*"Here are the mortal remains of Anita Garibaldi.")*

Still farther along the road, on the right, there is a lighthouse, the Faro di Roma.

It was given to the city in 1920 by an association of Italians who had immigrated to Argentina, as a gesture of affection for their old homeland. Why they thought Rome, 20 miles or more from the sea, needed a lighthouse is a mystery. Still, you must admit, it's a swell lighthouse, whose flashing beams of light are patriotically red, white, and green.

The passeggiata now begins to make a series of hairpin turns. At the middle of the first reverse, you'll be facing an imposing brick building with a papal insignia over the door. This is the Pio Romeno Pontifical College, established in 1937 to educate young Romanian clergymen. From 1948 to 1989, it had no Romanian students, but now, since the fall of Nicolae Ceauşescu's Communist regime in Romania, the college is active again.

After negotiating the major curves, you'll see the cream-colored buildings of the Bambino Gesù Pediatric Hospital. Across from the hospital's first entrance will be a graveled terrace with a fine view of Rome. Continue along the passeggiata, where you'll find a long stone wall on the left. Soon afterward, on the left and just before the second entrance to the hospital, you'll see the Renaissance Church of San Onofrio. You'll recognize it by its flight of steps on the left of the road, leading to the church's portico, lined by arches, with a bell tower rising behind the roofline. Fans of epic Italian poetry might like to know that in 1595, the great (but rather paranoid) Torquato Tasso sought refuge from his imaginary tormenters here, only to die in the cloisters the day before he was to be crowned poet laureate of Rome. But let us continue our walk.

Now, directly across the road away from the church steps, there is a narrow street, Salita di Sant'Onofrio. Turn right here, and follow the salita for about 300 yards. At the end of the salita there'll be a flight of stairs leading down. Take the stairs. At the bottom, you'll be on via del Gianicolo.

Turn right, and, after about 100 feet, carefully take the crosswalk to your left, across all the multiple lanes of traffic. Once across, look to your left, and you'll see the high, angled corner of a giant fortified wall, a bastion of the Leonine Wall surrounding the Vatican. Head for the wall, and just before you reach it, turn right into via di Porta Santo Spirito.

Continue through the grand marble arch ahead (it is, in fact, the Porta Santo Spirito), where the street name changes to via dei Penitenzieri; after about 200 yards, cross Borgo Santo Spirito into via dei Cavalieri del Santo Sepolcro, which, after 40 yards or so, will meet via della Conciliazione. Turn left, and you will see Saint Peter's Basilica straight ahead.

Via della Conciliazione, by the way, was begun under Benito Mussolini's rule in 1936. Completed in 1950, it involved the demolition of hundreds of homes and other structures that made up the densely populated center of the "Borgo" district, as well as the resettlement of thousands of residents.

You'll probably find that the great piazza in front of the church is enclosed by a fence. To find an open gate, you may have to circle around the colonnade (a semi-circular row of columns, four abreast) to the right. Just look for other people entering the piazza through the columns. Our first two fountains are in the square.

❧ 13 ❧

Mother Church's Twins
and New Water for Old Rome

Vatican Area

THIS WALK BEGINS IN PIAZZA SAN PIETRO.

The nearest Metro station to Piazza San Pietro is Ottaviano (line A).

By the way, I recommend that the following itinerary be followed over two days, since there is so much to see in Vatican City, and visiting our final fountain, the Pigna, requires that you purchase a ticket to the Vatican Museums. Once inside, you'll surely

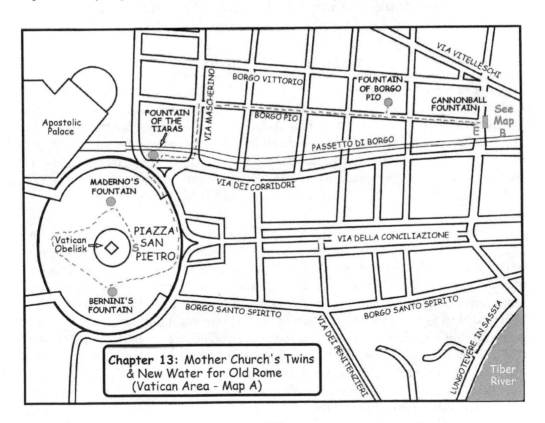

Chapter 13: Mother Church's Twins
& New Water for Old Rome
(Vatican Area - Map A)

want to spend several hours in this vast treasure house of wonderful things. So please see the second-day plan, which includes the museums, after the description of the Cannonball Fountain.

A few words about Saint Peter's Basilica and about Saint Peter's Square:

Once inside Piazza San Pietro, and facing the colossal façade, you may remember (or read in your guidebook) the statistics about the great church, the seat of Roman Catholicism: 610 feet long (715 feet including the porch), 375 feet wide, 450 feet high to the top of the dome. Almost six square acres in area, it can hold 20,000 seated worshipers and a standing crowd of 60,000. As for its construction, the figures are just as amazing: 120 years in construction, under the supervision of 10 architects, and lasting through the reigns of 31 popes.

But you will notice that from the piazza, Michelangelo's dome is barely visible, hidden by the height of the façade. In fact, most of what you see from the square was designed by just two men—well, three if you count the unknown Egyptian creator of the tall obelisk in the center. The strange Emperor Caligula brought the obelisk, which is 85 feet high, from Egypt in 37 AD and set it up in his garden, which later became the Circus of Nero. It was still standing when Pope Sixtus V ordered it moved to its present position in 1585.

The Twin Fountains of Piazza San Pietro (1614 and 1677)
ARCHITECTS: CARLO MADERNO AND GIAN LORENZO BERNINI

Maderno's Fountain

The enormous façade of the church—with its huge columns and pilasters, its marble balconies between them, its attic story surmounted by statues of Christ and his apostles—forms one end of the piazza. As you face the façade, to the right of the obelisk there is a large and graceful fountain, whose plume of *Acqua Paola* water shoots high in the air and then descends on—rather than into—an overturned marble basin, whose segmented convex surface breaks the flow into a glittering cascade, caught below in a larger basin. Both the church façade and the fountain were designed by one man: Carlo Maderno.

Of course, the basilica and its façade are, in terms of Roman history, rather new. The church replaces the original Saint Peter's Basilica, which was built by the order of Constantine the Great in 319 AD and endured until 1506, when the construction of today's great edifice began. And the fountain is also a replacement—for two previous fountains. One was there in medieval times, but little is known about it. It was superseded in 1490 by a large fountain of two granite vasques (basins), a larger and a smaller, but with limited water flow to fill the upper, smaller basin, which spilled into the lower. It wasn't until 1612, when powerful water pressure from the *Fontanone dell'Acqua Paola*, high on the slope of the Janiculum Hill, became available, that Maderno was able to replace the old, granite fountain with the spectacular display we see today. He completed the job in 1614.

The excellent water pressure, however, apparently became a somewhat mixed

Top: Maderno's Piazza San Pietro Fountain: Carlo Maderno's wonderfully showy fountain in Piazza San Pietro makes full use of the strong water pressure from the *Acqua Paola. Bottom:* The spectacular setting for Maderno's fountain wasn't there when the fountain was unveiled in 1614; Gian Lorenzo Bernini's colonnades weren't finished until 1667.

blessing at some point in the life of the *Acqua Paola* aqueduct. When it first came into service, the repaired aqueduct was fed by springs near Lake Bracciano, but in 1672 water from the lake itself was added to the mix. In the 1950s, one Vatican employee told a visiting writer that at certain times of the year he had to shut down the fountains to clear their pipes of millions of tiny eel fry, bred in Lake Bracciano's waters.[1] (I believe the lake water is now treated or filtered before being released into the aqueduct system.)

Bernini's Fountain

There is another fountain, almost identical to Maderno's, to the left of the obelisk as you face the church. It, too, has an upside-down basin above a larger vasque,

Bernini's Piazza San Pietro Fountain: Bernini must have admired Maderno's fountain, because he created this near-twin to balance the old fountain as part of his redesign of Piazza San Pietro.

along with a similarly powerful jet of water to create shimmering effects as it falls back on and then streams from the upper basin into the lower. It was installed to balance Maderno's fountain on the right, though it was not completed until 1677, sixty-three years later than its "twin."

It took the designer of the second fountain ten years—from 1667 to 1677—to complete the installation, rather than the two years Maderno required. But, looking around the piazza, it's easy to see why Gian Lorenzo Bernini might have needed the extra time. In 1657, Pope Alexander VII ordered him to redesign the whole piazza, to allow the largest possible number of people to receive the pope's blessing from the middle balcony of Maderno's church façade. In accomplishing this enormous task, Bernini created his greatest masterpiece as an architect.

The first area of Bernini's piazza is a trapezoid bounded by two rows of narrow buildings extending forward from the two ends of the façade, away from the church; the second area is elliptical, with two colonnades in the form of semi-circles marking the outer boundaries. Each colonnade is four Doric columns wide. However, the colonnades do not meet at the eastern end of the piazza. A curved pavement of travertine connects the two and marks where Vatican City ends and Rome begins. The

Bernini's Piazza San Pietro Fountain: It's clear that people come to Piazza San Pietro for a surprising variety of reasons. Bernini's fountain is in the background.

284 columns, and the buildings that connect them to the church, are topped with 140 statues of saints and martyrs.

Bernini explained the purpose of the design, with its two "arms" of columns: "Considering that Saint Peter's is almost the matrix of all the churches, its portico had to give an open-armed, maternal welcome to all Catholics, confirming their faith; to heretics, reconciling them with the Church; and to the infidels, enlightening them about the true faith."[2]

Bernini correctly foresaw a variety of visitors to Saint Peter's Square, but I suspect he would be amazed to see the crowds that gather there now: not just believers and heretics and infidels but also tourists from distances and places he could not have imagined, eager for selfies or Instagram images or to get a glimpse of the pope. We, of course, came in search of fountains, but I hope, while you are in Rome, that you can devote a day to exploring Saint Peter's Basilica. You can explore the magnificence of the interior, or climb up to the roof, or even ascend to the lantern of the dome (551 steps!) for an unequaled view of the city. Or you can descend into the "Scavi," an excavated necropolis under the church, to get a glimpse of Peter's tomb and several decorated Roman family crypts (though the Scavi tour must be booked weeks in advance at www.scavi.va).

But back to the fountains: The two are very similar, but a closer look reveals some interesting differences. In Maderno's fountain, the older of the pair, the upper basin (the upside-down one) and the top of the pedestal supporting it are made of a darker stone than that of Bernini's. The octagonal lower part of the pedestal has emblems honoring Pope Paul V carved in very worn relief: single crowned eagles or the pope's coat-of-arms (a crowned eagle above a dragon), with crossed keys above both.

Bernini's fountain, on the left as you face the church, has a younger inscription honoring Pope Paul VI, as well as Pope Clement X's coat-of-arms (a papal tiara and crossed keys above a shield emblazoned with six stars). There are also panels carved with entwined dolphins.

From Bernini's fountain, walk back toward Maderno's and continue through the colonnade, exiting from Saint Peter's Square. If you think of this semi-circular arm of the colonnade as part of a clock face, once outside the columns, you want to be at about two o'clock. There, you should see a long medieval stone wall with crenellations along the top, bearing the inscription Largo del Colonnato; near the wall and next to a door in the wall marked "Polizia di Stato," you'll find a small fountain wearing a number of carved "pope's hats." By the way, the stone wall is part of the secret Passetto di Borgo, an elevated walkway that the popes could—and did—use to reach Castel Sant'Angelo and safety when there was a threat to the Vatican. Pope Clement VII rode out the Sack of Rome in 1527 in Castel Sant'Angelo, while the troops of the Holy Roman Emperor, Charles V, laid waste to the city.

The Fountain of the Tiaras—La Fontana delle Tiare (1927)
Architect: Pietro Lombardi

In the first century AD, the Rome's first emperor, Augustus, divided the city into fourteen administrative districts, which he called *regiones*. This arrangement lasted

The Fountain of the Tiaras: Outside Piazza San Pietro, just beyond the northern arm of the colonnade, this neighborhood fountain symbolizes the Borgo *rione* with a stack of papal tiaras.

throughout the imperial age and into the medieval era, but by that time the term had morphed from *regiones* to *rioni*. The number of *rioni* fluctuated between twelve and fifteen over the centuries. In the eighteenth century, Pope Benedict XIV ordered that marble plaques be installed on the walls of houses at each *rione*'s border, and you can still see some of them today, though the number of districts has increased to twenty-two in modern times and the old signs no longer have legal meanings. Still, there are sentimental attachments to the old neighborhoods (and to old rivalries between them).

There were neighborhood fountains, too, after the papal restorations of the aqueducts, but by the twentieth century most had disappeared. In 1927, the City of Rome decided to create new fountains in some of the traditional *rioni* and, after a competition among architects, awarded a contract for ten small fountains, each to represent the history or traditions of its *rione*, to Pietro Lombardi, who wasted no time getting to work. By the end of 1927, he had completed nine fountains. The tenth was delayed by street repairs but was installed the next year. One of the ten is the Fountain of the Tiaras.

This fountain honors the *rione* of the Borgo, which during papal rule included

The Fountain of the Tiaras—*La Fontana delle Tiare*—is a handy source of excellent water for thousands of visitors. It was completed in 1927.

Saint Peter's and the Vatican. The fountain consists of a pedestal with three attached basins. Above each basin is a carved papal tiara, from each of which descend two carved keys, symbolically the keys of the Kingdom of Heaven that Christ gave to Saint Peter, the first pope. Water spouts into the basins from the upper part—the bow—of each key. Surmounting the three tiaras is another tiara in the center. The fountain is a user-friendly dispenser of drinkable water, either for those who want to drink from one of the six descending streams or for people who just want to fill up a container. On a hot day it is a welcome sight for tourists and pilgrims alike.

At the Fountain of the Tiaras, facing the wall, turn right and follow the Passetto di Borgo, the secret passage with the crenellated wall; after about 150 feet, you'll come to a double archway through the passage; turn left here into via del Mascherino and, after one block, turn right onto Borgo Pio, a pleasant street lined with pizzerias and trattorias. After the third block, on the left in Piazza del Catalone, there's a small fountain loaded with history.

The Fountain of Borgo Pio—La Fontana di Borgo Pio (ca. 1870)
ARCHITECT: UNKNOWN

Borgo Pio is one of the major streets of the old Borgo *rione*, and it runs from Vatican City toward Castel Sant'Angelo. About halfway between the Vatican and the castle, this curious small fountain can be found in a free-standing brick enclosure topped by a shallow pediment. From an iron spout, water falls into a travertine basin, and the stream is at a convenient height for drinking, washing your hands and face, or filling a water bottle. The water, according to an inscription above the spout, comes from the *Acqua Marcia* aqueduct. Back in the glory days of the Republic and the Empire, the *Aqua Marcia* was one of the most reliable of the ancient aqueducts that kept the baths and fountains of Rome filled; it was also one of the first aqueducts to serve the city, having been constructed under the supervision of the praetor Quintus Marcius Rex in 140 BC. However, the *Aqua Marcia* ceased to flow after the Empire fell.

The little Fountain of Borgo Pio—*La Fontana di Borgo Pio*—dates from the reign of Pius IX, just before the papacy lost Rome in 1870.

In the 1860s, Pope Pius IX sponsored the restoration of a part of the old *Aqua Marcia*, and this is the source of the water to the Borgo Pio fountain. However, the newly restored aqueduct was called the *Acqua Pia Antica Marcia*, rather than *Acqua Marcia*, in recognition of the pope's sponsorship. The little stream of water in this fountain, then, comes from the same source as the powerful jets and cascades that shower the water nymphs of the Fountain of the Naiads in Piazza Repubblica!

There is a marble relief above the Borgo Pio fountain's spout showing a papal crown and the crossed keys of Saint Peter. This papal insignia is a poignant reminder that this fountain must have been one of the last of the pope's works as ruler of Rome, because on September 20, 1870, the Italian army under the command of General Raffaele Cadorna captured Rome, putting an end to papal control of the city. Pius IX became a self-described "prisoner in the Vatican."

Now, continue on Borgo Pio for just a block and a half, where Borgo Pio ends at via di Porta Castello. Facing you across the street is a curious small fountain, with a distinctly martial flavor.

The Cannonball Fountain—La Fontana delle Palle di Cannone (1927)
ARCHITECT: PIETRO LOMBARDI

This second fountain of the Borgo *rione* is mounted on a wall bordering via di Porta Castello, very near the western flank of Castel Sant'Angelo. The castle was, in antiquity, the mausoleum of Emperor Hadrian, but from medieval times it served as a nearly impregnable fortress. As any good fortress must, it had a store of weapons with which the defenders could attack the besiegers. There is a courtyard in the castle known as the Cortile delle Palle, where the cannonballs were kept. When Pietro Lombardi designed this small fountain, he paid homage to the military might of the castle by making a small pyramid of cannonballs that dispensed water to people passing by! Beneath an arch made of stone and brick, ten cannonballs are stacked. The central ball has a carved face, and from its lips a stream of water falls into a basin below. There are two more cannonballs embedded in the sides of the arch, and water flows from these into two more basins.

I suggest that you visit the last two fountains in this chapter on another day, because one of them, the Pinecone Fountain (or "La Fontana della Pigna"), is within the Vatican Museums, and you will need a ticket to see it. It is an extraordinary work of art with a long and momentous history, so I believe it's worth the price. The museums are also worth dedicating most of a day to visit, and it's a good idea to purchase your tickets in advance and "skip the lines." In high season, lines for the Vatican Museums ticket office can reach for several blocks, and even in winter the wait can be agonizingly long. You can book tickets from the official Vatican Museums website (www.museivaticani.va).

It happens that the other fountain you have yet to visit is only a few steps from the Cipro Metro stop, the nearest station to the Vatican Museums. So it is convenient

The Cannonball Fountain: Another neighborhood fountain with a theme resides in a wall niche a few steps from Castel Sant'Angelo, which has served at times as a fortress. Its cannons are celebrated by *La Fontana delle Palle di Cannone.*

to take the Metro to the Cipro station (line A), have a look at the Fountain in Piazzale degli Eroi, and then walk to the museums.

So, to get from the Cipro station to the Fountain in Piazzale degli Eroi, exit onto via Cipro and turn right. Continue another 150 yards on via Cipro, and you'll enter Piazzale degli Eroi (Piazzale of the Heroes). Our fountain is in the center of the busy traffic circle. Be very careful as you approach it!

The Fountain in Piazzale degli Eroi—La Fontane in Piazzale degli Eroi, aka the Peschiera Fountain— La Fontana del Peschiera (1949)
Architect: Vittorio Piergiovanni

The water you see arching over this fountain has an interesting origin. The valley of the Velino River is below the hilltop town of Rieti, in Lazio, and, like a couple of other towns nearby, Rieti claims to be the geographical center of Italy. Narni and Terni, both within a few miles, hotly dispute this claim. Rieti and Terni were embroiled in another dispute about 2,300 years ago, this time about water—and,

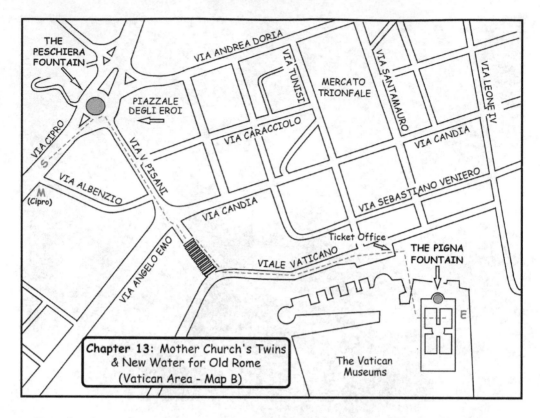

Chapter 13: Mother Church's Twins & New Water for Old Rome (Vatican Area - Map B)

indirectly, this ancient spat is related to the rather strange Peschiera Fountain in Rome.

From prehistoric times, the Velino valley was waterlogged. In fact, much of it was a shallow lake. During the Roman Republic, around 270 BC, Rieti citizens complained to the consul Curius Dentatus about the mosquitos that bred in the lake and marshes, as well as the fever (which we today call malaria) that sickened so many people. Curius Dentatus was a man of action, so it was not long before his engineers had diverted the course of the Velino so that it tumbled over a high cliff into another river below, the Nera. The Velino valley became a tillable flatland, ideal for a number of crops; the mosquitos disappeared; and the spectacular cataract where the Velino thundered over the cliff into the Nera became the highest manmade waterfall in the world. It still is.

The problem was that every time it rained, the swollen Nera River, burdened with the water from the Velino, flooded the downstream town of Terni. Eventually, Terni sued Rieti for damages. History doesn't record the verdict, but the waterfall is still there, though nowadays it turns turbines in a hydroelectric dam. (Twice a day, though, the water is allowed to tumble over its ancient spillway for the delight of picnickers in the park below. It's a grandly surreal experience to see a huge cataract suddenly appear, thundering down a series of cliffs, filling the valley of the Nera with mist. Go see it if you're ever near Terni: the *Cascata delle Marmore*. Check the website, www.cascatadellemarmore.info.)

But the province of Rieti is still naturally wet, with an abundance of springs and

The Fountain in Piazzale Eroi, aka the Peschiera Fountain—*La Fontana del Peschiera*—is named for the twentieth-century aqueduct that supplies it. Built in 1949, it's a bit of an ugly duckling, rather unfinished, because Italy had just emerged from World War II.

seeps, and it was here, a few miles from Rieti, that engineers working for A.C.E.A. (Rome's Water and Electricity Authority) found the source for a much-needed new aqueduct, the first since the *Acqua Pia Antica Marcia*. Work on the project began in 1938, and, although interrupted by World War II, the *Acqua Peschiera* was operational by the 1950s.[3] As it happened, 1950 was a jubilee year, and so A.C.E.A. rather hastily created a fountain in 1949 to serve as the *mostra* for the new aqueduct.

Constructed of concrete, the fountain consists of a large lower pool, within which an upper basin is surrounded by eight semi-circular basins, alternately large and small, projecting from a central structure whose widest concave vertical surfaces are decorated with shell-shaped settings for waterspouts. From the middle of the upper basin, tall leaping jets of water from unadorned nozzles arc into the lower basins.

To be frank, the fountain, though historically important, is an ugly duckling that never turned into a swan. Built in haste, the fountain is virtually devoid of applied ornamentation; tentative plans to improve (or at least decorate) the fountain have never been fulfilled. However, when in full flow, the water display can be impressive, a good reminder that the modern Peschiera aqueduct dwarfs the output of all the other existing aqueducts serving Rome. In fact, more than 80 percent of Rome's water supply nowadays comes from the *Acqua Peschiera* (or rather the Peschiera-Capore Pipeline, as it is now called, since water from a nearby spring system, Le Capore, has been added to the mix). Acea SpA (the current name of A.C.E.A.) has ambitious plans to add another pipeline, still from the Monte Nuria area a few miles from Rieti, which will double the volume of water reaching Rome, or so they say.[4] Let's hope that on that happy day, all the fountains in Rome can join the celebration.

With the fountain at your back, look toward via Cipro, the street from which you entered Piazzale degli Eroi. Now find the first street out of the piazzale to the left of via Cipro. This is via Vittor Pisani. Leave the piazzale on via Vittor Pisani. Soon, as you walk, you'll be able to see a set of stairs at the end of the street. This is our first objective. Just before reaching the stairs, via Vittor Pisani ends. Continue straight toward the stairs, and climb them.

At the top of the stairs, turn left on viale Vaticano; after about 200 yards, you'll see the imposing marble portal of the Vatican Museums across the street. Despite its welcoming appearance, the portal actually frames the exit—the ticket office and entrance are to the left, where a corner of the Vatican wall juts out from the building. Be sure to ask for a map of the museums, so you can find the Pigna Fountain and anything else you want to see in this vast complex. Don't miss the Raphael Rooms and, of course, the Sistine Chapel.

The Pinecone Fountain—La Fontana della Pigna (first century AD)
ARCHITECT: PUBLIUS CINCIUS SLAVIUS

The Fountain of the Pinecone—*La Pigna*—is certainly one of the oldest fountains still preserved in Rome, and it has a remarkable history. Today it stands in the Cortile della Pigna of the Vatican Museums. It was made in the first century AD, presumably by an artisan named Publius Cincius Slavius, since his name appears on the base of the sculpture. It is nearly 12 feet high, made of bronze, and was originally covered with pure gold. One medieval drawing shows it standing, like the finial of a lamp, atop the Mausoleum of Hadrian, which we know today as Castel Sant'Angelo. Another writer states that the fountain was once suspended in a grate that covered the oculus of the Pantheon. However, most sources agree that in antiquity it was in the Baths of Agrippa, or beside the Temple of Isis in the Campus Martius, very near today's church of *Santa Maria sopra Minerva*. Then, in the eighth century AD, the fountain was moved to the courtyard in front of the old Saint Peter's Basilica, the one built by the Christian emperor Constantine. It became the central feature of the *Cantaro*, a structure sheltering a fountain, where pilgrims could wash their hands and faces before entering the basilica. The Pigna probably replaced another fountain that had previously served the same function.

An elaborate enclosure for it was created: six porphyry columns with a sculpted marble covering. Among the decorations were two gilded bronze peacocks, taken

The Pinecone Fountain—*La Fontana della Pigna*. This enormous bronze pineapple from the first century AD is the oldest fountain in this book, and, strangely enough, we know who made it: Publius Cincius Slavius, a freed slave, who signed it.

from Hadrian's mausoleum. A thirteenth-century text states that water wept from tiny holes in the base of the pinecone's scales, though water actually flowed down the "cone" from a pipe in the top.

Pinecones, of course, suggest regeneration, rebirth, even perhaps resurrection, and, flowing with life-giving water, it must have been a powerful symbolic presence, especially flanked by the peacocks, traditionally linked with immortality.[5] In any case, the Pigna served its purpose elegantly for eight centuries. It was moved to its present location in 1608.

The Cortile della Pigna is part of what was once a long courtyard that connected the Vatican Palace with the Villa Belvedere (Innocent VIII's little getaway overlooking Saint Peter's). The courtyard, designed by Donato Bramante in 1505, was called, appropriately enough, the Cortile del Belvedere. Bramante died in 1514, before the project was complete, and Pirro Ligorio took over the job. Ligorio was the one who created the huge domed niche in which the fountain now sits—it's called the *Nicchione* ("Great Niche"). The Belvedere Courtyard was later divided in two when a wing of the Vatican Library was built across it, and the portion containing the pinecone was renamed the Cortile della Pigna.

Water doesn't flow from the pinecone these days. It sits on a base inscribed with a quotation from Dante's *Inferno*: "*La faccia sua mi parea lunga e grossa come La*

Pina di San Pietro a Roma," which means "His face seemed to me as long and broad as the pinecone of Saint Peter's in Rome." Dante was describing Nimrod, the great hunter from the Book of Genesis, a giant who is being punished in hell because he founded the city of Babel, whose tower offended God.

Below the quotation, water spouts into a basin from the mouth of a *mascherone*—a grotesque, mask-like relief in the stone base below *La Pigna*. There are two ancient Egyptian lions flanking the *mascherone*; they were carved in Egypt in the fourth century BC for Pharaoh Nectanebo II but came as spoils of war to Rome in antiquity, and they later spent some time spouting water for the Fountain of Moses. Above, on either side of the pinecone, you'll find the gilded peacocks from Hadrian's mausoleum that were the fountain's companions for so many centuries in the courtyard of the old Saint Peter's—or, rather, excellent copies of them. The originals are

The Pigna adorned the courtyard of old Saint Peter's for centuries, and it now resides in the Vatican Museums' Cortile della Pigna. The lions at its base are Egyptian, from the fourth century BC, the originals of those on the Fountain of Moses.

now in the *Braccio Nuovo*, the "New Wing" of the Chiaramonti Museum, one of the Vatican Museums.

There is a taxi stand along the Vatican wall on viale Vaticano, near the exit of the museums, if you need a ride to your lodgings after your visit. As you probably know, the Cipro Metro station is also nearby. If you want to continue on to our next fountain walk, go to Chapter 14.

❧ 14 ❧

A Walk in the Park

Villa Borghese Area

Since our last walk ended in the Vatican Museums, I suspect that you don't really want to hike all the way from the Vatican to Villa Borghese after trekking three miles or more of the museum corridors—and anyway, Borghese Park will probably require most of the day if you really want to enjoy it, so I advise getting there fresh in the morning. If you'd rather just wander and trust to serendipity, I understand. Also, if you want to visit the Galleria Borghese to see all the masterpieces there, be sure to make a reservation through the gallery's website (https://galleriaborghese.beniculturali.it/en/visita/info-biglietti). Booking ahead is mandatory.

However, to find most of the interesting fountains, I have a suggested itinerary.

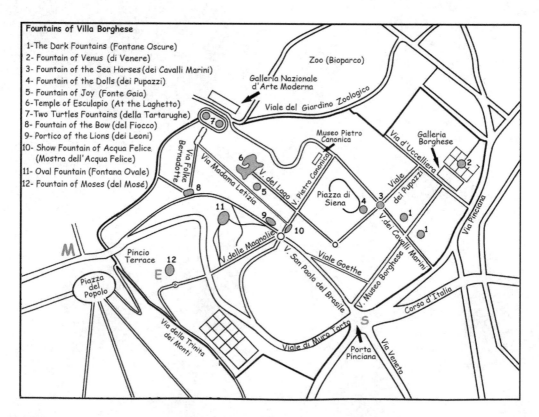

Fountains of Villa Borghese

1- The Dark Fountains (Fontane Oscure)
2- Fountain of Venus (di Venere)
3- Fountain of the Sea Horses (dei Cavalli Marini)
4- Fountain of the Dolls (dei Pupazzi)
5- Fountain of Joy (Fonte Gaia)
6- Temple of Esculapio (At the Laghetto)
7- Two Turtles Fountains (della Tartarughe)
8- Fountain of the Bow (del Fiocco)
9- Portico of the Lions (dei Leoni)
10- Show Fountain of Acqua Felice (Mostra dell' Acqua Felice)
11- Oval Fountain (Fontana Ovale)
12- Fountain of Moses (del Mosé)

Many of the roads and paths in the park are signposted, though some are not, and you may have to do some trail finding. You'll find maps on several signposts dotted throughout the park; they are also for sale in the gift shop in the basement of Galleria Borghese. You can visit the gift shop, ticket office and café without buying a ticket to the gallery; use the door underneath the double staircase.

There are several popular entrances to Villa Borghese Park. One, from Piazzale Flaminio, takes you on viale Giorgio Washington into the northwest section of the park. The street is busy with auto traffic and is not a recommended pedestrian entrance. Another (with which you will be familiar if you've followed the itinerary in Chapter 4) is up the stairway from Piazza del Popolo to the Salita del Pincio and on to the Pincio Terrace. Or you can enter the park through the Porta Pinciana at the north end of via Veneto. Finally, there's a gate off via Pinciana at the northeast corner of Villa Borghese, near Galleria Borghese. (There are other entrances from the north as well.)

But for our purposes today, let's begin at the Porta Pinciana gate.

First, a word or two about Villa Borghese itself:

There were famous gardens on the Pincian Hill long ago, when the Roman Republic still flourished. *Horti Luculliani*, they were called—the Gardens of Lucullus—and for centuries the very name evoked images of luxury, beauty, and bucolic peace. The gardens belonged to Lucius Licinius Lucullus, a general who, in the first century BC, won hard-fought victories over King Mithridates VI of Pontus (an ancient kingdom in what is now Turkey, on the southeast shore of the Black Sea). Lucullus returned to Rome with riches beyond measure—literally: so immense were the spoils of his wars that a complete accounting of them could not be made.

His gardens, lushly landscaped and filled with precious Greek sculptures, were so admired that long after Lucullus died and the Republic was replaced by the Empire, they remained highly coveted by the wealthiest and most powerful of Roman aristocrats. For example, according to Tacitus, Emperor Claudius' wife Messalina convinced her husband that the current owner of the gardens, Valerius Asiaticus, was guilty of adultery, sodomy, and official incompetence and should be executed—and, of course, have his gardens confiscated.[1]

I don't know whether Tacitus' account is true. Both Tacitus and Juvenal accuse Messalina of so many sins that, if they're telling the truth, she was a veritable superwoman of wickedness. It seems likely that they exaggerated a bit, but, in any case, on the orders of Claudius, she was later stabbed to death in her villa in the Gardens of Lucullus by a soldier of the Praetorian Guard—payback for plotting to overthrow the emperor in favor of her latest lover.

In the fourth century AD, during the empire's long decline, a wealthy aristocratic family called the Pincii built their Roman palace near where Lucullus' gardens and Messalina's villa once stood, and the whole area became known as the Pincian Hill. The name continued to be used throughout the medieval era and the Renaissance, and it still lives on today, though hardly anyone remembers anything about the family, except that the hill bears their name.

As Rome's glory faded, the noble palaces on the hill gave way to wild woodlands interspersed with vineyards, which, after the middle of the fourteenth century, belonged to the Augustinian monks of *Santa Maria del Popolo*. You can read about the founding of that church in Chapter 4, in which we visit the fountains of Piazza del Popolo.

By the sixteenth century, the groves and grapevines on the Pincio had been acquired by another wealthy and influential family, the Borghese. When Camillo Borghese became Pope Paul V in 1605 and gave his nephew Scipione a cardinal's hat, the future of the property took its most important turn.

Scipio Borghese, who leveraged his position with ruthless skill, became fabulously wealthy. He decided to create a 200-acre suburban retreat on the hill, for the use of his family and friends and to house his rapidly growing collection of artistic treasures. He commissioned landscaper Domenico Savino to create the gardens and architect Flaminio Ponzio to build an elegant mansion, which he (and his heirs) filled with works by the greatest artists of the Renaissance, Mannerist and Baroque eras.

Scipio probably never dreamed that the stars of this collection—sculptures by Bernini and Canova, paintings by Caravaggio, Titian, Raphael, Giovanni Bellini, Antonello da Messina and more—would be viewed by millions of commoners in his palace, now called the Galleria Borghese, much less that his secret gardens, lawns, groves of umbrella pines, statuary, gazebos, ponds and follies would become Rome's Central Park. But that's what happened: In 1903, the City of Rome acquired the property from the Borghese family, and today, in addition to Scipio's gardens, Romans and visitors alike can enjoy several museums, a carousel, pony rides, a puppet theater for kids and a replica of Shakespeare's Globe Theatre for adults. There is a "Casa del Cinema." There are rowboats available for rental, to paddle around on a lake containing a faux Greek temple. There is a zoo. The Pincio Terrace on the western edge of the hill has an unequaled view over Piazza del Popolo all the way to the Dome of Saint Peter's. There is an equestrian arena, lots of shady grass under the trees for picnics and frisbees, and pleasant trails for strolling, jogging, and dog walking. And there are fountains—lots of fountains.

Now, let's get started. Imagine that you are strolling north on the famous via Veneto, on your way to Villa Borghese from Piazza Barberini. When you reach the Porta Pinciana (an ancient gate in the Aurelian Walls), pass under the leftmost pedestrian arch. Notice that there are two grey, stone-block "gatehouses" ahead of you, each with a dragon relief on one side and an eagle sculpture on top. Dragons and eagles are symbols of the Borghese family, and the gatehouses remain from the days when the family owned this land. Use the crosswalk straight ahead to reach the leftmost gatehouse; then, turning right, use the crosswalk across two traffic lanes to reach the second gatehouse. Turn left and then right into the paved walking street next to the gatehouse. This is viale del Museo Borghese. There should be a map of Villa Borghese just to the right of the road, but, in any case, you'll know you're on the right road as soon as you see a marble statue of Lord Byron to your left. This road eventually ends at the Galleria Borghese, where Scipio's artistic treasures await if you've made a reservation. After a few minutes' walk along the way, you'll see the Aedicule della Musa—a small shrine containing the statue of a headless woman—on your right. The street leading away to the left is the viale Goethe, at the end of which is a grand sculpted monument to the great German poet (who was very fond of Villa Borghese during his two-year stay in Rome), but we will continue straight ahead toward the Galleria Borghese.

Farther on, past the intersection with viale dei Cavalli Marini, an unpaved pathway crosses at right angles to your road, leading in either direction—left or right—into a shadowed grove of Holm oaks. You may be able to discern the faint sound of falling water, and if you have time before your museum reservation, follow the sound in that direction. You can see a fountain among the trees in either direction; together they share a name: Le Fontane Oscure (the "Dark Fountains"). There, left or right, in the shade of the trees, you'll find a large basin, with two smaller bowls, on a stone column, spilling a cascade (if the water is turned on) into the bottom vessel. Around the fountain, in a broken circle, is a stone bench on which to sit at ease and contemplate the water.

The Dark Fountains—Le Fontane Oscure (early seventeenth century)
Architect: Giovanni Vasanzio

You've found one of the Dark Fountains—so called because of the deep and gloomy shade in which they sit. To find the other Dark Fountain, you must venture

The Dark Fountains, No. 1: This is one of the two "Dark Fountains"—*Le Fontane Oscure*—of Villa Borghese, so called because they are shadowed by great oaks and plane trees. This is the larger of the two, so you can call her *Fontana Oscura Una*.

into the woods on the other side of viale del Museo Borghese. They are much alike, though often only one of them has flowing water. If you turned right from viale del Museo Borghese, you are looking at the larger of the two.

A shady clearing in a quiet grove, with the cool sound of water splashing into a venerable basin, complete with stone seating worn smooth by twenty generations of backsides—what better place for a picnic?

These are the oldest fountains in Villa Borghese; it's said that perhaps they were present before the friars tended their grapevines on the hill. But in their current form, they date from the early seventeenth century and were designed by an architect named Giovanni Vasanzio, who also worked, along with Flaminio Ponzio, on Scipio Borghese's *Giardini Segreti* (Secret Gardens) beside the Galleria Borghese. Ponzio designed the palace itself, and when he died in 1613, Vasanzio (a native of Utrecht, whose real name was Jan van Santen) oversaw the completion of the building.

Return to viale del Museo Borghese and continue another 200 yards or so. You'll see the museum, Scipio Borghese's elegant seventeenth-century mansion containing his treasured collection, straight ahead, behind a balustraded forecourt. Enter the forecourt between the statues on either side of the gate. You'll notice that at the foot of each statue, a stern carved mask spouts water into a basin. You can consider these bonus fountains!

Whether you're touring the museum or not, our next fountain is around the back

The Dark Fountains, No. 2: Here is *Fontana Oscura Due*, the little sister of *Una*. She is left of viale del Museo Borghese if you are walking toward the museum, and *Fontana Oscura Una* is on the right.

of the mansion. Pass to the right of the building, on viale dei Daini, and you'll see a fenced garden to your right. It's called the Giardino dei Melangoli (Garden of Bitter Oranges), and it dates all the way back to the days of Scipio himself. Notice the small carved eagle spouting water in the center—another bonus fountain for you!

Once past the gallery building, look left, where you'll see another garden, this one surrounding the goddess of love.

Venus Fountain in the Sculpture Garden—*Fontana di Venere nel Giardino delle Sculture* (third century AD), installed c. 1613
ARCHITECTS: UNKNOWN THIRD-CENTURY ROMAN SCULPTOR AND GIOVANNI VASANZIO

Behind the Galleria Borghese building (originally called the Villa Borghese Pinciana), there is a rectangular garden of clipped hedges arranged in geometrical patterns around a circular pool. This garden was originally designed by Vasanzio in the early 1600s but has been much altered since that time. On a rocky mound in the

Venus Fountain in the Sculpture Garden: There were once elaborate formal gardens in the wooded area behind Galleria Borghese. The woods were dotted with classical sculptures. Venus and a few other figures survive from that time.

center of the pool is a statue of Venus, posed as if bathing from a spring that wells up in front of her. The sides of the garden are edged with statues and urns, with tall boundary markers (like Greek herms) guarding the corners. The boundary markers seem almost archaic, but scholars say they are the work of Pietro Bernini, assisted by his son Gian Lorenzo![2] Large planters (sometimes with shrubs inside) surround the pool. Most of the statues are concrete copies of ancient marble sculptures collected by the Borghese family over the years. Venus herself is made of concrete—the original marble figure was put in storage sometime in the 1990s, along with some of her garden companions.

Venus Fountain in the Sculpture Garden: The original third-century marble Venus is now stored in the Pietro Canonica Museum's basement; our twentieth-century copy still enjoys her bubbling spring, though.

You can see the original Venus, and many other statues that have now retired, in the basement of *Museo Pietro Canonica*, a few hundred yards away. The museum is free to enter and contains many splendid works by Pietro Canonica, an important nineteenth- and twentieth-century sculptor. The basement storage area is not part of the museum exhibit, however, so if you want to see the ancient works, you'll have to ask for permission. I'll tell you how to make a small detour there from our next fountain, if you're interested.

Heading for our next fountain, return to the front of the gallery, and stand at the bottom of the double staircase, with your back to the building. Don't go out through the forecourt. Follow the road to the right—this is viale dell'Uccelliera. As you go, you'll have Scipio Borghese's Giardini Segreti *(Secret Gardens) behind hedges on your right. They were made so that Scipio could privately entertain his friends surrounded by flowers and exotic plants.*

After about 150 yards, you'll see an ornate building on your right, topped with what look like four giant wire birdcages. That's why our street is viale dell'Uccelliera—it means "Birdcage Street." The building was built as an aviary and once was stocked with exotic birds. Turn left at the aviary building, onto a path into the woods called viale dei Pupazzi, which may or may not be signed. After about 300 yards, you'll come to a flight of stone steps; as you ascend, our next fountain—a famous one—will appear bit by bit, beginning with the top basins.

The Fountain of the Sea Horses—La Fontana dei Cavalli Marini (1791)
ARCHITECTS: CHRISTOPHER UNTERBERGER AND VINCENZO PACETTI

Three shallow, graceful stone bowls edged with carved acanthus leaves rise, largest to smallest, above a wide, sparkling, circular pool at ground level. A plume of water in the top basin overflows into the next, which then spills into the largest. Beneath are sculpted sea horses—*hippocampi*, they are called—partly submerged in the pool. These beautifully carved creatures support, with their intertwined, fishlike tails, the three flowing basins. Jets of water spout from between their hooves.

The hippocampus is a mythological creature with the head, neck, and forelegs of a horse and the body and tail of a fish—sort of like a male, equine mermaid. Oftentimes, as in this example, hippocampi also sport wings, though why sea horses need wings is a mystery. Just Pegasus envy, I guess. As you might imagine, Poseidon (or Neptune) often drives a team of hippocampi across the waves while riding in his sea chariot.

The fountain was begun in 1790 and completed in 1791, as part of the lengthy redesign of the villa begun by Marcantonio IV Borghese in 1766. It was designed by Christopher Unterberger, and the theme may have been suggested by an ancient cameo he received from Marcantonio as a gift. Unterberger was a painter, and neither a sculptor nor an architect, so the construction was undertaken by sculptor Vincenzo Pacetti.

Top: The beautiful Fountain of the Sea Horses—*La Fontana dei Cavalli Marini*—seems to arise slowly from its pool as you approach along viale dei Pupazzi from the Uccelliera. *Bottom:* The fountain's theme was suggested by an ancient cameo the designer, Christopher Unterberger, received as a gift from Marcantonio Borghese.

Pacetti and Unterberger's fountain has been enjoyed and admired by generations of visitors, and its imaginative structure and beautifully rendered carving caused at least one well-known, early twentieth-century writer and critic to assume it was the work of the preeminent sculptor of the Baroque era, Gian Lorenzo Bernini, though it was designed and built a century after Bernini died.[3]

The Fountain of the Sea Horses: The graceful Baroque figures were carved by the sculptor Vincenzo Pacetti, who rendered Unterberger's designs with such skill that many people believed they were the work of Bernini.

(I promised to tell you how to take a short detour to Museo Pietro Canonica, *so here goes—though be sure to come back here to continue our fountain walk!* **If you want to continue without visiting the Canonica museum, ignore this paragraph.** *For the museum: Face the fountain the way you came, and then turn right into* Viale dei Cavalli Marini. *Walk about 300 yards to the corner with viale Pietro Canonica. You'll know you're close when you see the so-called Temple of Antoninus and Faustina, a structure with columns and a broken pediment, to your right. It's not a real ruin—just eighteenth-century decoration. Antoninus Pius was a Roman emperor, and his wife's name was Faustina. Anyway, at this corner, turn left. Immediately look to your right, where you'll see a statue of an Italian World War I Alpine soldier and his mule. Behind the statues will be a building with crenellations along its roofline. This is the* Museo Pietro Canonica.*)*

Now, whether you visited the Canonica museum or not, let us continue, from the Cavalli Marini fountain, along viale dei Pupazzi about 100 yards or so. Here you'll see a small fountain overlooking an oval field of grass.

The Fountain of the Dolls—La Fontana dei Pupazzi (1792)
Architect: Vincenzo Pacetti

As part of Marcantonio IV Borghese's transformation of his family's Pincian Hill properties, his architects and landscapers created a large field, shaped like an ancient Roman amphitheater. It was also intended to evoke the Campo in Siena (the town from which the Borghese family originated), and so it is called the Piazza di Siena. Since 1922, the field has been used for horse shows and other sporting events, although the much larger Galoppatoio Equestrian Center in the park now hosts most riding competitions.

The small Fountain of the Dolls, overlooking Piazza di Siena, has an interesting history. The granite basin was originally part of a Fountain of Narcissus in the garden behind the Galleria Borghese. It dated from the time of Scipio Borghese himself, but Marcantonio's designers borrowed the basin and installed it on a pedestal, with some sculpted horses in the center, in its present position. Not long afterward, the horses were replaced by a marble group of cherubs playing with dolphins. Although the fountain was then called the *La Fontana degli Amorini* (after the cherubs), the group somehow became known as the *pupazzi* (dolls or puppets). I'm not sure exactly what the cherubs really looked like, because they were stolen in 1982 and never recovered. That was before digital photography, and apparently not many people wanted to waste their film on the little fountain, so I haven't found a good photo of it. I've seen a watercolor rendition by John Singer Sargent, but, frankly, it wasn't much help. By that time, it seems, the *pupazzi* had deteriorated badly anyway. Now water bubbles from a large stone in the center of the basin, but the fountain remains a cheerful and refreshing sight as you gaze out over the field.

Continue on viale dei Pupazzi for about 200 yards, and you'll come to what seems to be a small, circular Roman temple, with an empty pedestal in its center. This is the "Temple of Diana," and many a young lover literally puts his girl on a pedestal here, to take the requisite photo of his very own goddess. Anyway, turn right at the

The Fountain of the Dolls: The granite basin once belonged to a Fountain of Narcissus in the garden behind Galleria Borghese. When Narcissus was replaced by the Venus Fountain, the basin was moved here. The "dolls" (actually cupids) were stolen in 1982.

temple, onto viale della Casina di Raffaello. After 300 yards, cross viale Pietro Canonica and continue straight, through a gate in an iron fence, onto viale del Lago. You'll see another temple, ahead in the distance, with four columns across its façade; as you approach, you'll see that it stands on an island in a small lake. Before you get to the lake, though, look for a free-standing bronze statue to your left, with park benches around it, in a clearing.

The Fountain of Joy—La Fonte Gaia (1928)
ARCHITECT/SCULPTOR: GIOVANNI NICOLINI

Fonte Gaia (not to be confused with Jacopo della Quercia's monumental fountain in Siena) is sometimes called the *Fontana dei Satiri* (Fountain of the Satyrs). But I think *Fonte Gaia*, which means Fountain of Joy, or Joyful Fountain, describes the true spirit of the work. Nicolini's bronze fountain on a marble plinth is set in the peaceful woods near the *Laghetto*, the ornamental lake created around 1785 by Marcantonio's imported Scots landscaper, Jacob More. Two mythical woodland creatures, a satyr couple, are happily at home among the trees, grasping hands to make a swing for their little son, who sits contentedly on their linked wrists, clutching

The Fountain of Joy (also known as the *Fonte Gaia*) shows a satyr couple from the days of pagan innocence, playing happily with their young son, in a poignant bronze work by Giovanni Nicolini.

a bunch of grapes to his chest. A Latin inscription—*Fons canit vitae laudem murmure his* ("The fountain's murmur sings the praises of life")—is carved on the plinth. Unfortunately, it seems the murmuring water has been turned off for years—a pity, because this Art Nouveau masterpiece would be even more delightful if the water were actually murmuring.

Having admired the satyr couple and their son, it's time to enjoy the lake and the fountain nymphs who flank the island temple.

The Temple of Esculapio Fountain—La Fontana del Tempio di Esculapio (1792)
ARCHITECTS: CHRISTOPHER UNTERBERGER, ANTONIO ASPRUCCI, VINCENZO PACETTI, AND AGOSTINO PENNA

The *Laghetto* (Jacob More's large ornamental lake) is just a few steps from *Fonte Gaia*. Here you can relax and watch flocks of seagulls, ducks, geese, and other

The Temple of Esculapio Fountain consists of a faux Greek temple on an artificial island in an artificial lake, with water nymphs filling the lake from their overturned urns. It works—especially from a boat.

waterfowl search for food in the shallows. If you want a closer look at the Greek temple on its little island near the lake's far shore, you can rent a rowboat and admire the structure's Ionic columns, as well as the tympanum in its pediment, whose carved reliefs show the arrival of the sacred snake of Asclepius (*Esculapio* in Italian) on the Isola Tiberina (Tiber Island) in Rome.

Inside the structure, framed by the columns, is an ancient statue (perhaps from Augustus' mausoleum) of Asclepius, son of Apollo. He was the Greek god of medicine. Asclepius was born in the Greek town of Epidaurus, and so, according to the ancient writer Livy, the Romans sent a delegation there in 293 BC, seeking relief from a devastating plague. In Epidaurus, they captured a snake (a creature sacred to Asclepius) and brought it back to Rome. There, as their ship sailed up the Tiber, the snake slithered into the water and swam to Isola Tiberina, where the Romans built a temple to the god, and the plague abated. (If you took the detour to Ponte Fabricio in Chapter 12, on the way to Santa Cecilia in Trastevere, you crossed Tiber Island.)

Although the original temple was destroyed after the fall of the Empire, Isola Tiberina is still home to a hospital, the *Ospedale Fatebenefratelli.* Can there be a better name for a hospital run by monks? Do well, brothers! The temple here in the *Laghetto* was built as a salute to the lost temple on Isola Tiberina. On either side of the temple, on the banks of the little island in the *Laghetto*, are statues of water

Top: The Temple of Esculapio Fountain: This nymph seems unconcerned about the Esculapian snake wrapped around the wooden staff she's holding. She may be a friend of Mercury, who carried a wand encircled with snakes—the *caduceus*, a symbol of healing. *Bottom:* Some unknown admirer seems to have given this ancient lady a modern potted plant to keep her company.

nymphs, pouring water into the lake. Collectively, the nymphs constitute the working part of *La Fontana del Tempio di Esculapio.*

Looking across the lake toward the temple, circle left around the shore of the lake, and, near the boat rental landing, you'll see ahead an arch across a path, with some statuary on top. Cross under it. This is the Arch of Septimius Severus (not to be confused with the much larger arch, in the Roman Forum, dedicated to the emperor). Once through the arch, you'll be on via Madama Letizia, which, after less than 200 yards through the trees, will open up into Piazzale Paolina Borghese. Walk to your right, past a bronze statue. (The piazzale changes its name as you walk through it.) Now, at the bottom of a long slope, you'll see the neoclassical façade of a grand building, the Galleria Nazionale d'Arte Moderna, which has a huge collection of nineteenth- and twentieth-century art, by all the usual suspects—Modigliani, Calder, de Chirico, Kandinski, Pollock. Somehow Antonio Canova slipped in! Check museum information at www.lagallerianazionale.com. It's worth a day, if you have time. Anyway, walk toward the building, through the parking lot ahead, descending a couple of levels as you go. Near the bottom, flanking the wide piazza below, you'll see two fountains, one on either side of the stairs.

The Two Turtle Fountains—Le Due Fontane delle Tartarughe (1911)
Architect: Cesare Bazzani

These twin fountains are also sometimes called the Fountains of Valle Giulia because they overlook Valle Giulia, a low area between the Giardino del Lago in Borghese Park and the Parioli hills in north-central Rome. The Galleria Nazionale d'Arte Moderna, below and across a wide street, is housed in a splendid neoclassical palace designed by architect Cesare Bazzani. The museum building was begun in 1911, the year in which Rome celebrated the fiftieth anniversary of the unification of Italy by hosting an International Exhibition of Art. No doubt to spruce up the city for the exhibition, Bazzani designed the two fountains to decorate one of the terraces of his monumental staircase between Villa Borghese and the gallery. He may have been inspired to use turtles on the rims of his lower basins by the famous sixteenth-century turtle fountain in Piazza Mattei. One of the fountains was, in 1916, the inspiration for the composer Ottorino Respighi's tone poem "The Fountain of Valle Giulia at Dawn," in his most famous symphonic work, *The Fountains of Rome.*

From the Turtle Fountains, retrace your steps up the slope and back into Piazzale Paolina Borghese. When you reach the point where viale Madama Letizia starts back toward the Arch of Septimius Severus (you'll see the arch at the end), do not head for the arch. Instead, take the next street to the right of viale Madama Letizia, which is viale Folke Bernadotte. After about 200 yards, between the intersection of viale Folke Bernadotte and two other streets, you'll see a tall stone arch above an overflowing basin. This is our next fountain.

Top: The Two Turtle Fountains: Flanking a monumental staircase from Villa Borghese to the *Galleria Nazionale d'Arte Moderna*, this is one of two fountains from 1911, when Rome hosted an International Exhibition of Art. *Bottom:* Composer Ottorino Respighi wrote a tone poem about one of the Turtle Fountains in his most famous symphonic work, *The Fountains of Rome*, which proves that even turtles can be inspirational.

The Fountain of the Bow or the Fountain of Asclepius—
La Fontana del Fiocco (1833)
ARCHITECT: LUIGI CANINA

The translation of the Italian name is somewhat puzzling. Perhaps it is intended to refer to a rainbow created by a powerful spray of water in the sunshine—*fiocco* can mean "bow"—although the usual Italian word for rainbow is *arcobaleno*. An Italian friend speculated that *fiocco* might refer to a decorative bow, suggested by the five streets that converge, ribbon-like, on the piazza surrounding the fountain. *Fiocco* can also mean several other things, including "flake," though how that describes a fountain is obscure (at least to me).

The fountain was built between 1830 and 1833 to provide a spectacular entry to Villa Borghese from Piazzale Flaminio. Atop a jumbled stone ridge rising from a sparkling irregularly shaped pool is a marble basin from which a jet of water spouts, falling back into the basin, which overflows into the pool. At the other end of the rocky ridge is a tall masonry arch. The center of the arch is conspicuously empty; the two exterior sides of the arch are each adorned with a female figure standing on an attached plinth. One is Juno, and the other is Clotho, the Spinner—one of the

The Fountain of the Bow or the Fountain of Asclepius: Also known as the *Fontana del Fiocco*. *Fiocco* can mean "flake," "bow," "arch," and "ribbon," among other things. The arch used to contain a statue of Asclepius.

Fates. Clotho seems to have lost her head. Atop the attic of the arch is an earthenware eagle.

There was once an ancient, second-century statue of Asclepius in the center of the arch, one of the Borghese collection treasures. In 1986, it was removed and put into storage in the Pietro Canonica Museum in the park, and a copy was put in the arch. On the night of October 15/16, 2003, a vandal completely destroyed the copy. Ever since, the arch has been empty. Rome's *Sovrintendenza Capitolina ai Beni Culturali* (Capitoline Superintendence of Cultural Heritage) has proposed using 3-D digital imagery of the surviving original to produce a cement copy, so perhaps one day the Roman god of health will once again be ready to welcome visitors to the park.

Standing at the foot of the Fountain of the Bow, looking over the pool and the basin toward the front of the arch, the street passing the right side of the arch (with bus stops on either side) is viale Fiorello la Guardia. Follow this street past the arch. Almost immediately, you'll see Egyptian-style obelisks on either side of the street, each with its own accompanying "gateway" of two short towers with a columned loggia in between. Carved lions beyond the gateways complete the ensemble. These are the Propilei Egizi, or "Egyptian Gates," though they are no more Egyptian than I am. They were installed in 1827 when Prince Camillo Borghese acquired more land west of them to add to his park.

The Fountain of the Bow or the Fountain of Asclepius: The fountain can be a pleasant place to sit and daydream, especially if it's a beautiful day in spring. The Asclepius statue, by the way, was vandalized and destroyed in 2003.

After another 400 yards or so, passing the Museo Carlo Bilotti *on your left, you'll see another low building with a loggia—well, actually an arcade—and some more lions to your left; this time, there's also a fountain.*

The Portico of the Lions—Il Portico dei Leoni (late eighteenth and early nineteenth centuries)
ARCHITECTS: ANTONIO ASPRUCCI AND LUIGI CANINA

The Portico of the Lions is another "gate" on viale Fiorello La Guardia, near the *Museo Carlo Bilotti* (the former Aranciera di Villa Borghese). By the way, the *Museo Carlo Bilotti* (www.museocarlobilotti.it) contains eighteen intriguing, rather spooky canvases by the godfather of surrealism, Giorgio de Chirico. Admission is free.

But back to the Portico of the Lions—it is part of a wall behind which is the Giardino del Lago. There is a garden area between the street and the portico building, featuring a small pool with a little plume of water in the center. The portico itself is in the form of a low, arcaded gateway. The semi-circular space behind the columns contains sarcophagi, tombstones, and other inscribed fragments—and presumably a

The Portico of the Lions is a gateway, decorated by a fountain featuring lions and pools, that once led into the Giardino del Lago.

The Portico of the Lions: I suspect that this Egyptian-looking lion, probably made in the late eighteenth century by Antonio Asprucci, was inspired by the Nectanebo lions we've met before, on the Fountain of Moses and the Pigna.

doorway through the wall. In front of the building are four handsome granite lions, spouting water into basins. Antonio Asprucci began the construction as part of Marcantonio IV Borghese's revamping of the villa gardens, and after his death Luigi Canina completed the project.

As you pass the Portico of the Lions, you are only about 100 feet from a traffic circle straight ahead, Piazzale delle Canestre. As you approach the circle, note in particular a wall bordering the street that enters the circle to your left. The street is viale Pietro Canonica, and the wall, at the corner, contains and supports a very interesting fountain ensemble.

Show Fountain of the Acqua Felix— *Mostra dell'Acqua Felix (1611)*
Architect: Antonio Asprucci

In 1586, the architect Giovanni Fontana completed construction of the *Acqua Felice* aqueduct for Pope Sixtus V (Felice Peretti). Giovanni's brother, Domenico Fontana, supervised the construction of an elaborate fountain on the Quirinal Hill in Rome that featured triumphal arches, a giant statue of Moses summoning

The Show Fountain (or *Mostra*) of the *Acqua Felice* marks the point where the seventeenth-century branch line of the *Acqua Felice* aqueduct reached the Villa Borghese. Notice the ancient sarcophagus panel on the wall, depicting a lion hunt.

water from a rock, and several Egyptian lions spitting water into huge basins. This was the original *mostra*, or show fountain, for the new aqueduct, and more information about it can be found in the "Fountain of Moses" entry in Chapter 2. The *mostra* for the *Acqua Felix* in Borghese Park is a very different, though related, fountain. *Felix* is Latin for *Felice*.

In 1610 (or perhaps 1611), Scipio Borghese asked Giovanni Fontana to extend a branch line of the *Acqua Felice* into Scipio's estates on the Pincio—he needed water to support the gardens he had commissioned from Domenico Savino. Fontana's new water line terminated near today's Piazzale delle Canestre, inside Villa Borghese at the south end of viale Pietro Canonica. Apparently, Scipio and Giovanni were content just to water the plants and have some ornamental water features around the estate, but in the late eighteenth century Marcantiono IV Borghese decided to redesign the property in the "English manner." He hired the architect Antonio Asprucci to construct and update buildings, monuments, and fountains; he also imported a Scottish painter and landscape designer named Jacob More to create a grand park with groves of exotic North American trees and a large ornamental lake (the *Laghetto*). Among Asprucci's updates was the creation of a *mostra* at the point where Giovanni Fontana's branch of the *Acqua Felice* terminated in the park.

Asprucci's creation is a section of stone wall, ornamented with four Ionic pilasters and the fragmentary front panel of an ancient sarcophagus, depicting a lion

The Show Fountain of the *Acqua Felice*: Roman fountains often depict lions, as I'm sure you've noticed. This one, for a change, doesn't look Egyptian. He does look like he's pretty annoyed about that lion hunt down below.

hunt in relief. Below and to the sides of the sarcophagus are two waterspouts in the form of dragon heads (or perhaps turtle heads—it's difficult to tell) protruding from collars of rough stones. The water is caught in shell-shaped basins. Atop the wall is a raised platform, on which the figure of a great, crouching lion appears to look with displeasure on the lion hunt below him.

Standing with the Mostra dell'Acqua Felice *to your left, looking across Piazzale delle Canestre, the street leading straight out of the circle is viale delle Magnolie; the street leaving the traffic circle to the right is viale Fiorello La Guardia. Cross the traffic circle and bear right on La Guardia. On your left, you should see a small, kiosk-style café with outside seating. I hope it's still there, in case you need some refreshment. Less than 100 feet from where viale La Guardia leaves the circle, and just past the café, you should see a paved pathway marked "viale della Fontana Rotonda" that heads left and downhill into a grove of trees. Soon another path will intersect with yours, just before you reach a sizeable pond ahead of you, but keep going straight to the pond. Notice that the path divides into a circle around the water.*

The Oval Fountain—*Fontana Rotonda, aka Fontana Ovale or Fontana della Peschiera (1908)*
ARCHITECT: UNKNOWN

This large fountain, which looks more like a small pond, fills a depression in the ground surrounded by green lawn. Water spurts from a stone "island" in the pond. The depression was caused by excavations during the creation of viale delle Magnolie, which connects Villa Borghese with the Pincio. The water in this fountain's "pond" comes from the *Acqua Peschiera*, and it serves as a reservoir for other uses in the park. The gently sloping banks, covered with grass, are a favorite area for picnics and sunbathing.

When you are ready to leave the Oval Fountain, return to the path you arrived on, viale della Fontana Rotonda, but turn right at the first intersection onto viale Tarragona. Viale Tarragona ends at via delle Magnolie, which will take us onto the Pincio Terrace and then out of Villa Borghese. Turn right on via delle Magnolie; after a few hundred feet, you'll come to a wide pedestrian overpass above a multi-lane motorway. The wide, flat surface of the overpass is sometimes a venue for in-line skating competitions. Beyond the overpass is the Pincio extension of Villa Borghese, and via delle Magnolie becomes via dell'Obelisco. There'll be a café/bar on the right, La Casina

The Oval Fountain—*La Fontana Ovale*—like all the park's fountains nowadays, is fed by the Peschiera aqueduct, and it serves as a reservoir for various uses in Villa Borghese.

dell'Orologio. As promised by the street name, after about 200 yards you'll come to a circular piazza with a pink granite obelisk in its center. The obelisk was commissioned by Emperor Hadrian in memory of his young favorite, Antinous, who, in 130 AD, mysteriously drowned in the Nile. It was found in the sixteenth century near the ancient Porta Maggiore gate, spent some time in the Vatican, and in the nineteenth century was erected on the Pincio by Pope Pius VII. When you reach the obelisk, look to your right through the trees; you should be able to spot the low basin of a small fountain about 200 feet from the obelisk. If not, walk directly right, at right angles from the road, and you'll see it: the marble figure of a woman, surrounded by greenery.

The Fountain of Moses on the Pincio—La Fontana del Mosè sul Pincio (ca. 1805)
Architect/Sculptor: Francesco Laboureur

There are two Roman fountains known colloquially as "The Fountain of Moses." The *Fontana dell'Acqua Felice*, a monumental fountain on the Quirinal Hill that serves as the *mostra* for the *Acqua Felice*, is often called the Fountain of Moses because of the sculpture of the prophet in its central arch.

However, this small fountain on the Pincio recounts the biblical story, in Exodus, of how the pharaoh's daughter discovered the infant Moses, asleep in a basket, hidden in the bulrushes alongside the Nile. If you are lucky when you visit, you may find that the lush plants (I'm not sure that they're actually bulrushes) surrounding the baby have been trimmed; otherwise, the child is not visible—proof, I suppose, that neoclassical sculpture and deferred garden maintenance is not always a happy combination.

Return to the obelisk, and continue out of the piazza on via dell'Obelisco. Keep going straight ahead, and you'll soon be on the left (or southern) edge of the Terrazza del Pincio, which you'll recognize from the stone balustrades ahead, at the edge of the Pincian Hill. Here you have a choice:

First choice: If you turn right at the end of via dell'Obelisco, into a short, tree-lined lane, it will lead to the wide, graveled main section of the terrace. Almost directly across the terrace, look for an iron gate, from which steps descend down. Go down the steps. From the bottom, you can follow the Salita del Pincio down the hill to viale Gabriele d'Annunzio; turn right and follow the street as it makes a hairpin turn back on itself. (You'll see an ancient stone tub in a dry basin at the turn; this is the Fontana della Vasca, placed here in the nineteenth century. It may have come from the Baths of Caracalla, and it may have served a few years in Piazza Farnese as a decoration, but I'm not certain.)

Just after the turn, you'll find steps leading downward into Piazza del Popolo. Take the steps into the piazza, and then turn right. The Flaminio Metro station is just across four lanes of traffic from the Porta del Popolo, leading out of the piazza, so you can take the Metro back to your lodgings. Or there's a taxi stand in Piazza del Popolo right where via del Babuino exits the piazza.

Second choice: If you turn left and follow viale Adamo Mickievicz (which becomes via della Trinità dei Monti after about 100 yards), you'll have a fine panoramic view of Rome from a small, semi-circular belvedere (viewpoint) where the roads meet. You'll notice a bronze monument to the Cairoli brothers, heroes of the Risorgimento, there. (You may remember the fountain in Piazza Cairoli, which we visited during our Chapter 8 tour of the Roman ghetto fountains.) Continue on via Trinità dei Monte to the left, along the edge of the Pincian Hill. You'll pass the Villa Medici and the Fountain of Trinità dei Monti. After less than 1,000 yards, you'll be at the top of the Spanish Steps, at the bottom of which you can find the entrance of the Spagna Metro station, to the right.

Turn to Chapter 15 for our last group of fountains.

The Fountain of Moses on the Pincio depicts the moment in the Book of Exodus when the pharaoh's daughter finds the infant Moses hidden among the bulrushes along the Nile. If you look closely, you can see little Moses among the greenery.

❧ 15 ❧

Scattered Treasures

Here and There

There are five important or otherwise interesting fountains that cannot easily be grouped with others, whether geographically or thematically, so in this chapter I will try to tell their stories. As for walking, our best bet is to begin from some point—Metro station, well-known landmark, and so on—that is reasonably near whichever fountain we're seeking, and then walk from there, since it's not feasible in every case to walk from fountain to fountain, because of the distances between them.

So, our map for Chapter 15 does not show routes to or from all the fountains. It is a wider view of Rome with the locations of our last five fountains marked, just so you know where in the city to look for them.

Here are the starting locations for the fountains in this chapter. There are walking directions under each fountain's entry, but here, in short, are the beginning points:

For the Fountain in Piazza San Giovanni in Laterano, start at the San Giovanni Metro stop (lines A and C).

For the Fountain of the Amphorae, start at the Piramide Metro stop (line B).

For the Triton Fountain in Piazza Bocca della Verità, start from Piazza Bocca della Verità.

For the Mascherone of Santa Sabina, start from the Triton Fountain in Piazza Bocca della Verità.

For the Fountain of the Frogs, start from Piazza Buenos Aires.

And now for our first fountain.

The Fountain in Piazza San Giovanni in Laterano, aka the Fountain of the Lateran Obelisk— La Fontana nella Piazza San Giovanni in Laterano, aka La Fontana dell'obelisco Lateranense (1607)
Architect: Domenico Fontana (attributed)

Let's begin at the San Giovanni Metro stop (lines A and C). No matter what exit you use from the station, if you look around, you will see a magnificent stretch of the

234

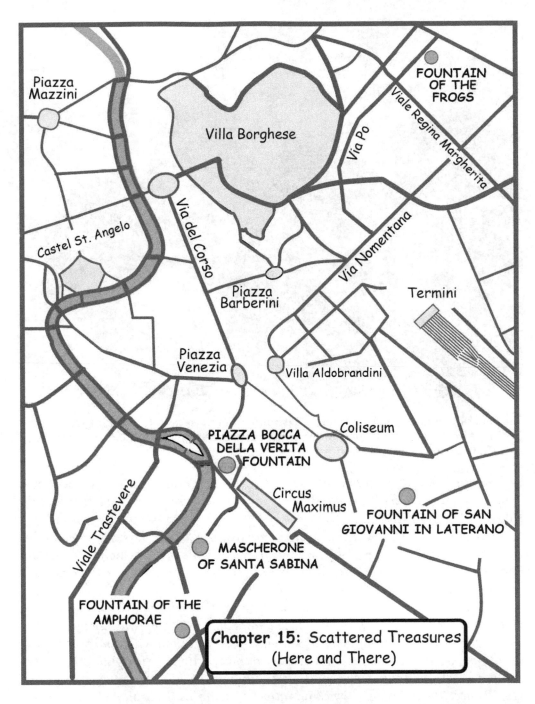

Piazza Mazzini

Villa Borghese

FOUNTAIN OF THE FROGS

Via Po

Viale Regina Margherita

Castel St. Angelo

Via del Corso

Via Nomentana

Piazza Barberini

Termini

Piazza Venezia

Villa Aldobrandini

Coliseum

PIAZZA BOCCA DELLA VERITA FOUNTAIN

Circus Maximus

FOUNTAIN OF SAN GIOVANNI IN LATERANO

Viale Trastevere

MASCHERONE OF SANTA SABINA

FOUNTAIN OF THE AMPHORAE

Chapter 15: Scattered Treasures (Here and There)

third-century Aurelian Walls, with a huge white marble arch (Porta San Giovanni) in the center and a number of other, more plain-Jane arched openings to accommo-date the multiple traffic lanes passing through the wall. Notice that there are two round towers in the wall, left of Porta San Giovanni. There is a pedestrian-sized opening in the wall just to the right of the towers. I recommend using the left-hand sidewalk, bordering the wide Piazzale Appio that leads to the wall, to reach the

The Fountain in Piazza San Giovanni in Laterano sits at the base of the tallest Egyptian obelisk in the world. It stood in Egypt to honor Thutmose III for two thousand years before being brought to Rome.

pedestrian opening. (There is a stoplight-controlled crosswalk across via Appia Nuova, where it enters Piazzale Appio, if you are not already on the left side of the street.)

Once through the wall, you'll see the great white façade of the Basilica of San Giovanni in Laterano to your left, with its fringe of stone apostles along the roofline. The church is flanked on its right by the walls of the Lateran Palace. There are triangular patches of lawn on either side of a cobbled carriageway leading to the main door of the basilica. Take the outer sidewalk beside the right-hand lawn, following it all the way around the basilica and the Lateran Palace. On your way, though, look to your right—you'll see what looks like an apse from a church with a large mosaic in its half-dome. This is an eighteenth-century reconstruction of the eighth-century Triclinium Leoninum from Pope Leo III's state dining room in the original, ancient Lateran Palace. The building to which it is attached contains the Scala Santa, a flight of 28 steps that pilgrims climb on their knees in memory of Christ's Passion. They are believed by the faithful to be the steps Jesus climbed to his trial before Pontius Pilate, brought to Rome from Jerusalem by Saint Helen, Emperor Constantine's mother. For details, check www.scala-santa.com.

Once past the flank of the palace, you'll see a tall obelisk. Our fountain is at its base.

Before we examine the fountain, here is some background about the great church it serves:

The *Archbasilica del Santissimo Salvatore e dei Santi Giovanni Battista ed Evangelista in Laterano* (better known to us as the Church of Saint John Lateran) is the Diocese of Rome's cathedral church, as well as the Pontifical Seat, meaning that it is the pope's main church, taking precedence over even Saint Peter's Basilica. The basilica was dedicated by Pope Sylvester in 324 AD, just a dozen years after Constantine defeated Maxentius at the Milvian Bridge. This makes it the oldest public church in Rome.[1] The original building was toppled by an earthquake at the end of the ninth century; its replacement burned down, was repaired, burned down again in the fourteenth century, and was then rebuilt. In the middle of the seventeenth century, the interior was restored in a refined Baroque style by Francesco Borromini. It has been altered many other times over the centuries but is still a magnificent and mighty presence. The bronze doors in the center of the front façade, green with age, are much older than the church; they came from the Roman Senate House— the *Curia*—and date to the first century AD. Pope Alexander VII had them moved to Saint John Lateran in 1660.

There are other important buildings in Piazza San Giovanni in Laterano. One of them is the Lateran Palace, which was once a papal residence; many years before that, in the first century AD, it was home to a Roman family called the *Plautii Laterani*, which is why this area is known in Italian as *Laterano*. The building, of course, underwent many restructurings during the almost 1,500 years before its last major facelift in 1589. Actually, it was a lot more than cosmetic surgery: Domenico Fontana, working for Pope Sixtus V, removed almost all of the old building and constructed a fine Renaissance residence for the pope.

Although the basilica, its fifth-century baptistry, and the Lateran Palace are in Rome, not in the Vatican, they have extraterritorial status from the Italian state and have been properties of the Holy See ever since the Lateran Treaty of 1929. (Under the terms of this agreement, the Kingdom of Italy recognized Vatican City as an independent state.)

Just beyond the northwest corner of the Lateran Palace, there is that tall Egyptian obelisk—in fact, the tallest Egyptian obelisk in the world. It was made for Thutmose III and his grandson Thutmose IV around 1500 BC and stood near the Temple of Amun in Karnak for nearly two millennia. It was brought to Rome by Emperor Constantius II in the fourth century AD and erected in the *spina* (the long central barrier of Roman racetracks, around which chariots raced) of the Circus Maximus. After the fall of the Roman Empire, the obelisk fell, too, and the accretions of time covered it. It was discovered in three pieces in 1587 and, on the orders of Pope Sixtus V, hauled to Piazza San Giovanni in Laterano, where Domenico Fontana somehow erected it, engineering wizard that he was! (Sixtus V was a man who had difficulty taking "no" for an answer.)

Now, for the fountain itself: In 1603, Pope Clement VIII ordered the construction of a fountain at the foot of the obelisk. Just who was responsible for the project is a mystery,[2] though some people think it was Domenico Fontana. It is interesting that the fountain took about four years to complete, but during that time three different popes sat on the throne of Saint Peter, and all three wanted their family symbols included on the fountain. The first, of course, was Clement VIII, whose family name was Aldobrandini, one of whose emblems was the Maltese cross; the second was Leo XI of the Medici clan, and the Medici, of course, liked to be identified with the Florentine lily; the third was Paul V, a Borghese, and among the traditional Borghese images are eagles and griffins.

The construction of the fountain began in 1603, and Clement VIII died in March 1605. Leo XI succeeded him in April but caught a chill and died less than a month later. Paul V took over in May and reigned for nearly 16 years.

The fountain has three steps leading up to a semi-circular lower basin extending from a stone slab that rises in front of the obelisk's base. The sides of the slab are decorated with carved scrolls. At each side of the basin, grotesque dolphin-like creatures spout water into it; above them, a smaller, shell-shaped basin receives water from two griffins flanking it. Above the shell basin is a square carved frame holding a papal tiara and Saint Peter's keys in high relief, and atop the frame sits a sculpted eagle with widespread wings. The stone slab is topped with a cornice decorated with a frieze of two repeated motifs: an egg-and-dart course above a row of Maltese crosses.

The Aldobrandini Maltese crosses are there, along with the Borghese eagles and griffins. But where are the Medici lilies? I'm afraid I can't tell you, because no

The Fountain in Piazza San Giovanni in Laterano: Three different popes ruled during the four years it took to build the fountain, and they all wanted their family emblems on it. Check the text and see whether you can find them.

one seems to know. They were there for a couple of hundred years, part of a sculpture group of Saint John the Evangelist, seated, reading a book, flanked by large Florentine lilies, almost like armrests for his chair. The whole sculpture, which sat on the table-like surface above the egg-and-dart frieze and the Maltese crosses, disappeared in the early nineteenth century. Some say it was struck by lightning and the broken pieces taken away by scavengers, never to be found. All that's left is a seventeenth-century engraving by an unknown artist.[3]

You may want to return to the San Giovanni Metro stop to begin the trip back to your lodgings, or, if you want to visit our next fountain, you can take the Metro from San Giovanni to Termini, and change to Metro line B. Your destination is the Piramide Metro station, from which we'll go in search of the Fountain of the Amphorae.

The Fountain of the Amphorae—*La Fontana delle Anfore* (1927)
Architect: Pietro Lombardi

Fortunately for us, the Piramide Metro stop (line B) not only lands us reasonably close to our next fountain but also is near some truly remarkable remnants of history.

The Fountain of the Amphorae—*La Fontana delle Anfore*—was made in 1927 by Pietro Lombardi to memorialize the slender terracotta jugs in which Roman wine and olive oil were shipped in antiquity.

You'll see them right away when you exit the station (which is attached to the Ostiense rail station). As you step out into Piazzale Ostiense, look for an ancient gate structure with two round towers topped by square crenellations. This is the Porta San Paolo, once part of the third-century Aurelian Walls. Walk a little farther into the square, and you'll spot a huge pyramid made of marble, as tall as the old gate. This is the Pyramid of Gaius Cestius, built as a mausoleum for a prominent politician who died around 12 AD, when Caesar Augustus ruled Rome. Head out of the square between Porta San Paolo and the pyramid, on the sidewalk closest to the pyramid. You'll be on via Raffaele Persichetti, which quickly becomes via Marmorata. The reddish walls to your left enclose the Cimetero Acattolico (Non-Catholic Cemetery), where, back in the day, non–Catholics were buried outside the city walls. John Keats and Percy Shelley, among many other famous people, are buried there. Keats, who died tragically young at twenty-five, asked that in place of his name, his gravestone should say only "Here lies one whose name was writ in water." The house where Keats died is now a museum, in Piazza di Spagna, dedicated to both poets. You can find the museum information in Chapter 3.

The cemetery is a hauntingly beautiful place, and if you want to take a small detour, you can visit by turning left at via Caio Cestio, just where the red wall makes a left turn. You'll find the entrance through the wall after about 200 yards. A donation toward the maintenance of the cemetery is requested. Visit www.cemeteryrome.it for more information.

But we're bound for the Fountain of the Amphorae, so we will continue straight on via Marmorata for four blocks and turn left into via Aldo Manuzio. One block later, you'll see the wide, tree-lined Piazza Testaccio open up to our right, with a unique and well-loved fountain in the center.

I called this fountain unique. "Bizarre" might be an even more apt description, and I think I'd better explain: Two thousand years ago, perhaps even earlier, there were enormous warehouses on the left bank of the Tiber, about where the Ponte Testaccio crosses the river into Trastevere. All the grain imported from Egypt to feed the city was stored there, along with many other imported foodstuffs, including wine. One absolutely essential item for the ancient Romans was, of course, olive oil, and not only for food. It also fueled their lamps, lubricated their cart wheels, served as a base for perfume, and even helped clean their bodies, for soap, as we know it, didn't exist at that time. Romans would go to the baths and have a massage, during which their bodies would be coated with olive oil; afterward, they would go out to the *palaestra* (exercise yard), work up a sweat, and then have an attendant scrape off the oil and sweat and dirt with a curved blade called a *strigil*.

Over the years, millions of *anfore* (*amphorae* to you and me)—long, slender terracotta jugs with handles at the top ends and tapered, pointed bottoms—arrived at these warehouses filled with wine or olive oil or other foods. There, they were emptied into huge storage vats. The used amphorae, made of porous terracotta, retained the residue of their liquid contents and could not be reused, so they were smashed and the pieces deposited on a pile of previously used and broken amphorae. Over time, this pile of pottery grew to a hill—a *big* hill, 120 feet high, covering about

220,000 square feet—over five acres. Today, mostly covered with a skin of blown soil, it's one of Rome's most recognizable hills. It's called Monte Testaccio, and the surrounding neighborhood is, naturally, called Testaccio. The name is derived from the Latin word for broken pottery, *testae*.

In 1924, the Municipality of Rome held a competition for five fountains, to be placed in the central piazzas of recently created Roman neighborhoods. One of the contracts was won by a young architect named Pietro Lombardi. As it happens, he created one of Rome's most-loved modern fountains and started a career of fountain design that adorned more than a dozen districts with clever and handsome creations honoring local traditions.

The *Fontana delle Anfore* is made of travertine. In the center of a base five steps high, a tall tower rises, sculpted to look like a stack of ancient Roman amphorae arranged for loading in a ship's hold. From the lower half of the tower, four rectangular basins extend like spokes. At the inner end of each basin is carved the SPQR motto of the city of Rome, surmounted with a ram's head. The outer end of each rectangle is shaped like an arch, with a relief image of an amphora, from which a stream of water issues. Another stream of water arcs into the basin from the opposite surface of the arch. At each inner angle of the basins, where they attach to the central structure, a small basin fits into the angle, and above it water streams into the small basin from a spigot in the central tower.

When the fountain was put into service in 1927, it was located in the main square of the neighborhood, Piazza Testaccio, where it became a local favorite, especially with children, who liked to play on the steps between the basins. However, a severe problem of subsidence in the piazza began to destabilize the fountain, so in 1935 it was moved, with considerable difficulty, to Piazza dell'Emporio, near the Tiber, at the end of Ponte Sublicio. That is where I first saw the fountain in 2008, when my photographer wife took a couple of photos.

We didn't visit the fountain again until 2016, when we decided to try for some better pictures. So we made our way to Piazza dell'Emporio, only to discover that the very sizeable travertine fountain, as big as a small house, had disappeared like Brigadoon, leaving only an empty grassy mound in its place. When we inquired at a nearby bar, the barman knew nothing about the fountain (to be generous, let's assume he was new in the area) and tried to direct us to the Trevi.

We found it again, of course. In 2015, after 80 years, the fountain had returned to its original home. The transfer was a complex and fascinating process, which was documented in a video you can find on YouTube.[4] The structure was disassembled into more than 350 numbered pieces and then transported to the center of the piazza, where it was carefully cleaned and reassembled, while a modern hydraulic system was installed to ensure that all the water features worked once again. A lighting system was installed as well, to light the interiors of the rectangular basins. At the re-inauguration on January 24, 2015, a large and happy crowd filled the piazza to celebrate.

After we found the fountain again in 2016, we sat on a bench at the side of the square and watched with pleasure the local children climbing the steps, posing for their friends, and using the fountain as a soccer goal.

The Fountain of the Amphorae: The previous photograph shows the *Fontana delle Anfore* in 2016. This photograph shows the fountain where we first saw it in 2008. Check the text for the fountain's peripatetic history.

The Triton Fountain in Piazza Bocca della Verità— La Fontana dei Tritoni in Piazza Bocca della Verità (1717)
ARCHITECTS: FRANCESCO CARLO BIZZACCHERI, FRANCESCO MARATTI, AND FILIPPO BAI

We'll begin a mini-walk for two fountains at our next, rather elegant fountain. There is no nearby Metro stop for this one, though the Bocca della Verità bus stop on via Luigi Petroselli is served by multiple bus lines, including numbers 44, 83, 170, and 716. Check www.atac.roma.it for your route. (Your destination is Piazza Bocca della Verità.)

The fountain stands in a piazza across the street from an ancient church, the *Basilica di Santa Maria in Cosmedin*, and both the piazza and the fountain owe their names (at least in part) to the church. Built in the eighth century, in a part of Rome that was then inhabited primarily by Greeks (this was during the Byzantine rule of Rome, when the city was governed by popes who owed their positions to the Eastern Roman emperor in Constantinople), the church was decorated in the eastern style, with icons, lots of colorful mosaics, and (an Italian touch) floors of intricate Cosmatesque marble inlay. It was so elaborately decorated that it earned the adjective

The Triton Fountain in Piazza Bocca della Verità: Hundreds of tourists risk their fingers in an old *mascherone*'s "Mouth of Truth" in the church porch across the street. He'll bite you if you're a liar!

phrase "in Cosmedin," from the Greek *kosmidion*, meaning "ornate." The church has had several restorations over the years, of course: one of them in the twelfth century (when the fine Romanesque campanile was added); another in the eighteenth, when the church was "Baroqued"; and still another in 1899, when most of the Baroque work was removed. The campanile is the tallest medieval bell tower in Rome, at 111.5 feet. In the church's porch hangs an ancient drain cover, carved like a giant face, with a slot for a mouth. Following an ancient tradition, crowds of visitors take turns sticking their hands in the slot, braving the old story that a liar's hand put into the *Bocca della Verità*—the "Mouth of Truth"—will be bitten off.

The fountain, located in the nearby piazza named for that old-fashioned lie detector in the church porch, was commissioned by Pope Clement XI in 1715. It was inspired by Gian Lorenzo Bernini's Triton Fountain in Piazza Barberini, though the lower basin's shape is an eight-pointed star in acknowledgment of the Albani family crest, which seems to alternate between featuring a six-pointed star and one with eight points. (Clement XI's birth name was Giovanni Francesco Albani.)

In the center of the star-shaped pool, a rocky crag rises, dotted with carved vegetation, as if the plants are growing from fissures in the stone. Atop the crag, two Tritons (mythological sons of Poseidon and Amphitrite), kneeling with their

The Triton Fountain in Piazza Bocca della Verità: The fountain was built for Clement XI in 1715 and features two Tritons holding a shell-shaped basin. The church, Santa Maria in Cosmedin, is a well-preserved eighth-century structure, slightly Byzantine in spirit.

fishlike lower limbs entwined, support a vaguely shell-shaped basin, which has two shields bearing the Albani family coat-of-arms. One of the symbols on the Albani shield is a stylized group representing three mountains, a device in heraldry called a *trimonio.* At the top of the fountain, a sculpted, three-dimensional trimonio (now nearly unrecognizable because of mineral deposits) rises from the middle of the shell-shaped basin, from which a plume of water issues, falling back to feed the fountain's display.

The piazza is supplied with benches, nicely positioned on patches of lawn divided by box hedges. Here you can rest after having endured the Mouth of Truth's nerve-wracking test of your veracity (and perhaps having taken a look inside the historic church). You'll see nearby in the square two ancient Roman temples. The round one is the Temple of Hercules Victor, and the rectangular one is the Temple of Portuna.

Now, on to our next destination. From the fountain, with the Santa Maria in Cosmedin church across the street on your left, head for the next street corner. Cross to the church side of the street, and then, just a step to your right, cross the busy, multi-lane via della Greca at the stoplight-controlled crosswalk. Now turn left and head uphill on via della Greca. After about 150 yards, there'll be a smaller road—Clivo dei Publici—angling away uphill to the right. Clivo means a sloping path, and this slope is up the side of the Aventine Hill. After climbing (mostly between old stone walls) about 400 yards, you'll come to an intersection where the pavement widens and the main road curves slightly to the right. You'll see a large building with multiple levels and a bell tower on your left, with a whiteish, arched marble entry. This is the Convent of Sant'Antonio, home to a community of Camaldolese nuns, who regularly provide meals to the poor. Clivo dei Publici narrows and turns sharply left, skirting the convent. The main road's name changes to via di Santa Sabina, and that's the route you will take.

(If you like, you can take a short—about 100 yards or so—scenic detour before continuing. Look at the green area, beneath a few umbrella pines, left of the convent. This is the Roseto di Roma—Rome's Rose Garden. You'll see a gate in the metal fence surrounding it, as well as a paved pathway, via di Valle Murcia, which bisects the garden and leads to Piazzale Ugo La Malfa, with a monument honoring the late Italian politician. The garden is normally open from 8:00 a.m. to 8:00 p.m.; from Piazzale La Malfa, you'll find a fine view over the Circus Maximus to the ancient ruins on the Palatine Hill before you return to via di Santa Sabina.)

However, returning from the Rose Garden and continuing along via di Santa Sabina: After walking another 300 yards or so, you'll see a metal gate (usually open during the day) in the brick wall to your right. Beyond it is the Giardino degli Aranci (Garden of the Oranges), one of the loveliest of Rome's secret places, in the shadow of the Basilica of Santa Sabina. The orange trees in the garden shade a grassy lawn, often dotted with bright fallen fruit. A gravel path through the grove leads from the gate to a stone terrace, from which there are splendid views past the Tiber, all the way to the Dome of Saint Peter's.

It might be a good time, while you relax on one of the terrace's stone benches, to tell you a bit about the ancient and noble church whose garden we're enjoying. Then we can go see our fountain—and perhaps afterward the church itself.

The church is the *Basilica di Santa Sabina all'Aventino*. It was founded in 425 AD by a Christian bishop named Peter of Illyria (better known as Presbyter Peter) on the site where a woman named Sabina once lived in the first century AD. Her house was next to a very old, ruined Temple of Juno, but Sabina was a Christian who maintained a forbidden *titulus* (Christian house-church) in her home. She was beheaded during the rule of Emperor Vespasian.

When Presbyter Peter built the basilica named for Sabina, he reused 24 fine fluted columns with Corinthian capitals from Juno's ancient temple next door. These columns still divide the aisles from the nave. The apse is decorated with a fresco from 1559, which seems to have copied the theme of the original fifth-century mosaic (now lost) that once was there. It shows Christ seated on a hillside with various figures, including the two thieves who were crucified beside him, while below sheep graze on the green grass. There is a door, as old as the church, made of dark cypress wood, in the narthex of the church, with carved panels telling sacred stories, including one of the oldest crucifixion scenes known to exist.[5]

The orange trees in the garden are said to have been planted long ago by Dominican monks, following the lead of Saint Dominic, who, in the thirteenth century, brought an orange tree sapling from his native Spain and planted it in the church cloister. There is a hole in the narthex wall through which you can see that very tree—or at least one of its descendants.

When you are ready to visit our fountain, return to the gate through which you entered the garden, but, rather than exit, turn right and follow the path along the wall, and then pass through the tall arched gate of an intersecting wall.

Beyond the gate, look to your right. Attached to the wall you just came through, you'll find our fountain.

The Mascherone of Santa Sabina—Il Mascherone di Santa Sabina, aka Il Mascherone del Giardino degli Aranci (1593—reinstalled 1936)
ARCHITECTS: GIACOMO DELLA PORTA AND ANTONIO MUÑOZ

In front of the high stone wall that separates the tiny Piazza Pietro d'Illiria from the orange grove, and the grove from the church, is an ancient marble basin with high walls, rather like a bathtub—probably, in fact, once used in a Roman bath. It sits in a rectangular drain pool with sloping sides. Behind the basin, in an arched niche, is a giant face made of marble, spouting an arc of water into the "bathtub." The stern face, with deep-set eyes, beetling, bushy eyebrows, a lumpy nose, and long, flowing moustaches, was carved in 1593 by Giacomo della Porta to decorate

Mascherone of Santa Sabina: In the small piazza next to the handsome and very ancient (fourth century) Basilica of Santa Sabina, the fountain features a grotesque mask carved by Giacomo della Porta in 1593.

a watering trough for cattle in the Campo Vaccino ("Field of Cows"), part of the ancient Forum, which in those days had not been excavated and where cattle grazed among the stony tops of buried monuments.

The cattle fountain was removed in 1816, and the mask was later used, in 1827, to decorate another fountain, this time located at Porto Leonino on the Tiber. When the port was demolished in 1890, the mask was stored until 1936, when the architect Antonio Munõz paired it with the ancient "bathtub" and created the fountain that now welcomes visitors to the Garden of the Oranges.

Standing in front of the fountain, facing away from it, the side entrance to the Basilica of Santa Sabina is ahead and to your right, behind a porch of three arches supported by two stone columns. There is another structure of brick extending at right angles to the left from the church. To reach the narthex, where the famous cypress door can be found, go through the brick arch closest to the church corner and turn right. You will enter the narthex, which is a kind of portico for the church, and near the farthest end you'll find the ancient door, framed in marble.

After you've enjoyed the garden and the fountain and the church, there is one other delight here on the top of the Aventine. As you exit from Piazza Pietro d'Illiria (the small piazza in front of the church), turn right onto Piazza di Sant'Alessio and walk about 300 yards or so. You'll come to Piazza dei Cavaliere di Malta. On the

Mascherone of Santa Sabina: Beyond the wall in which the mask is set, there is one of the loveliest spots in Rome, the Giardino degli Aranci, where bright fallen oranges dot the grassy lawn, and a terrace offers views from the Aventine all the way to the Dome of Saint Peter's.

right-hand side of the piazza, there's a dark green, wooden door in a large ornamental gate. The keyhole in this door is quite famous, because if you close one eye and look through the hole, you'll see a vista of trees, rooftops, and the Dome of Saint Peter's, like an image in a camera obscura, *framed perfectly in an arch of greenery. Note: You'll probably have to wait in line.*

The Fountain of the Frogs—La Fontana delle Rane (1927)
Architect: Gino Coppedè

Now, though, it's time to consider our last fountain, which is miles away, in a very unusual neighborhood north of Rome's historic center. Two of Rome's tram lines, numbers 3 and 19, stop nearby on via Regina Margherita at Piazza Buenos Aires; the

The Fountain of the Frogs—*La Fontana delle Rane*—marks the central piazza of a quirky and delightful neighborhood developed by Gino Coppedè in the early twentieth century.

bus stop where via Po enters Piazza Buenos Aires is served by bus lines 63, 83 and 92. Check with www.atac.roma.it for your best route.

Via Po enters Piazza Buenos Aires from the southwest, and it exits out of the piazza with a new name: via Tagliamento. If you get off your public transport in Piazza Buenos Aires, find via Tagliamento and follow it one block to where it crosses via Arno. You'll see an enormous, highly eclectic archway, with a roadway beneath, leading diagonally away from the intersection. Pass under the arch on via Dora, and continue toward the fountain straight ahead, into the one and only Coppedè Quarter.

In 1916, the *Società Anonima Edilizia Moderna* commissioned an architect named Gino Coppedè to design a residential complex in the Trieste area of Rome. I'm not sure the society members fully understood just what they were about to unleash on the neighborhood, but the collection of palazzi and villas and apartment buildings that sprang up over the next decade was so extraordinary—well, actually strange, startling, and somehow irresistible—that to this day it is famous as its own unique "district"—the *Quartiere Coppedè*.

There's that grand entrance arch you just passed under, spanning via Dora and connecting two halves of a large apartment complex whose façade sprouts Mannerist nudes, Romanesque and Renaissance loggias, Baroque balcony corbels, and medieval grotesques—all in travertine or marble. Above the apex of the arch is a huge *mascherone*, solemnly eyeing all comers, and hanging from the center of the

The Fountain of the Frogs: Trust Coppedè to find unique sources from which to spout water. The fountain has undergone renovation and cleaning since this photograph was taken.

arch is a giant Art Deco chandelier. Beyond the arch, there's a fountain we'll examine shortly, sitting in the middle of a traffic circle called Piazza Mincio; beyond the fountain is another typically unpredictable Coppedè structure, *Villino delle Fate* (the House of the Fairies). The term *eclectic* simply doesn't do it justice. There are brick arches, stone arches, half arches, loggias whose columns have capitals of every classical order, and more. There are tiles. There are Art Nouveau wrought-iron balconies. There are walls painted with Florentine cityscapes, Venetian galleys, and portraits of Dante and Boccaccio. There is also a wall-mounted sundial.

I suppose it must be wrong, somehow, to admit it, but the place is delightful. Coppedè built another 40 or so more structures nearby, in the same exuberant style.

One thing Coppedè understood was that every proper Roman neighborhood since the days of Marcus Agrippa (who built hundreds of fountains in the city when he was Augustus' water commissioner) had to be centered around a fountain. I seem to see Coppedè, in my mind's eye, pondering a theme: "Let's see—mythological gods and goddesses ... nah, been done. What about horses or dolphins or Tritons? Or lions, maybe? How about giant naked river deities, with long beards? Putti? Seductive water nymphs? Or, no, wait.... I have it! Frogs!"

So, in the middle of Piazza Mincio, you'll find *La Fontana delle Rane* (the Fountain of the Frogs), forming a centerpiece for the busy traffic roundabout. The area

The Fountain of the Frogs: These *atlantes* or *telemons*—male figures in architecture that hold up part of a structure—are so covered with mineral deposits in this picture that they are hardly recognizable. Happily, they have undergone a thorough scrubbing recently.

around the Coppedè Quarter is rather posh, and there are numerous foreign embassies nearby, so as you attempt to cross the street to the fountain, remember that the driver bearing down on you may have diplomatic immunity.

Once across, you'll be standing beside a large lower basin, roughly 33 feet in diameter, made of cement. In its center, a somewhat smaller basin rests on a sizeable pillar, with four travertine masks placed around the pillar's top, to help support the upper basin, on whose rim eight small frogs sit. They are poised as if to jump into the basin, while at the same time spouting water. In the center, a bell-shaped sculpture emits a plume of water upward from its top.

In the lower basin, four large sculptural groups surround the central pillar. Each consists of two muscular kneeling men, bearing on their backs one half of a giant bivalve shell, while ejecting water into the lower pool through pursed lips; in each shell is a large frog, also filling the pool with streams of water from both nostrils.

The fountain has recently undergone a woefully overdue restoration and cleaning; this process included consolidating the soil beneath the lower basin, which had been sinking on one side. I'm sure Gino Coppedè didn't foresee his fountain tilting, but he might have enjoyed the idea—*the Leaning Fountain of Piazza Mincio*. After all, Coppedè's work was always a little … well … sideways.

Now, cari compagni, we've found the last fountain of our last walk together, and I'm sure you can find your own way home! We have, if I've not miscounted, made our way by street, alley, path, lane, ramp and stair to eighty fountains in many different corners of Rome, with lots of stops and detours along the way. The wonderful thing is that there are two thousand or more fountains in Rome and plenty of reasons to follow (and occasionally stray from) the paths between them.

Alla Prossima Volta!

Chapter Notes

Introduction

1. Venturi and Sanfilippo, *Fountains of Rome*, 21–24.
2. Morton, *The Fountains of Rome*, 108.

Chapter 1

1. Twain, *The Innocents Abroad*, 301.
2. Lombardo, *Vedute delle Fontane Rinascimentali di Roma*, 46.
3. Falda and Venturini, *Selected Plates from the Classic "Le Fontane di Roma" 1660–1675*, 8.

Chapter 2

1. Venturi and Sanfilippo, *Fountains of Rome*, 62.
2. Morton, *The Fountains of Rome*, 228, 230.
3. Mattei, "Mario Rutelli, My Great-Grandfather."
4. Ostrow, "Discourse of Failure in Seventeenth-Century Rome," 267.
5. Morton, *The Fountains of Rome*, 127, 130.
6. Loomis, *The Book of the Popes*, 77.
7. Barber, *Pilgrim's Rome*, 90.

Chapter 3

1. Lombardo, *Vedute delle Piazze di Roma*, 742.
2. Hintzen-Bohlen and Sorges, *Art & Architecture*, 226.
3. Lombardo, *Vedute delle Fontane Barocche di Roma*, 73.
4. Morton, *The Fountains of Rome*, 116.

Chapter 4

1. Woodyard, "Nero's Ghost, 1885–1905." This is one version of the legend, quoted or paraphrased (from nineteenth-century sources) by a very clever and entertaining blogger.

Chapter 5

1. Falda and Venturini, *Selected Plates from the Classic "Le Fontane di Roma" 1660–1675*, 15.
2. Sovrintendenza Capitolina, "Fountain of the Porter."
3. Morton, *The Fountains of Rome*, 154.

Chapter 6

1. Morton, *A Traveller in Rome*, 286 (citations refer to the Da Capo edition).
2. Morton, *The Fountains of Rome*, 156.

Chapter 7

1. Lombardo, *Vedute delle Fontane Rinascimentali di Roma*, 57.

Chapter 8

1. Hazlitt, *Notes of a Journey through France and Italy*, 280–281.

Chapter 9

1. Ranogajec, "The Pantheon."

Chapter 10

1. Philostratus, *The Life of Apollonius of Tyana, Volume II*, 6:32. According to Philostratus, Domitian killed Titus by persuading him to eat the flesh of a poisonous fish called a "sea-hare," a method of murder also used (per Philostratus) by Nero. Philostratus, however, was by no means a reliable historian. Still, there are hints of suspicion about Domitian's treatment of Titus in other ancient texts. Suetonius, in his *Life of Domitian*, states that he forbade treatment for his older brother when Titus was suffering his fatal illness.

2. Lombardo, *Vedute delle Fontane Barocche di Roma*, 50–51.

3. Morton, *A Traveller in Rome*, 292.

4. Enggass and Brown, *Italy and Spain, 1600–1750*, 110 (translation from Filippo Baldinucci's 1682 *Vite del Cavaliere G.L. Bernino*).

5. Shi, "Monuments as Symbols." The symbolic meanings of the sculpted elements of the fountain are, of course, open to many interpretations. I have speculated freely about them, but I found Shi's thoughtful paper very helpful.

6. Venturi and Sanfilippo, *Fountains of Rome*, 90.

Chapter 11

1. Singer, *Giordano Bruno: His Life and Thought*, 179–180.

2. Knox, "Giordano Bruno."

3. Martínez, "Was Giordano Bruno Burned at the Stake for Believing in Exoplanets?"

4. Lombardo, *Vedute delle Fontane Barocche di Roma*, 35.

Chapter 12

1. Macaulay, *Lays of Ancient Rome and Other Poems*, 49. The Etruscan city of Clusium, from which Lars Porsena set out to reinstall the Tarquin monarchy (if the old story is true), was located where today's town of Chiusi can be found, in Tuscany, just south of Lake Trasimeno.

2. Futrell and Scanlon, *The Oxford Handbook of Sport and Spectacle in the Ancient World*, 268–269.

3. Norse, *The Roman Sonnets of G.G. Belli*. (This edition of Norse's translations has a preface by William Carlos Williams. The sonnets translated by Anthony Burgess, it seems, were used in his novel *Abba Abba*.)

4. Rinne, *The Waters of Rome*, 146–148.

Chapter 13

1. Morton, *A Traveller in Rome*, 340.

2. Biblioteca Apostolica Vaticana, *Codice Chigiana*, H, II, 22.

3. Rinne, *The Waters of Rome*, 230.

4. Acea SpA, "The Peschiera-Capore Pipeline Doubles."

5. Greenlee, "Quod Vocatur Paradiso," 7–8.

Chapter 14

1. Tacitus, *Annals of Imperial Rome*, 231–251.

2. Campitelli, *Skira Guides: Villa Borghese*, 43.

3. MacVeagh, *Fountains of Papal Rome*, 185.

Chapter 15

1. Hintzen-Bohlen and Sorges, *Art & Architecture*, 348.

2. Morton, *The Fountains of Rome*, 253.

3. Lombardo, *Vedute delle Fontane Barocche di Roma*, 8–9.

4. URL for the video: https://www.youtube.com/watch?v=ZV8-jp2ZRU8.

5. Macadam, *Blue Guide Rome*, 244.

Bibliography

Acea SpA. "The Peschiera-Capore Pipeline Doubles." Gruppo.acea.it. Accessed October 3, 2021. https:// www.gruppo.acea.it/en/stories/sustainability-territory/peschiera-pipeline-guarantees-water-in-rome.

Alighieri, Dante. *The Inferno*. Translated by Henry Wadsworth Longfellow. New York: Barnes & Noble, 2003.

Barber, A.B. *Pilgrim's Rome: A Blue Guide Travel Monograph*. London: Blue Guides/Somerset Books, 2012.

Biblioteca Apostolica Vaticana, *Codice Chigiana*, H, II, 22.

Campitelli, Alberta. *Skira Guides: Villa Borghese*. Translated by Timothy Stroud. Milan: Skira Editore S.p.A., 2003.

Enggass, Robert, and Johnathan Brown. *Italy and Spain, 1600–1750: Sources and Documents*. Englewood Cliffs: Prentice-Hall, 1970.

Falda, Giovanni Battista, and Giovanni Francesco Venturini. *Selected Plates from the Classic "Le Fontane di Roma" 1660–1675*. Mineola, NY: Dover, 2014.

Fiore, Kristina Herrmann. *Guide to the Galleria Borghese*. Rome: Gebart, 1998.

Futrell, Alison, and Thomas Francis Scanlon. *The Oxford Handbook of Sport and Spectacle in the Ancient World*. Oxford: Oxford University Press, 2021.

Greenlee, Justin. "Quod Vocatur Paradiso: The Pigna and the Atrium at Old St. Peter's." *Athanor* 32 (2014): 7–15.

Hazlitt, William. *Notes of a Journey through France and Italy*. London: Hunt and Clarke, 1826.

Hintzen-Bohlen, Brigitte, and Jürgen Sorges. *Art & Architecture: Rome and the Vatican City*. Könemann, 2005.

Knox, Dilwyn. "Giordano Bruno." *The Stanford Encyclopedia of Philosophy*, edited by Edward N. Zalta (Summer 2019 Edition). Accessed August 29, 2021. https://plato.stanford.edu/entries/bruno/.

Lombardo, Alberto. *Vedute delle Fontane Barocche di Roma*. Rome: Palombi Editori—Il Nartece, 2007.

_____. *Vedute delle Fontane Rinascimentali di Roma*. Rome: Palombi Editori—Il Nartece, 2007.

_____. *Vedute delle Piazze di Roma*. Rome: Palombi Editori, 2002.

Loomis, Louise Ropes, trans. *The Book of the Popes: Liber Pontificalis*. New York: Columbia University Press, 1916.

Macadam, Alta. *Blue Guide Rome*. Taunton, Somerset, UK: Somerset Books, 2010.

Macaulay, Thomas Babington. *Lays of Ancient Rome and Other Poems*. New York: James Miller, 1872.

MacVeagh, Mrs. Charles. *Fountains of Papal Rome*. New York: Scribner's, 1915.

Martínez, Alberto A. "Was Giordano Bruno Burned at the Stake for Believing in Exoplanets?" *Scientific American*. Accessed August 29, 2021. https://blogs.scientificamerican.com/ observations/was-giordano-bruno-burned-at-the-stake-for-believing-in-exoplanets.

Mattei, Paolo. "Mario Rutelli, My Great-Grandfather." Italian Ways. Accessed February 5, 2017. www. italianways.com/mario-rutelli-my-great-grandfather-interview-with-francesco-rutelli.

Morton, H. V. *The Fountains of Rome*. New York: Macmillan, 1966.

_____. *A Traveller in Rome*. London: Methuen, 1958; Boston: Da Capo Press, 2002.

Norse, Harold, trans. *The Roman Sonnets of G. G. Belli*. London: Perivale Press, 1974.

Ostrow, Steven F. "The Discourse of Failure in Seventeenth-Century Rome: Prospero Bresciano's 'Moses.'" *The Art Bulletin* 88, no. 2 (2006): 267–291.

Philostratus. *The Life of Apollonius of Tyana, Volume II*. Translated by F. C. Conybeare. Loeb Classical Library. Cambridge: Harvard University Press, 1912. Kindle.

Pulvers, Marvin. *Roman Fountains: 2000 Fountains in Rome, a Complete Collection*. Rome: L'Erma di Bretschneider, 2002.

Ranogajec, Paul A. "The Pantheon." Khan Academy. Accessed June 29, 2021. https://www.khanacademy. org/humanities/ap-art-history/ancient-mediterranean-ap/ap-ancient-rome/a/the-pantheon.

Rinne, Katherine Wentworth. *The Waters of Rome*. New Haven: Yale University Press, 2011.

Shi, Mark. "Monuments as Symbols: The Piazza Navona and Bernini's Fountain of the Four Rivers." Art History Presentation Archive (Summer 2007). Accessed October 5, 2021. http://honorsaharchive. blogspot.com/2007/09/monuments-as-symbols-piazza-navona-and.html.

Singer, Dorothea Waley. *Giordano Bruno: His Life and Thought, with Annotated Translation of His Work on the Infinite Universe and Worlds*. New York: Henry Schuman, 1950.

Sovrintendenza Capitolina. "Fountain of the Porter." Accessed May 25, 2021. www.sovraintendenzaroma. it/content/fontana-del-facchino-0.

Tacitus, Cornelius. *The Annals of Imperial Rome*. Translated by Michael Grant. Dorchester: Dorset Press, 1984.

Twain, Mark. *The Innocents Abroad, or The New Pilgrims' Progress*. Hartford, CT: American Publishing Company, 1869.

Venturi, Francesco, and Mario Sanfilippo. *Fountains of Rome*. New York: Vendome Press, 1996.

Woodyard, Chris. "Nero's Ghost, 1885–1905." *Mrs Daffodil Digresses* (blog). Accessed August 12, 2021. https://mrsdaffodildigresses.wordpress.com/2019/03/15/neros-ghost-1885-1905.

Index

CPSIA information can be obtained
at www.ICGtesting.com
Printed in the USA
LVHW060205290323
742929LV00015B/139

9 781476 689241